AMERICAN CRIMINAL PROCEDURES

AMERICAN CRIMINAL PROCEDURES

James F. Anderson

Bankole Thompson

CAROLINA ACADEMIC PRESS

Durham, North Carolina

Library of Congress Cataloging-in-Publication Data

Anderson, James F.
  American criminal procedures / by James F. Anderson, Bankole
Thompson.
      p.   cm.
  ISBN-13: 978-1-59460-237-5
  ISBN-10: 1-59460-237-9
  1. Evidence, Criminal--United States. 2. Searches and seizures--United
States. 3. Arrest--United States. I. Thompson, Bankole. II. Title.

  KF9660.A76 2006
  345.73'05--dc22

                                        2006017475

CAROLINA ACADEMIC PRESS
700 Kent Street
Durham, North Carolina
Tel: (919) 489-7486
Fax: (919) 493-5668
www.cap-press.com

This book is dedicated to the efforts of everyone who toils to make justice a reality in the American criminal justice system.

Contents

PREFACE

The purpose of this text is twofold: first, to acquaint the reader with certain individual rights due every American citizen; and second, to educate the reader on the legal aspects and processes that customarily unfold when citizens' constitutional rights are challenged. More important, the text provides the reader with the legal procedures that guide the criminal justice system in general and the actions of police officers in particular. The book devotes specific attention to the safeguards and practices that police officers must adhere to while discharging their sworn duty to uphold the U.S. and state constitutions. Essentially, the book presents a comprehensive examination of the legal aspects and procedures guaranteed to criminal offenders when they are processed through the justice system. More specifically, it lists constitutional amendments defining what rights are given defendants, along with a chronology of pertinent U.S. Supreme Court cases that provide the Court's rulings and interpretations of the rule of law as it pertains to individual rights and to rules governing law-enforcement practices.

The book is intended to be the primary text for undergraduate and graduate students enrolled in Criminal Procedures or a similarly titled college course. It is written in a concise and straightforward style and provides many examples so that students need not have prior knowledge of the subject matter. While some of the language may appear esoteric to non-criminal justice majors, it will be familiar to students who know the terminologies used by law-enforcement officers, judges, lawyers, probation and parole officers, and other agents of the justice system.

American Criminal Procedures, a text well-researched and up-to-date, is composed of nine chapters that provide readers with an understanding of the criminal justice system, the legal rights of the accused, and the procedures that follow when individual rights (or freedoms) are at issue in the system.

Chapter 1 introduces the student to the American court system. Specifically, it examines the United States dual court system, which consists of both state and federal courts. It distinguishes between the jurisdictions of both systems and demonstrates how cases are tried before state and federal courts. Moreover, it presents the laws that protect individual freedom and liberty as well as those that govern police behavior. Such laws typically include the U.S. Constitution, state constitutions, case- or judge-made law, as well as criminal law. The chapter also discusses the amendments to the Constitution-including those in the Bill of Rights-that protect the interests of the criminally accused.

Chapter 2 addresses the processes involved in the justice system. It briefly introduces the student to the operations of police, courts, and corrections. Then, more specifically, it discusses the salient experiences of a suspect-turned-defendant. In this chapter, special attention is given to pretrial activities such as the initial appearance, the preliminary hearing, the grand jury, the arraignment, and plea-bargaining procedures. The chapter also explains the processes of the trial phase as well as posttrial procedures such as sentencing. Finally, the chapter explains the appeals process and the process of filing a habeas corpus claim.

Chapter 3 introduces the reader to an essential standard-of-proof concept called probable cause-with which police officers, lawyers, and judges are intimately familiar. Probable cause is very important since it governs many aspects of policing. The chapter posits that many police procedures are contingent upon establishing this standard of proof. For example, according to the Fourth Amendment, probable cause must be established before warrants may be issued allowing legal searches and seizures and before arrests can be made. The chapter also discusses the consequences of failing to establish probable cause. More specifically, it discusses the importance of probable cause to the state's case.

Chapter 4 defines the exclusionary rule and recounts its history, beginning with case law on the federal and state levels. The chapter further establishes what is admissible and what is inadmissible under the rule and provides the guidelines to which police officers must adhere in order to use evidence obtained from an arrest to gain a lawful conviction. The chapter also examines concepts such as the fruit of the poisonous tree doctrine and the silver platter doctrine. In addition, the chapter explores the advantages and disadvantages of the exclusionary rule. It also examines the modification of the rule by exceptions and the impact of such exceptions on law-enforcement practices in particular and on the criminal justice system in general. Some exceptions to the exclusionary rule discussed in this chapter include the plain view doctrine; good faith; the inevitable discovery rule; search incidental to a lawful arrest; and the purged-taint exception. In its final section, the chapter discusses the future of the exclusionary rule.

Chapter 5 examines another concept central to conducting police work-reasonable suspicion. It argues that this level of proof is needed before an officer can conduct a stop and frisk. The chapter presents the leading cases in the area, along with other cases that have reaffirmed the courts' position on the issue. It further provides a detailed analysis of the procedures associated with a stop and frisk and indicates when a suspect is free to leave the presence of an officer who has briefly stopped and frisked the individual. The chapter also addresses the possible consequences to officers who use a legitimate stop to go on a "fishing expedition" of the suspect's personal effects. In fact, the chapter argues that police cannot haphazardly or arbitrarily stop and detain citizens without legitimate justification. However, if police officers can establish reasonable suspicion, they are legally allowed to make brief stops to ask questions and conduct a pat down of the suspect's outer garments for their own self-protection. Moreover, the chapter addresses investigatory automobile stops, automobile stops based on pretext, the use of drug-courier profiles, racial profiling, and other factors that may invalidate stops and frisks.

Chapter 6 defines a search and a seizure. It provides the legal limits involved in a search and examines two types of searches: those with warrants and those without warrants. It further focuses on the process involved in procuring a valid, or legal, search warrant. For example, it provides the procedures an officer must follow to obtain a warrant-such as filing an affidavit stating why there is probable cause that a particular person has engaged in a specific crime or why evidence can be found at a certain location. After filing the affidavit, the officer must provide sworn testimony to probable cause and seek a detached magistrate who must also find probable cause. At this point, a search warrant is issued commanding the officer either to arrest the suspect or to go to the stated location and retrieve the evidence. The chapter also discusses the legality of wiretaps as well as searches of people, houses, automobiles, and borders. In addition, it addresses searches made without warrants, especially those incidental to a lawful arrest, including consent searches.

Chapter 7 defines an arrest. It examines the leading cases that have established the point at which a person is considered under arrest and not free to leave the control of a police officer. It further distinguishes between a valid and an invalid arrest and explains the consequences of each. Through case history, the chapter presents the procedures used to make a valid arrest. It also indicates the procedures that must follow an arrest: most important, the suspect must be given the Miranda warnings to avoid self-incrimination and to safeguard his or her rights under the Fifth Amendment. In addition, the chapter connects the due process clause in the Fifth Amendment with the suspect's right to an attorney guaranteed by the Sixth Amendment. The chapter devotes special attention to the legal consequences of false arrest and false imprisonment.

Chapter 8 presents the procedures for interrogating suspects who are in police custody-either in the field or at the station house. The chapter distinguishes between confessions and admissions. Moreover, it provides case law and a large number of court decisions establishing the guidelines which officers must follow when questioning a suspect about his or her involvement in a crime. The chapter gives special attention to and more detailed information about a suspect's rights as spelled out in Miranda as well as in the Fifth and Sixth Amendments. The chapter also examines the importance of the suspect's having an attorney present so that the suspect will not be coerced or deceived into making incriminating statements that can be used to gain a criminal conviction. Finally, the chapter examines voluntary and involuntary confessions and their admissibility in court.

Chapter 9 examines the types of identification procedures police often use before a trial in order to identify a suspect and connect that suspect to a crime. The chapter examines several procedures, including station-house lineups, showups, and photographic arrangements. It further examines the constitutionality of such practices and indicates critical moments in the processes when a suspect needs the assistance of an attorney representing his or her legal interests. It also addresses the use of Deoxyribonucleic Acid Tests, or DNA profiling.

About the Authors

James F. Anderson is currently a professor of Criminal Justice and chair of the Criminal Justice Department at East Carolina University. He was formerly professor of Criminal Justice and Criminology at the University of Missouri-Kansas City in the Department of Sociology, Criminal Justice, and Criminology. He was also associate professor of Police Studies at Eastern Kentucky University. Professor Anderson received his master's degree in Criminology from Alabama State University and his Ph.D. degree in Criminal Justice from Sam Houston State University. He was a Doctoral Fellow at the National Institute of Justice in Washington, D.C., where he engaged in a comparative recidivism investigation of CRIPP participants, regular probationers, and parolees in Harris County, Texas. His research interests include the areas of police liability, criminal procedure, crime and public health, criminological theory, and legal aspects of criminal justice. He is the author of several articles and five books. Chief among them are Legal Rights of Prisoners: Cases and Comments and Criminological Theories: Understanding Crime in America.

Bankole Thompson is currently one of the judges of the Special Court for Sierra Leone, a United Nations-backed war crimes tribunal. He was formerly dean of the Graduate School at Eastern Kentucky University, from which he is currently on leave of absence as a professor of Criminal Justice. He was also associate professor of Criminal Justice at Kent State University, Ohio. Judge Thompson holds the degrees of MA, LLB, Ph.D. (in Law) from the University of Cambridge, England. In his native country of Sierra Leone, he first served as state prosecutor and then as judge of the High Court of Sierra Leone. He was also a founding member of that country's Law Reform Commission. In addition, he became legal officer for the Mano River Union, West Africa. His specialties are comparative constitutional law, comparative law, and international criminal law. He was the first African to hold the David Brennan Chair of Comparative Constitutional Law at the Akron School of Law, Ohio. He has to his credit several articles, book chapters, and two recently published books, The Constitutional History and Law of Sierra Leone (1961-1995) and The Criminal Law of Sierra Leone.

AMERICAN CRIMINAL PROCEDURES

CHAPTER 1

The Court System and Legal Rights

Focal Points

- The United States Dual Court System
    - The State Court System
    - The Federal Court System
- The Trial and Appellate Processes
- The Territorial Effect of Judicial Decisions
- The Doctrine of Stare Decisis
- The Exclusivity of Federal and State Jurisdictions
- Jurisdiction and Venue Distinguished
- Origins of Rights
    - Constitutions
    - Statutes
    - Case Law
    - Subordinate Legislation
- The Incorporation Doctrine
- Background
- Doctrinal Approaches
    - The Concept of Fundamental Rights
    - Rights Amenable to Incorporation
    - Rights Not Amenable to Incorporation
    - Nationalization of the Bill of Rights

INTRODUCTION

America is a nation of laws that govern every aspect of the human experience (Adler, Mueller, & Laufer, 2006). In fact, the rule of law is the instrument that prevents lawlessness and promotes civility. When crimes are committed, the social balance that characterizes civil society is disrupted; therefore, the law functions to heal social injury and remove the need for victims to seek personal revenge, since the law shifts the responsibility of exacting retribution to the state (Bohm & Haley, 2005; Fuller, 2006; Albanese, 2005; Fagin, 2005).

When offenders commit crime, the criminal justice system has the difficult task of dispensing justice to both offenders and victims. However, the lion's share of legal rights is provided to offenders while victims' rights go ignored, as evidenced by the term *criminal justice* rather than *victims' justice* and by the many constitutional safeguards and protections afforded to criminal defendants. Disparate treatment is perhaps given to defendants since their freedom is in jeopardy, or even their lives, depending on the gravity of their crimes, since some crimes carry the death penalty. Therefore, the United States grants defendants every opportunity to prove their innocence. When legal issues emerge in America, they are addressed in a court having the geographical and subject-matter jurisdiction to hear the case (Bohm & Haley, 2005; Fuller, 2006; Albanese, 2005; Fagin, 2005). To ensure that justice is served, the court system allows for an appeal if it can be shown that a procedural mistake was made which disadvantaged a defendant. When such a mistake occurs, the defendant is entitled to a new trial or a reversal of a lower court's decision. In fact, some of these cases may be appealed to the highest court in the land, the U.S. Supreme Court.

One fundamental feature of the American legal system is the duality of its court system. There are the federal courts, on the one hand, and the state courts, on the other. It is sometimes said that the American judicial system is plural in character. But it is more accurate to characterize it as a dual judicial system. In the context of the criminal jurisdiction of the American judiciary, it is noteworthy that criminal cases may be tried in the federal courts and in the state courts if the act constitutes a crime under both jurisdictions. However, because the primary responsibility for the maintenance of law and order is a state or local function, most criminal cases are tried in the state courts. Hence, this chapter is divided into several parts. Part One examines such basic facets of the United States legal system as the dual nature of the court system. Part Two provides the trial and appellate processes. Part Three discusses the territorial effect of judicial decisions. Part Four explains the doctrine of stare decisis. Part Five addresses the exclusivity of federal and state jurisdictions.

Part Six presents the distinction between *jurisdiction* and *venue*. Part Seven covers the juridical origins of rights. Part Eight explains the incorporation doctrine.

PART ONE:
THE UNITED STATES DUAL COURT SYSTEM

As already noted, a key feature of the organization and structure of the American legal system is the duality of its court system—comprising state and federal courts. State crimes are prosecuted in state courts, whereas federal crimes are prosecuted in federal courts (del Carmen, 2001; Reid, 1996). State crimes are criminal acts proscribed at the state and local levels, whereas federal crimes are those proscribed at the federal level—more precisely, by Congress. Certain acts constitute both state crimes and federal crimes and thus may be tried at both state and federal levels.

At the federal level, the court system comprises the United States Supreme Court, the United States courts of appeals, and the U.S. district courts. At the state level, courts are classified hierarchically into supreme courts, intermediate appellate courts, trial courts of general jurisdiction, and trial courts of limited jurisdiction. But this hierarchical structure is not inflexible. There is some variation. First, states usually have one state supreme court, which renders final decisions in cases involving the laws of the state and its constitution. However, Texas and Oklahoma depart from the general pattern. Each of those states has two courts of last resort, one exercising civil jurisdiction and the other criminal jurisdiction. Second, states usually have intermediate appellate courts. Yet, here, too, the pattern is not rigid, since only thirty-five of the fifty states have such courts. In states with no intermediate appellate courts, cases on appeal go directly from the trial courts of general jurisdiction to the states' supreme courts (del Carmen, 2001). Third, below the intermediate appellate courts, states have trial courts of general jurisdiction. In some states, they are categorized according to judicial specialization in areas such as probate, juvenile justice, and commercial and domestic relations. Specifically, they bear such names as "circuit courts," "district courts," or "courts of common pleas." Interestingly, in New York, the trial court of general jurisdiction is called "the supreme court."

At the bottom of the state judicial pyramid are the courts known as courts of limited jurisdiction. They are sometimes referred to as lower or inferior courts (in contrast to superior courts). As their name implies, their jurisdiction is restricted. Legally, they can hear and determine only specific types of cases—for example, minor civil matters and crimes described as misdemeanors, punishable with a short term of imprisonment or a moderate fine or both. They carry such names as "magistrates' courts," "police courts," "justices of the peace courts," and "municipal courts."

At the federal level, there is a distinct trifurcation of courts, beginning with the United States Supreme Court at the apex of the federal judicial pyramid. Its constitutional importance is entrenched by Article III of the United States Constitution in these terms: "The Judicial Power of the United States shall be vested in one supreme court, and in such inferior courts as the Congress may from time to time ordain and establish." The Court is composed of a chief justice and eight associate justices, all of whom are nominated and appointed by the president of the United States with the "advice and consent" of the Senate. The justices enjoy life tenure and can be removed only by impeachment, the implication being that their life tenure is subject to good behavior. Figure 1.1 illustrates the current (2006) composition of the U.S. Supreme Court. More specifically, it provides the names and ranks of the one chief justice and the eight associate justices. It gives the date of their appointment, followed by the president who nominated them for the bench. It also gives the university where they received their legal training, along with their political affiliation. Legal scholars argue that once nominated and confirmed by the Senate, justices are more likely to decide cases coming before the Court along party lines. If this proves to be the rule, it is conceivable that with the composition of the current Court, many of the civil liberties and freedoms that Americans enjoy could either be seriously curtailed or overturned by the Court's conservative majority. Recently, many citizens have expressed their concerns over whether the Court will overturn *Roe v. Wade*.

Figure 1.1 The Composition of the United States Supreme Court

Name	Rank	Appointed	Appointed by	Education	Political Affiliation
John Roberts, Jr.	Chief Justice	9/29/2006	George W. Bush	Harvard	Conservative
John P. Stevens	Associate Justice	12/19/1975	Gerald R. Ford	Northwestern	Liberal
Antonin Scalia	Associate Justice	8/26/1986	Ronald Reagan	Harvard	Conservative
Anthony Kennedy	Associate Justice	2/18/1988	Ronald Reagan	Harvard	Conservative
David H. Souter	Associate Justice	10/9/1990	George Bush	Harvard	Moderate
Clarence Thomas	Associate Justice	10/23/1991	George Bush	Yale	Conservative
Ruth B. Ginsburg	Associate Justice	8/10/1993	William Clinton	Columbia	Liberal
Stephen G. Breyer	Associate Justice	8/3/1994	William Clinton	Harvard	Liberal
Samuel A. Alito	Associate Justice	1/31/2006	George W. Bush	Harvard	Conservative

The U.S. Supreme Court is the final appellate tribunal in the federal system. Its basic function is to interpret federal laws and the U.S. Constitution. Below the U.S. Supreme Court, at the intermediate level, are the United States courts of appeals consisting (based on 1999 statistics) of a total of 179 judges officiating in thirteen different regions of the country. Like the U.S. Supreme Court justices, the judges of the U.S. courts of appeals are nominated and appointed by the president of the United States for life, with the "advice and consent" of the Senate. Their life tenure is likewise subject to good behavior, so they, too, are impeachable. The judges usually sit in panels of three for the purpose of normal judicial appellate work. However, they may sit in panels of five (i.e., en banc) as the complexity of the issues on appeal before them dictate. Third in the federal judicial hierarchy are the United States district courts. They are located in ninety-four judicial districts. The total number of judges who officiate in those courts is approximately 646. Each state has at least one judicial district, but some states have as many as four (del Carmen, 2001). Like the U.S. Supreme Court justices and the judges of the U.S. courts of appeals, they are nominated and appointed by the United States president for life, with the "advice and consent" of the Senate. Their life tenure is likewise subject to good behavior. They hear and determine cases involving violations of federal criminal laws. They also try civil cases that meet specified criteria.

Appended, as it were, to the U.S. district courts is a body of judicial officials collectively designated the U.S. magistrates and established primarily to relieve the heavy judicial workload on the U.S. district courts. The U.S. magistrates have limited jurisdiction, such as trying minor offences and misdemeanor cases punishable by incarceration for one year or less. They are also authorized to grant bail, issue arrest and search warrants, and review habeas corpus petitions.

PART TWO: THE TRIAL AND APPELLATE PROCESSES DISTINGUISHED

Like most major world legal systems, the American legal system, in its organizational structure, makes a clear distinction between the trial process and the appellate process. This distinction is important, and it exists at both the state and federal court levels. A key feature of trial courts is that they try the facts of the case, arrive at certain findings of fact, and reach appropriate conclusions of law based on these findings. Specifically, in the context of a criminal trial, the case is usually tried by a judge and a jury, and rarely by a judge alone (such a trial is called "a bench trial"). The trial process involves the determination of the facts of the case based on the evidence adduced by the adversarial parties, namely, the prosecution and the defense. By applying principles of law to the facts of the case, the judge or jury determines the outcome of the case—usually either a conviction or an acquittal. In this last phase of the trial process, the appellate process becomes implicated, which means that an aggrieved party in a trial court can appeal his or her case to an appellate court, whose responsibility—and, in essence, core function—is to expound authoritatively on the law through the method of interpretation. Specifically, the appellate process involves both a determination and a remediation of errors of law that may have taken place during the trial phase or the sentencing phase of a criminal case. However, there is no presentation or evaluation of evidence in the course of the appeal process.

Like a trial court, an appellate court does arrive at a decision. It may either affirm, reverse, or reverse and remand the decision of the lower court. "To affirm" means that the decision of the lower court is upheld. "To reverse" means that the decision of the lower court is overturned or vacated. "To reverse and remand" means that the lower court's decision is reversed but that the court is afforded the opportunity of hearing further arguments and of making another decision.

Part Three: The Territorial Effect of Judicial Decisions

It is an elementary principle of law that judicial decisions given within the framework of national or municipal legal systems are limited territorially as to their binding force and legal effect. This principle has its counterpart in the sphere of international law in the form of the doctrine of extraterritoriality, which asserts that judicial decisions are generally not enforceable outside the geographic boundaries of the adjudicating tribunals. For example, the decisions of American courts cannot automatically have legal binding effect outside the geographic boundaries of the United States. Put slightly differently, a judicial decision is authoritative and has precedential value for future cases only within the geographic limits of the area in which the court is vested with the authority to adjudicate. Specifically, the decisions of the U.S. Supreme Court on questions of federal law bind all courts within the boundaries of the country since the entire nation is under the jurisdiction of the Court as the highest national tribunal. In contrast, decisions of the U.S. courts of appeals have legal binding effect or force of law only within the territorial compass of the circuits in which they are located. For example, the decisions of the First Circuit Court of Appeals are legally binding within Maine, Massachusetts, New Hampshire, Rhode Island, and Puerto Rico—areas within its jurisdictional scope.

By analogy, decisions rendered by state courts are, generally, legally binding within the particular state, except that state supreme court decisions are recognized as extending beyond state borders. One tremendous practical consequence of a dual system of courts is the probability of conflicting decisions on legal issues that come before the courts for resolution. This probability is one reason for justifying the mechanism of appeal. In effect, inherent in the appellate process is the capacity to eliminate or resolve conflicting decisions on legal questions.

A final feature of the appellate process worthy of note is its response to the question: How should adjudicating bodies be guided when there is no settled or authoritative law on an issue in dispute in a given area? Where an issue arising before a court has not been litigated before in that forum or jurisdiction, the courts have always been guided by the spirit of judicial pragmatism; that is, they seek persuasive guidance from another forum or jurisdiction. Furthermore, where, in the opinion of a particular court, its previous decisions no longer seem to represent the preponderant view of the law, it may, consistent with the notion of the law as a dynamic and evolving institution, choose to revise or reinterpret such decisions.

Part Four: The Doctrine of Stare Decisis

A prominent feature of Anglo-American jurisprudence is what is quaintly called *stare decisis*. It is a Latin phrase which means "to stand by the things decided." The doctrine has its origin in the common law system as distinct from the civil law system. In essence, stare decisis is the doctrine of precedent, under which it is necessary for a court to follow earlier judicial decisions when the same points arise again in litigation (del Carmen, 2001; Black, 1999; Lile, Redfield, Wambaugh, Sunderland, Mason, & Cooley, 1914). However, when we say that a judicial decision has precedential value for future cases similarly circumstanced, such precedent relates only to those cases over which the particular court has jurisdiction. For example, the decisions of the Fifth Circuit Court of Appeals are of precedential value only in respect to the states of Texas, Louisiana, and Mississippi—all within the territorial jurisdiction of the court (del Carmen, 2001).

How does the doctrine of precedent operate? Generally, the rationale behind the doctrine is the need for stability in the law, but the doctrine also recognizes the need for flexibility in the law. In effect, though it is desirable for courts to adhere to the principles of decided cases and apply them to future cases coming before them, it is equally desirable for courts to have the flexibility to overrule their previous decisions when the interests of justice dictate the adoption of such a judicial option. Technically, therefore, it is important to distinguish between the reason for the decision or the principle upon which it is predicated and the expositions of the judges on issues that are not part of the actual ruling. The reason for the decision or holding of the court is called the *ratio decidendi*, whereas the statements, opinions, or comments not necessary for the decision are referred to as the *obiter dicta*. For clarity and precision in understanding case law, it is necessary not to confuse the dicta with the reason for the court's holding or decision. A good illustration of the difference between the two is the statement in *Carroll v. Carroll*:

> If it [the point of law commented on in the opinion] might have been decided either way without affecting any right brought into question, then, according to the principles of the common law, an opinion on such a question is not a decision. To make it so, there must have been an application of the judicial mind to the precise question necessary to be determined, to fix the rights of the parties, and to decide to whom the property in contestation belongs. And, therefore, this court, and other courts organized under common law, has never held itself bound by any part of an opinion, in any case, which was not needful to the ascertainment of the right or title in question between the parties.

PART FIVE: THE EXCLUSIVITY
OF FEDERAL AND STATE JURISDICTIONS

In any federal system of government, it becomes imperative when one examines the jurisdiction of the courts to make a clear distinction between the jurisdiction of the federal courts, on the one hand, and the jurisdiction of the states' courts, on the other. The jurisdiction of a court is its authority to hear and decide a case. Such authority is usually vested in the court either by the constitution or the statute creating the court. The impression is sometimes created that the existence of both federal and state jurisdictions raises the juristic specter of double jeopardy, freedom from which is constitutionally guaranteed every person charged with a crime in the United States. This impression stems from the possibility under the American legal system of an act constituting a crime under both state law and federal law at a given time. The reasoning is that such concurrent federal and state jurisdiction over the crime means that an accused will be put in peril twice for the same offense. This argument, however, constitutes a legal misconception. The true position in law is that there is no double jeopardy here because of the dual-sovereignty concept, which posits that the federal and state governments are considered sovereign each in their own right. Hence, when the act with which a suspect is charged constitutes a violation of both federal and state criminal laws, he or she can properly be tried for the same offense under both jurisdictions. The two sovereignties decide which jurisdiction should have priority in trying the accused, though it is common practice for the sovereignty that first obtains custody of the suspect to try him or her first.

As articulated in *United States v. Lanza*, the doctrine of dual sovereignty states that "an act denounced as a crime by both national and state sovereignties is an offence against the peace and dignity of both and may be punished by each." The ruling was reaffirmed in *Bartkus v. Illinois* and in *Abbate v. United States*. In *Bartkus*, the defendant was tried first in federal court for robbery of a federally insured savings and loan bank. After a federal acquittal, he was tried and convicted in a state court for the same crime. The reverse situation occurred in *Abbate*: a state trial preceded a federal trial for the same act. The difference, however, was that in *Abbate* both trials resulted in a conviction. At the appellate level, the decisions of both federal and state courts were upheld as constitutionally valid on the grounds that a defendant's conduct "may impinge more seriously on a federal [state] interest than a state [federal] interest." The U.S. Supreme Court in *Bartkus* put this aspect of the matter in the dual-sovereignty context with the observation that a contrary decision could allow a defendant who has been convicted of a federal civil rights offense, punishable with no more than a few years' imprisonment, to evade state prosecution for homicide charges. In the same vein, the Court in *Abbate* indicated that the defendants were contending that their state convictions, "resulting in three months' prison sentences[,] should bar this federal prosecution which could result in a sentence of up to five years."

PART SIX:
JURISDICTION AND VENUE DISTINGUISHED

American courts are organized on the basis of two key concepts. One is *jurisdiction*; the other is *venue*. There is always a tendency to confuse them. Jurisdiction, as already noted, is the authority conferred on a court to hear and decide a case. A court's jurisdiction is usually determined by either the country's or state's constitution or by any specific law establishing the court. There are three main types of jurisdiction for the purposes of the administration of justice—namely, geographical, subject-matter, and hierarchical. Jurisdiction, in the geographical sense, implies the authority to adjudicate cases with reference to specified political boundaries (for example, a metropolitan or urban area, a judicial district, or a provincial area) (Thompson, 1999). Jurisdiction in respect to subject matter implies that a court may be limited to hearing and deciding only certain types of cases—for example, juvenile cases, commercial lawsuits, domestic or family relations, probate matters, or bankruptcy disputes. Hierarchical jurisdiction, as its name implies, is predicated upon the distinction between the original jurisdiction and the appellate jurisdiction. The former refers to the jurisdiction of a court to hear and decide a case at the first-instance level. In essence, the court tries the case by finding the facts and by applying principles of law to the said facts to reach a legally supportable decision. The latter refers to the jurisdiction of a court to review the decision of a court of original jurisdiction for errors of law.

The concept of venue, as distinct from the concept of jurisdiction, is predicated upon location. The rationale behind this concept is that adjudication of legal disputes must take place where, in the case of a crime, it was committed or where, in the case of a civil lawsuit, a party resides. However, the law permits a change of venue when the interests of justice so demand. The classic illustration of the law's policy to allow a change of venue in the sphere of criminal adjudication is excessive or prejudicial pretrial publicity that might make it difficult to impanel an impartial jury.

PART SEVEN: ORIGINS OF RIGHTS

Constitutions

The rules and principles governing criminal procedure in the United States derive largely from four basic sources: the federal and states' constitutions, statutes, judicial decisions, and rules of court. In most legal systems of the world, the most authoritative source of rights, freedoms, and privileges enjoyed by human beings is the fundamental law referred to as the constitution. Hence, a nation's constitution is the primary source of legal norms and values for that nation. It is from this perspective that the United States Constitution can be seen as the most authoritative legal instrument embodying the basic rights, freedoms, and privileges accorded a person accused of crime before a court in the United States. The most prominent of such rights is the presumption of innocence. Specifically, the constitutional norms governing the procedural aspects of a criminal trial in the United States are collectively referred to as the Bill of Rights. It incorporates the first ten amendments to the U.S. Constitution and has been judicially recognized as containing key procedural safeguards guaranteed to every person facing criminal prosecution in the United States. In a work of this nature, it is imperative to recall some of these constitutional provisions. They are as follows:

Amendment I: "Congress shall make no law respecting an establishment of religion, or prohibiting the free exercise thereof; or abridging the freedom of speech, or of the press, or the right of the people peaceably to assemble, and to petition the Government for a redress of grievances." The First Amendment protects freedom of religion, freedom of speech, freedom of the press, freedom of assembly, and freedom to petition the government for redress of grievances.

Amendment II: "A well regulated militia, being necessary to the security of a free State, the right of the people to keep and bear arms, shall not be infringed." The Second Amendment grants the right to keep and bear arms.

Amendment IV: "The right of the people to be secure in their persons, houses, papers, and effects, against unreasonable searches and seizures, shall not be violated, and no Warrants shall issue, but upon probable cause, supported by oath or affirmation, and particularly describing the place to be searched, and the person or things to be seized." The Fourth Amendment protects citizens against unreasonable searches and seizures.

Amendment V: "No person shall be held to answer for a capital, or otherwise infamous crime, unless on a presentment or indictment of a Grand Jury, except in cases arising in land or naval forces, or in the Militia, where in actual service in time of War or public danger; nor shall any person be subject for the same offense to be twice put in jeopardy of life or limb; nor shall be compelled in any criminal case to be a witness against himself, nor be deprived of life, liberty, or property, without due process of law; nor shall private property be taken for public use without just compensation." The Fifth Amendment affords the right to a grand jury indictment for a capital or other serious crime, protection against double jeopardy, protection against self-incrimination, and the prohibition against the taking of life, liberty, or property without due process of law.

Amendment VI: "In all prosecutions, the accused shall enjoy the right to a speedy and public trial, by an impartial jury of the State and district wherein the crime shall have been committed, which district shall have been previously ascertained by law, and to be informed of the nature and cause of the accusation; to be confronted with the witnesses against him; to have compulsory process for obtaining witnesses in his favor, and to have the assistance of counsel for his defense." The Sixth Amendment provides the right to a speedy and public trial, the right to an impartial jury, the right to be informed of the nature and cause of the accusation, the right to confront witnesses, the right to summon witnesses, and the right to have assistance of counsel.

Amendment VIII: "Excessive bail shall not be required nor excessive fines imposed, nor cruel and unusual punishments inflicted." The Seventh Amendment guarantees protection against excessive bail and protection against cruel and unusual punishment.

In addition to the Bill of Rights is an important constitutional safeguard:

Amendment XIV: "All persons born or naturalized in the United States and subject to the jurisdiction thereof, are citizens of the United States and of the State wherein they reside. No State shall make or enforce any law which shall abridge the privileges or immunities of citizens of the United States; nor shall any State deprive any person of life, liberty, or property, without due process of law; nor deny to any person within its jurisdiction the equal protection of the laws." The Fourteenth Amendment ensures the right to due process and the right to equal protection.

Because of its federal-government structure, the United States today has fifty separate state constitutions, several of which incorporate bills of rights similar to the federal Bill of Rights, providing for guarantees of protection against deprivation of rights by state governments. As a matter of constitutional law, the states' constitutions must conform in letter and spirit to the provisions of the U.S. Constitution. A key doctrine of constitutional consistency between the states' constitutions and the Constitution of the United States is that if a state's constitution or state law guarantees a defendant fewer rights, freedoms, and privileges than those guaranteed at the federal level, such restriction will be declared unconstitutional and the provisions of the federal Constitution will prevail. For example, when a state constitution, for some inexplicable reason, compels a defendant to testify to the extent of abrogating his federally protected privilege against self-incrimination, such a provision will be declared unconstitutional as an infringement of the Fifth Amendment privilege against self-incrimination. However, the requirement of consistency between state constitutions and the federal Constitution does not imply a perfect constitutional alignment. It is permissible for the constitution of a state to provide greater protection for defendants than is provided at the federal or national level.

Statutes

Besides constitutional provisions as a source of procedural rights in the application of American criminal law, there is another key source of such rights—namely, statute law. It should be emphasized that in the context of the American federal system, statutes are enacted by states as well as by Congress. The enacted laws relevant for the enforcement of criminal law are designated procedural laws. Therefore, statute law—at both state and federal levels—is a primary source of American legal procedure covering the pretrial, trial, and posttrial phases of a criminal case. Both state and federal statutes on criminal procedure often cover the same rights, freedoms, and privileges guaranteed an accused person—but in greater detail. Three key illustrations of this simultaneous coverage are the right of an accused person to have counsel during trial, the right of a convicted person to have counsel during a probation hearing, and the right to a jury trial. The first is guaranteed by the U.S. Constitution, but it may also be guaranteed under federal or state statute, which has equal binding force in criminal proceedings. The second is not guaranteed by the Constitution, but many states provide for this right. The third, the right to a jury trial, is not guaranteed by the Constitution in juvenile cases, but it may be granted under state law (del Carmen, 1995).

Case Law

For the purpose of understanding case law as a source of legal rights, whether substantively or procedurally, it must be acknowledged that the common law does not work from preestablished truths of universal and inflexible validity. Its method is inductive and it draws its generalizations from particulars (Cardozo, 1921). Hence, in the context of Anglo-American jurisprudence, the decisions of judges emanating from their adjudicating function create case law. As the term *case law* suggests, a particular decision or a collection of particular decisions generates law—that is, rules of general application (Ginsburg & Janklow, 2003). Precisely stated, case law is the law as enunciated in cases decided by the courts. Despite the historical juridical affinity between case law and common law, contemporary Anglo-American jurisprudence differentiates between them in this respect: common law is a historical product of the ancient and unwritten laws of England and in the context of criminal adjudication in the United States today, it has no precedential value in the administration of criminal justice at the state level; in contrast, case law does have precedential value within the territorial jurisdiction of the court that issued the opinion.

Subordinate Legislation

Of some significance, too, is the function of subordinate legislation, or simply, rules and regulations in creating legal rights. All that needs to be mentioned here is that rules specifically formulated by state and federal courts in exercise of their supervisory authority over the administration of criminal justice have the force of law and constitute legal rights—especially in the context of providing procedural safeguards for persons who are suspected or accused of criminal offenses. Essentially, rules in this sense supplement or fill gaps in state and federal criminal procedural codes.

PART EIGHT: THE INCORPORATION DOCTRINE

Background

In the context of what has become known as the incorporation controversy in respect to the sources of legal rights, two key issues have arisen for judicial determination. The first and more general one is whether the Bill of Rights in the U.S. Constitution guarantees protection against infringement of individual rights by the federal government or whether it restricts governmental actions at the state and local levels. The second and more specific issue is what constitutional rights, freedoms, and privileges are to be incorporated into the due process clause of the Fourteenth Amendment to the U.S. Constitution and are therefore to be applicable to the states. Historically, it is of some interest that the federal Constitution was ratified by thirteen states in 1789 and that the Bill of Rights only became an integral part of the Constitution in 1791. The initial view regarding the first issue was that the Bill of Rights applied only to federal governmental actions and that state governmental actions were subject to state constitutional and statutory limitations. The second issue relates to Section 1 of the Fourteenth Amendment, part of which is presented below:

> No State shall make or enforce any law which shall abridge the privileges and immunities of citizens of the United States, nor shall any State deprive any person of life, liberty, or property, without due process of law; nor deny to any person within its jurisdiction the equal protection of the laws.

The controversy concerning this Amendment has centered on whether this part of the Amendment, succinctly referred to as "the due process clause," has incorporated most of the provisions of the Bill of Rights. The United States Supreme Court has authoritatively laid the issue to rest by acknowledging the incorporation doctrine. However, four main varieties of the doctrine have emerged as judicial preferences.

Doctrinal Approaches

The first preference is referred to as "the selective incorporation approach," or the "honor roll position," as it is sometimes called. According to this approach, only those rights considered "fundamental" are amenable for incorporation under the due process clause of the Fourteenth Amendment to render them applicable to state criminal proceedings. Predicated upon this approach, the U.S. Supreme Court has articulated three main criteria for determining whether to incorporate a right under the due process clause. These are (1) whether a right falls within the category of those "fundamental principles of liberty and justice which lie at the base of our civil and political institutions," (2) whether the right is "basic in our system of jurisprudence," and (3) whether the right can be characterized as a "fundamental right essential to a fair trial." Selective incorporation is the preponderant approach.

The second preference is total incorporation. The doctrinal thrust of this position is that the Fourteenth Amendment's due process clause should be interpreted as incorporating all the rights granted by, and embodied in, the first ten amendments to the U.S. Constitution. This preference is judicially credited to Justice Hugo Black in his separate concurring opinion in *Duncan v. Louisiana*. This approach, in essence, advocates the incorporation of all the provisions in the Bill of Rights.

The third preference is referred to as "the total incorporation plus approach." As its name implies, it is an extension of the second preference. It asserts that, in addition to extending all provisions of the Bill of Rights to the states, other rights ought to be added. Justice William O. Douglas was the main advocate of this approach. However, it is not a popular viewpoint.

The fourth preference is the case-by-case incorporation approach. Also known as the "fair trial approach," its main focus is a scrutiny of the facts of a specific case in order to determine whether that case, due regard having been given to the peculiarity or uniqueness of the facts, should be brought within the constitutional ambit of the due process clause of the Bill of Rights. It has been observed that this approach poses the problem of the unpredictability of the application of the Bill of Rights.

The Concept of Fundamental Rights

In the context of comparative law, misgivings have been expressed as to the wisdom and efficacy of incorporating fundamental rights into modern constitutions. McIntyre (1966) once observed thus: "The ideal Constitution … would contain few or no declaration of rights though the ideal system of law would define and guarantee many rights. Rights cannot be declared in a Constitution except in absolute and unqualified terms, unless they are so qualified as to be meaningless." Under the American constitutional system, the U.S. Supreme Court has defined fundamental rights as those "of the very essence of a scheme of ordered liberty" and as "principles of justice so rooted in the traditions and conscience of our people as to be ranked as fundamental." Though such assertions may sound theoretical and conceptual, the Court's pragmatic approach will entail an examination, on a case-by-case basis, of which rights are amenable for incorporation.

Rights Amenable to Incorporation

Guided, as already noted, by a cautious and pragmatic approach and using the selective incorporation method, the Court has progressively held amenable to incorporation the rights set forth below:

First Amendment provisions for freedom of religion, speech, assembly, and petition for redress of grievances (*Fiske v. Kansas*, 274 U.S. 380 [1927])

Fourth Amendment protections against unreasonable arrest, search, and seizure (*Wolf v. Colorado*, 338 U.S. 25 [1949])

Fifth Amendment protection against self-incrimination (*Malloy v. Hogan*, 378 U.S. 1 [1964])

Fifth Amendment prohibition against double jeopardy (*Benton v. Maryland*, 395 U.S. 784 [1969])

Sixth Amendment right to counsel (*Gideon v. Wainwright*, 372 U.S. 335 [1963])

Sixth Amendment right to a speedy trial (*Klopfer v. North Carolina*, 386 U.S. 213 [1967])

Sixth Amendment right to a public trial (*In re Oliver*, 333 U.S. 257 [1948])

Sixth Amendment right to confrontation with opposing witnesses (*Pointer v. Texas*, 380 U.S. 400 [1965])

Sixth Amendment right to an impartial jury (*Duncan v. Louisiana*, 391 U.S. 145 [1968])

Sixth Amendment right to a compulsory process for obtaining witnesses (*Washington v. Texas*, 388 U.S. 14 [1967])

Eighth Amendment prohibition against cruel and unusual punishment (*Robinson v. California*, 370 U.S. 660 [1962])

Rights Not Amenable to Incorporation

Despite the recognition of these legal protections in the federal criminal process, states are under no constitutional or statutory obligation to grant a person accused of crime either the Fifth Amendment right to a grand jury indictment or the Eighth Amendment prohibition against excessive bail and fines.

Nationalization of the Bill of Rights

A key feature of contemporary American criminal law resulting from the selective incorporation process insofar as it applies to the Fourteenth Amendment's due process clause is what has been succinctly characterized as the "nationalization" of the Bill of Rights. In effect, the Bill of Rights, as a legal instrument, is today applicable throughout the United States.

REFERENCES

Adler, F., Mueller, G., & Laufer, W. (2006). *Criminal justice: An introduction* (4th ed.). New York: McGraw-Hill.

Albanese, J. S. (2005). *Criminal justice* (3rd ed.). New York: Allyn and Bacon.

Black, H. C. (1999). *Black's law dictionary with pronunciations* (5th ed.). St. Paul, MN: West.

Bohm, R. M., & Haley, K. N. (2005). *Introduction to criminal justice* (4th ed.). New York: McGraw-Hill.

Cardozo, B. N. (1921). *The nature of the judicial process.* New Haven: Yale University Press.

del Carmen, R. V. (1995). *Criminal procedure: Law and practice* (3rd ed.). Belmont, CA: Wadsworth.

del Carmen, R. V. (2001). *Criminal procedure: Law and practice* (5th ed.). Belmont, CA: West/Wadsworth.

Fagin, J. A. (2005). *Criminal justice.* New York: Allyn and Bacon.

Fuller, J. R. (2006). *Criminal justice: Mainstream and crosscurrents.* Upper Saddle River, NJ: Prentice Hall.

Ginsburg, J. C., & Janklow, M. L. (2003). *Introduction to law and legal reasoning.* New York: Foundation Press.

Lile, W. M., Redfield, H. S., Wambaugh, E., Sunderland, E. R., Mason, A. F., & Cooley, R. W. (1914). *Brief making and the use of law books* (3rd. ed.). St. Paul, MN: West.

McIntyre, W. D. (1966). *Colonies into commonwealth.* London: Blanford Press.

Reid, S. T. (1996). *Criminal justice* (4th. ed.). Chicago: Brown and Benchmark.

Thompson, B. (1999). *The criminal law of Sierra Leone.* Lanham, NY: University Press of America.

Cases Cited

Abbate v. United States, 359 U.S. 187 (1959)
Bartkus v. Illinois, 355 U.S. 281 (1958)
Benton v. Maryland, 395 U.S. 784 (1969)
Carroll v. Carroll, 57 U.S. 275 (1853)
Duncan v. Louisiana, 391 U.S. 145 (1968)
Fiske v. Kansas, 274 U.S. 380 (1927)
Gideon v. Wainwright, 372 U.S. 355 (1963)
In re Oliver, 333 U.S. 257 (1948)
Klopfer v. North Carolina, 386 U.S. 213 (1967)
Malloy v. Hogan, 378 U.S. 1 (1964)
Pointer v. Texas, 388 U.S. 14 (1967)
Robinson v. California, 370 U.S. 660 (1962)
United States v. Lanza, 260 U.S. 377 (1922)
Washington v. Texas, 388 U.S. 14 (1967)
Wolf v. Colorado, 338 U.S. 25 (1949)

CHAPTER 2

The Criminal Justice Process

Focal Points

- Pretrial Process
    - Filing of a Complaint
    - Arrest
    - Booking
    - Initial Appearance Before a Magistrate
    - Setting of Bail
    - Preliminary Hearing
    - Prosecutorial Decision to Charge
    - Grand Jury Indictment and Information Differentiated
    - Arraignment
    - Plea by Defendant
- Trial Process
    - Selection of Jurors
    - Opening Statements
    - Presentation of Case for the Prosecution
    - Presentation of Case for the Defense
    - Rebuttal Evidence
    - Closing Arguments
    - Judge's Instructions to Jury
    - Jury Deliberations
    - Verdict
- Posttrial Process
    - Sentencing
    - Appeal
    - Habeas Corpus

INTRODUCTION

After crimes are committed, victims turn to the criminal justice system to dispense justice. Specifically, victims expect the system to punish perpetrators of crimes in order to restore the condition that existed prior to their victimization (Bohm & Haley, 2005; Fuller, 2006; Albanese, 2005; Fagin, 2005; Tobolowsky, 2000; Fattah, 1986). However, when such restoration is not possible, victims typically ask that justice be served—that is, they want the perpetrators to receive what is due to them according to the dictates of the law. But exactly *what* is due to offenders when they commit crimes? As mentioned earlier, America is a nation of laws—as demonstrated by the U.S. Constitution, state constitutions, state and local statutes, and other laws. In addition to these, each state has a model penal code that defines *crime*, so when offenses are committed, state prosecutors know what charges to bring against offenders (Fuller, 2006; Fagin, 2005).

While victims desire justice, the best that the criminal justice system can deliver in some cases is having the interest of justice served: occasionally the guilty go free because they plea-bargained successfully, or because charges were dismissed against them since police had operated outside of the scope of their authority, or because police could not collect enough evidence to bring a case to trial. The interest of justice is served because of the process that holds offenders accountable for their actions. When the process works, the victim and the offender will have their day in court.

This chapter focuses on the entire spectrum of the American criminal justice system as a mechanism of social control. In doing so, it examines the three major phases of the administration of criminal justice in the United States. Part One explains the pretrial phase. Part Two explains the trial phase. Part Three explains the posttrial phase. Specifically, the chapter covers such key steps in the process as the filing of a complaint, the arrest, the initial appearance, bail, the preliminary hearing, the grand jury indictment, the arraignment, the plea, jury selection, the presentation of the case for the prosecution, the presentation of the case for the defense, the judge's instructions to the jury, jury deliberations, the verdict, and sentencing.

PART ONE: PRETRIAL PROCESS

Filing of a Complaint

Usually, the criminal justice process in common law jurisdictions begins with what is technically called a *complaint*. In the United States, a complaint may be filed either by the complainant or by a police officer who has investigated and gathered information about the commission of a crime or who has actually witnessed its commission. The complaint provides the factual basis or substratum for issuing an arrest warrant. When the suspect has been arrested without a warrant, the complaint is prepared and filed at the defendant's initial appearance before the magistrate, usually by the arresting officer.

Arrest

American criminal procedure distinguishes between two kinds of arrest: an *arrest with a warrant* and an *arrest without a warrant* (also referred to as a "warrantless arrest"). An arrest is made *with* a warrant when a complaint has been presented to a magistrate for the issuance of a warrant based on probable cause that justifies its issue. In other words, the complainant has established probable cause that a crime was committed and that it was the accused who committed it. In contrast, a warrantless arrest is effected in two situations. First, an offense is committed in the presence of a police officer. Second, a citizen is authorized to make an arrest when a crime has allegedly been committed. In several states a *citation* and a *summons* are alternative modes of bringing a person before a court for a crime. A citation is an order issued by a court or a law-enforcement officer and directed to the person named in the citation to appear in court at a specified time to answer to the criminal charge or charges specified therein. A summons, as its name implies, is a writ directed to the sheriff or other appropriate court official requiring him or her to notify the person named therein to appear in court on the specified date to answer the complaint made or alleged in the summons. When the person against whom either legal process is filed fails to appear in court, an arrest warrant will then be issued.

Booking

The next step in the pretrial process is technically referred to as *booking*. It takes place at the police station, where an entry is made in the police register of arrests setting out the suspect's name, the time of arrest, and the offense allegedly committed. Before the actual booking, the suspect is searched for any weapons or any evidence connected with the alleged crime. His or her personal effects are then inventoried. If the offense is serious, the suspect may also be photographed and fingerprinted. Before or after booking, the suspect is usually placed in a *lockup* (a place of detention run by the police department in major cities) or in a jail (in smaller cities where no lockups are necessary). After the formal booking process, the suspect may be allowed to make a telephone call (usually to a lawyer or a family member) and even, in some jurisdictions, to post bail if the offense is minor. If bail is not posted, the suspect remains in detention until his or her initial appearance before a magistrate.

Initial Appearance Before a Magistrate

When, after the police investigation, the prosecution holds the opinion that there exists sufficient evidence which would lead a reasonable person to conclude that the suspect committed the alleged crime, the prosecutor decides to file formal charges. Usually, the suspect will then be taken before a magistrate for what is technically referred to as an *initial appearance*. The purpose of the initial appearance is to have the court determine whether there is probable cause to charge the suspect with the alleged crime. Therefore, due process dictates that a suspect who has been detained must be brought before a magistrate without unreasonable delay. Usually, the initial appearance is brief and involves the following: the magistrate verifies the name and other personal details of the suspect, informs the suspect of the formal charge against him or her, and informs the suspect of his or her constitutional rights—now succinctly known as the "Miranda warnings." These rights are usually given as follows:

You have a right to remain silent.

Anything you say can be used against you in a court of law.

You have the right to the presence of an attorney.

If you cannot afford an attorney, one will be appointed for you prior to questioning.

You have the right to terminate this interview at any time.

The suspect may also be informed of other rights granted by statute, which may vary from state to state. One is the right to a preliminary hearing. Another is the right to a speedy hearing. A third is the right not to incriminate oneself. Despite the variety of procedures among jurisdictions concerning the initial appearance, the process of appointing counsel begins at this stage. If a defendant has already retained counsel, his counsel may appear with him or her at the initial appearance. If the alleged offense is a misdemeanor, the defendant may choose to plea guilty at this stage. If the defendant does not plea guilty or such a plea is not permissible (when, for example, a defendant is charged with a felony), the defendant is informed of the next stage of the proceedings.

Setting of Bail

In legal theory, bail may be defined as "the security required by the court and given the accused to ensure that the accused appears before the proper court at a scheduled time and place to answer the charges brought against him or her" (del Carmen, 2001). In plain language, bail is the money or property posted by the defendant (or a surety) to guarantee that he or she will appear at trial. If the defendant does not appear, the money or property will be forfeited (Reid, 1996). From a societal perspective, whether the defendant is released or detained pending trial is critical because public confidence in the justice system is eroded when persons charged with serious crimes are released pending trial and during their period of release they commit other serious crimes. There is one problematic aspect about granting or denying bail in the context of the protection of the defendant's right to liberty: although, in legal theory, the purpose of granting bail is to ensure that the defendant appears for his trial, in practice, denying bail can be used as a form of preventive detention to preclude the release of a defendant who may otherwise be dangerous to society or whom the magistrate or judge may be averse to releasing. The concept of preventive detention received judicial endorsement by the United States Supreme Court in *United States v. Salemo*. In that case, the Court held as constitutional a provision of the Federal Bail Reform Act of 1984 empowering federal judges to deny pretrial release to persons charged with certain serious felonies when they find that no combination of release conditions can reasonably assure the community of safety from such individuals if they are granted bail.

The procedures for granting or denying bail vary among jurisdictions. Generally, however, a hearing is required, and the defendant is entitled to the benefit of counsel at the hearing. In the federal system, expedition is essential: the hearing must take place within twenty-four hours of the arrest. In some state jurisdictions there are statutory provisions specifying which types of offenses are bailable. In others, statute laws specify some of the factors to be considered by a magistrate in arriving at a bail decision. One final feature of the bail process worthy of mentioning is the statutory authority in a number of states empowering a judicial official to release an accused person on his or her own recognizance, that is, without monetary bail. Such a release is usually permitted when an accused person has strong ties in the community and seems quite likely to appear for trial. If the accused person "jumps bail," as it is usually put, a warrant will be issued for his or her arrest.

Preliminary Hearing

In the American criminal justice system, a person accused of a felony is usually entitled to a preliminary hearing or examination, which takes place at both federal and state levels. However, the hearing is not required in all states. Usually, it follows the initial appearance of the accused. In some jurisdictions, it is normally conducted between one and two weeks after the initial appearance. In order to guide the appropriate officials, the U.S. Supreme Court held in *Riverside v. McLaughlin* that detention of a suspect for forty-eight hours without a probable-cause hearing is presumably reasonable. Though some of the key features of a preliminary hearing resemble those of a trial, it differs significantly in its objective, which is primarily to ascertain whether there is probable cause to support the charges brought against the accused. If probable cause is not established, the charges are dismissed. The rationale behind a preliminary examination is to ensure that serious charges which are legally unsustainable owing to a lack of evidence are precluded from coming to trial—not only to protect individuals from harassment and possible injustice from the justice system but also to obviate the possible erosion of public confidence in the criminal justice process. Above all, a preliminary hearing eliminates the possibility of huge financial expenditures in prosecuting cases where, from an evidentiary perspective, there are no realistic prospects of convictions.

A probable-cause hearing also serves two other purposes, though of an ancillary nature. They are *discovery* and *binding over*. Discovery is a procedure whereby either party in a case is given the opportunity to obtain information in the possession of the other party necessary or helpful in developing that party's case. The targeted materials in the discovery process are those of an evidentiary nature or others specified by law. Some jurisdictions use a preliminary hearing to determine if the accused will be "bound over" for a grand jury hearing, which will be held only if there is a finding of probable cause. Other jurisdictions use a preliminary hearing to determine whether the accused should be "bound over" for trial instead of a grand jury hearing. At the preliminary hearing, the prosecution presents sufficient evidence to enable the magistrate to determine probable cause. Normally, the preliminary hearing is conducted in public, in accordance with both the First Amendment right to freedom of the press to cover such hearings and the right of the public to be informed of them. The hearing may be conducted in a closed session if the defendant shows that he or she cannot get a fair hearing without one. Defen-

dants may waive the preliminary hearing, but such a waiver must be a knowing and intelligent one (Reid, 1996).

A preliminary hearing is not required when (a) an indictment has been preferred against the defendant prior to the preliminary hearing, (b) the charge
is a misdemeanor, and (c) the accused has waived his or her right to a preliminary hearing. After the preliminary hearing, the magistrate may (a) "hold
defendant to answer," if he or she finds probable cause, (b) discharge the defendant if he or she does not find probable cause, or (c) reduce the charge
when a reduction is warranted by the findings of the hearing.

Prosecutorial Decision to Charge

The prosecutorial decision to charge a person believed to have committed
a crime is clearly an important, if not the most important, law-enforcement
power under the American criminal justice system. From a legal perspective,
not only is it immense and discretionary; it also has tremendous practical significance for the liberty of the individual. Indeed, U.S. Supreme Court Justice
Robert Jackson observed that "the prosecutor has more control over life, liberty and reputation than any person in America." In the context of exercising
this power, the gravity of the crime or crimes involved enhances the prosecutorial function in the decision to charge and correspondingly diminishes the
role of the police with whom the accused has made the initial contact in the
criminal justice system. In exercising this power, the prosecutor has the option of deciding not to prosecute. However, once the prosecutor decides to
prosecute, he or she must determine the appropriate charge or charges to be
preferred. A key factor in this determination is that many criminal statutes
overlap in the gravity of offenses and in the degrees of such gravity. Some offenses are defined according to the degree of gravity—for example, first-degree or second-degree murder. When the suspect has committed a number of
crimes, it is within the prosecutor's discretion to decide which charges to bring
in each case. There is no requirement that the suspect be charged with all the
alleged crimes. The public expects that this discretion will, as a rule, be exercised prudently and in the interests of justice. Hence, even after a suspect has
been charged, it is within the prosecutor's discretion to file a *nolle prosequi*
seeking a dismissal of the charges if the interests of justice so demand.

Grand Jury Indictment and Information Differentiated

In most common law jurisdictions, the prosecution of a serious crime begins with the filing of an accusatory document or instrument. In the United

States, the official accusation for a felony begins in one of two ways: one is a *grand jury indictment*; the other is what is technically known as an *information*.

In the federal judicial system, grand jury indictments are required for the prosecution of capital or otherwise infamous crimes, subject to the exceptions specified in the Fifth Amendment (del Carmen, 2001). At the state level, the grand jury is usually composed of no fewer than twenty-three persons, though some states allow grand juries composed of fewer members. Originally, the number of jurors required to reach a decision was a majority; today, however, some states require the vote of more than a majority (del Carmen, 1995). A grand jury proceeds to hear the evidence presented by the prosecutor and to determine whether there is probable cause to approve the indictment presented by the prosecutor. Hence, the proceeding begins with the submission by the prosecutor to the grand jury of the bill of indictment, which is, in essence, a written accusation of the crime. The prosecutor then presents the evidence in support of the accusation. The person named in the bill of indictment has no right to present evidence at the hearing, though he or she may, at the discretion of the jury, be permitted to do so. The person also has no right to counsel at the hearing, since the proceeding is not a trial but an investigation. The grand jury's deliberations are conducted in secret in order to safeguard an accused person from unfair and prejudicial publicity if the deliberations fail to establish probable cause.

After the deliberations, if the required number of jurors finds that the evidence presented by the prosecution establishes probable cause and warrants the approval of the bill of indictment, the jury will endorse it as a "true bill" of indictment. Thereafter, it will be filed with a court having jurisdiction to try the case. If the jury does not find probable cause, the bill of indictment will be disregarded and a "no bill" will be issued.

As already noted, an information is the alternative mode of charging a person believed to have committed a crime. This mode obtains if there is no requirement for a grand jury indictment. An information is required in some states, although there are variations in these states as to which felonious charges are to be preferred by a grand jury indictment. The procedure for preparing an information is relatively straightforward: Once the prosecutor has decided to bring specific charges against a suspect or an accused, formal charges must be filed. The law specifies where and how those charges are to be filed with the court. Accordingly, the prosecutor prepares an information— a document that names a specific person and specific charges against the person.

Arraignment

After either an indictment or an information has been filed in court, a hearing is scheduled before a judge or magistrate. This hearing is technically referred to as the *arraignment*. At the hearing, the defendant is identified, and the judge or magistrate reads the indictment or information to the defendant, informs the defendant of his or her constitutional rights, and asks the defendant how he or she pleads to the charge or charges. If the defendant pleads not guilty, a date is set for trial. If he or she pleads guilty, a date is set for formal sentencing. If the charges are less serious, the judge or magistrate sentences the defendant at the arraignment. In some jurisdictions, a defendant is permitted to enter a plea known as *nolo contendere* (literally meaning, "I do not contest it")—which, legally, is equivalent to a plea of guilty.

Plea by Defendant

In the legal sense, a *plea* is the answer by an accused person in court to the charges contained in either the indictment or the information. The American criminal justice system provides three options. The first is a plea of not guilty. The second is a plea of guilty. The third is a plea of nolo contendere, literally meaning, as just noted, "I do not contest it." In the jurisdictions of some states, there is a fourth option, namely, the plea of not guilty by reason of insanity. What, briefly, are the legal effects of each of these pleas? According to the law, by pleading not guilty, the accused is deemed to have put himself or herself on trial. The plea, therefore, places the entire case for the prosecution in issue. The prosecution has the burden of proving beyond a reasonable doubt each essential element of the offense. If the indictment charges more than one count and the accused pleads not guilty to some or all of the counts, a jury is then impaneled to decide the ultimate question of the accused's guilt or innocence. In some cases, however, the prosecution may opt not to proceed with the trial except for those counts to which the accused has pleaded guilty, if he or she has pleaded guilty. In effect, there are two main options available to the prosecution: (i) to offer no evidence regarding the count or counts in question or (ii) to request that the count or counts in question remain in the court's file and marked "not to be proceeded with unless by leave of the court."

Once a plea of not guilty is entered, the case is set for trial, as a rule, within two or three weeks in order to give the prosecution and defense adequate time to prepare their respective cases. When the defendant refuses to plead or the court is not certain of the defendant's plea, the court will enter a plea of not guilty. Between the filing of the plea of not guilty and the start of the trial, the defendant's attorney often files a number of written applications or motions with the court, notably a motion for the suppression of evidence allegedly illegally obtained. If the defendant pleads guilty, the records must show that the plea was voluntary and unequivocal and that it was made with the defendant's full understanding of its consequences. The case of *Boykin v. Alabama* set the legal precedent that a plea of guilty is invalid if the plea was not made with the defendant's full understanding of its consequences. When a defendant pleads guilty voluntarily and knowingly, he or she waives the constitutional rights (i) to trial by jury, (ii) to confront witnesses against him or her, and (iii) not to incriminate himself or herself.

An *inducement* does not necessarily invalidate a plea of guilty. For example, a plea of guilty can be held valid when it was made in the hope of avoiding the death penalty. A plea of guilty can also be held valid if there is some basis on the record supporting its validity even though the defendant continues to assert his or her innocence. When an accused pleads guilty to some counts and not guilty to others, the judge postpones sentencing for the counts to which the accused has pleaded guilty and proceeds with the trial for the counts to which the accused has pleaded not guilty.

By pleading nolo contendere, the defendant accepts the penalty without admitting guilt. The plea has the same effect as that of a plea of guilty. But one legal benefit accrues to the defendant: the plea will not be construed as an admission of guilt for imposing civil liability on the defendant in subsequent civil litigation arising out of the same facts and circumstances constituting the criminal charge or charges to which he has entered the plea. This type of plea is available in federal courts as well as in the courts of about half of the states—usually for minor or less serious offenses or at the discretion of the judge.

A plea of guilty may sometimes emerge from a *plea bargain* (or *plea negotiation*, as it is otherwise called). It is one of the most prominent but controversial facets of American criminal justice (Regoli & Hewitt, 1996). The preponderant view is that plea bargaining is an essential ingredient of the American criminal justice process since it reduces the number of cases that go to trial. Only a few jurisdictions—notably, Alaska and some counties in Louisiana, Texas, Iowa, Arizona, Michigan, and Oregon—have abolished it. Generally, pleas of guilty emerging from a plea bargain are the results of an arrangement among the prosecutor, the defense attorney, the accused, and the judge. By such a bargain, the accused pleads guilty to reduced charges in exchange for a lenient sentence—that is, a lighter sentence than the judge would normally give after conviction at trial (Anderson & Newman, 1998; Adler, Mueller, & Laufer, 2006).

Part Two: Trial Process

Selection of Jurors

In American criminal justice, the Sixth Amendment guarantees every person accused of crime the right to a trial by an impartial jury. To effect this right, a panel of jurors is assembled according to established procedures under state law. In twenty-three out of the fifty states, a jury list is compiled by utilizing a list of registered voters and a list of persons with driver's licenses. After compilation, the jury commissioner sends out letters of notification to prospective jurors with instructions to report at a specific time and place for possible jury duty (del Carmen, 2001). The laws in most states provide exemptions from jury service, mainly on grounds such as undue hardship, poor state of health, and status as officer of the court. Several states also exempt persons in certain occupations from jury duty, including doctors, dentists, members of the clergy, elected officials, police officers, firefighters, teachers, and sole proprietors of businesses (del Carmen, 2001; Reid, 1996). In legal theory, jurors must be representative of the community. This requirement has been the subject of subtle legal interpretations. In *Taylor v. Louisiana*, the U.S. Supreme Court observed:

> [J]uries must mirror the community and reflect the various distinct groups in the population. Defendants are not entitled to a jury of any particular composition, but the jury wheels, pools of names, panels, or venires [lists of persons summoned to serve in the jury pool for a particular case] from which juries are drawn must not systematically exclude distinctive groups in the community and thereby fail to be reasonably representative thereof.

The reality in jury representation is that both parties in the case strive to impanel jurors sympathetic to their case. This has led to the controversial practice of utilizing consultants in the jury-selection process for the trial of a particular case. Before the final selection is made for a particular trial, prospective jurors are usually questioned to ascertain whether there are grounds for challenging them as to partiality, bias, or prejudice. The procedure for such challenge is technically known as *voir dire*, meaning "to tell the truth."

Two main types of challenge are permissible: *challenge for cause* and *peremptory challenge*. In a challenge for cause, the challenging party raises an objection to the selection of a juror on such legal grounds as the following: the person is ineligible as a voter in the state or county where the court has jurisdiction; the person has been indicted for or convicted of a felony; the person is insane; the person is a prospective witness for either party in the matter; the person served in the grand jury that issued the indictment; the person has already formed an opinion on the case; the person is in favor of or biased against the accused. Peremptory challenges are objections to the selection of a juror for no stated reason. They are discretionary on the part of each side. The permissible number of such challenges varies from state to state and depends on the gravity of the alleged offense. Specifically, the number of peremptory challenges increases with the gravity of the offense. For example, each side may be allowed six peremptory challenges if the offense is a misdemeanor and twelve if the offense is a felony. There are no set numerical limits. For example, there may be as many as sixteen or twenty peremptory challenges in capital cases. One problematic aspect of such challenges is that they might be made on the grounds of race or gender. However, the U.S. Supreme Court has ruled that peremptory challenges predicated on race or gender are unconstitutional.

Opening Statements

In the American criminal justice system, after the jury has been impaneled for the trial of an indicted person, the prosecution begins with an opening statement. The opening statement is very important and should therefore be well-crafted and convincingly delivered. It is designed to provide the jury with an overview of the case. In outlining the case for the prosecution, the prosecuting attorney is expected to explain to the jury the charges as contained in the indictment and to indicate that the role of the judge is to rule on any points of law. The opening statement should also address the issue of the *burden of proof*: the prosecution must prove the case against the accused beyond a reasonable doubt. In addition, the statement should concisely summarize the facts upon which the prosecution relies and the evidence which the prosecution intends to present in support of the factual allegations. The statement should also outline the evidence which each of the main witnesses is expected to give. Not permissible in the prosecution's opening statement are opinions, conclusions, references to the character of the accused, argumentative issues, and references to matters concerning which evidence will not be proffered. Likewise, the prosecution's opening statement must not contain inflammatory or prejudicial comments. The defense, too, has the right to make an opening statement, immediately after the prosecution's. The same principles and restrictions governing the opening statement of the prosecution apply to that of the defense. The opening statement of the defense is designed to stimulate the jury to listen attentively to possible answers the defense may have to the charges made in the indictment.

A defense attorney may waive the right to make an opening statement until after the prosecution has presented its evidence. The tactical value of an opening statement by the defense immediately after the prosecution's opening statement is controversial. There are two main viewpoints on the issue. One is that the defense should not create the impression in the minds of the jury that it bears any burden of disproving the prosecution's case. The other is that a failure by the defense to make an opening statement may imply a weak or nonexistent defense. The better option, however, seems to be for the defense to make an opening statement after the entire evidence for the prosecution has been presented. As a matter of law, if the defense attorney intends to present evidence concerning the facts of the case other than, or in addition to, that of the defendant, he or she is not entitled to make an opening statement. If the only evidence for the defense is presented by the defendant and/or witnesses concerning the defendant's character, the defense attorney also has no right to make an opening statement.

Presentation of Case for the Prosecution

After the prosecution's opening statement, followed by the opening statement of the defense (if the defense exercises that option), the prosecution will present evidence to support the charge or charges in the indictment and specifically to prove the underlying factual allegations. In the federal jurisdiction and in all states' jurisdictions, most of the evidence takes the form of the testimony of witnesses—also known as *testimonial evidence*. Before testifying, witnesses are sworn to tell the truth. If they do not tell the truth, they may be prosecuted. Expert witnesses may also be called. In addition, it is permissible to present other types of evidence, notably documentary evidence and real or physical evidence. Regarding the prosecution's presentation of the evidence, the prosecutor begins by questioning his or her witness in a process referred to as *direct examination*. Next, the defense attorney *cross-examines* the witness or, with leave of the judge, reserves the right to do so later. If the defense attorney cross-examines the witness, the prosecutor may then question the witness in a process called *redirect examination*. If that happens, the defense may then question the witness again in a process called *recross-examination*.

Presentation of Case for the Defense

After the prosecution has closed its case, the defense presents its case. But before the defense presents its evidence, special issues may arise for the judge to determine. Two such issues are worthy of note. The first is that the defense attorney may exercise the legal option of filing a motion for acquittal of the defendant. Such a motion is usually designed to impact significantly the outcome of the trial. In essence, a motion for acquittal is a submission by the defense that the defendant is entitled to a judgment of acquittal on the grounds that the prosecution has failed to establish a prima facie case against him or her. A *prima facie* case is one established by sufficient evidence—that is, evidence which would justify conviction. It can be rebutted by evidence already adduced by the other side. In presenting a motion for acquittal, the defense attorney may contend that the prosecution has not provided any evidence to prove a necessary ingredient of the alleged crime—for example, malice aforethought in a charge of first-degree murder. By its very nature, this type of motion is an issue of law for the judge, not the jury, to rule upon. If the judge denies or overrules it, the defense has the option of presenting evidence in support of its case. However, the defense may repeat the motion at the close of the entire case—that is, when all the evidence has been presented. This is usually done during the defense attorney's closing address. The second legal option which the defense may exercise is to file a motion for a mistrial, alleging errors of law such as the introduction of inflammatory evidence or prejudicial remarks by the trial judge.

If none of these legal options succeed, the defense attorney presents the evidence for the defense in the same sequence as that for the prosecution. The defense attorney questions his or her witness by direct examination. Next, the prosecution cross-examines the witness. If he or she desires, the defense attorney then questions the witness by redirect examination. The prosecution then recross-examines the witness, if necessary. Of great importance in the trial process is the defendant's right not to testify, as guaranteed by the Fifth Amendment. If the defendant exercises his or her right not to testify, such an option cannot, as a matter of law, be the subject of adverse comment by either the prosecution or the judge. Historically, in early English common law, from which United States law is derived, persons accused of crime were not considered competent to testify because they were regarded as having a vested interest in the outcome of the case. In addition to other witnesses, the defense may call character witnesses—those who testify about the good character of the defendant. If this option is exercised, the prosecution is entitled to call witnesses to testify about the defendant's bad character.

Under American criminal law, the diverse defenses open to the defendant include infancy, intoxication, duress, involuntary action, entrapment, execution of public duty, legal impossibility, self-defense, defense of others, acting under authority of law, and insanity.

Rebuttal Evidence

After the defense has closed its case, the prosecution may present evidence in rebuttal. *Rebuttal evidence* is designed to attack the credibility of the testimonies of witnesses or of any evidence presented by the defense concerning facts that have been in dispute among witnesses at the trial. Essentially, rebuttal evidence is direct, additional, contrary evidence. It is invariably used by the prosecution if the accused relies on the defense of *alibi*, whereby a person charged with a crime contends that he or she was not at the crime scene when the crime was committed. In addition, if a witness denies having a reputation for untruthfulness, the witness's answer can be rebutted by direct, limited, contrary evidence. The defense, too, may exercise this option.

Closing Arguments

In most jurisdictions, after the presentation of evidence in rebuttal, each side presents a *closing argument*—first the prosecution and then the defense. The prosecution is then given the opportunity to put forward a final argument in rebuttal of the case of the defense. The rationale behind the prosecution's second opportunity to present a closing argument derives from the fundamental principle of American criminal law that the prosecution bears the burden of proving the case against the accused beyond a reasonable doubt. In terms of content, both the prosecution and the defense must avoid going beyond the evidence adduced in court and the possible reasonable inferences to be drawn from the evidence. The prosecution should also be guided by the norm "not to persecute but to prosecute," as was emphasized by the U.S. Supreme Court when defining the prosecutorial function in *Berger v. United States*. In that case, the Court observed that the prosecutor's role

> is not that [he] should win a case, but that justice shall be done.... [H]e may prosecute with earnestness and vigor; indeed, he should do so. But, while he may strike hard blows, he is not at liberty to strike foul ones.

If the prosecution exceeds permissible bounds in its closing argument, the issue of prejudicial errors may arise, justifying a declaration of a mistrial. Unless the defense decides to waive its right to a closing argument, the argument should outline its case on the basis of the evidence it has presented in refutation of the case for the prosecution. The defense attorney should also argue the defense upon which the defendant has relied to disprove the charge. Strategically, the closing argument for the defense is important for two reasons: first, its emphasis on the burden of proof—namely, that the prosecution must prove its case beyond a reasonable doubt in respect to all the ingredients of the alleged crime; and second, its legal submission that the prosecution has failed to discharge that burden. The closing argument of the defense should comprise forceful analyses of the deficiencies in the evidence adduced by the prosecution and of the inferences to be drawn from them from the defense perspective, as well as a persuasive presentation of any specific defenses put forward in support of its case.

Judge's Instructions to Jury

After all the preceding steps in the trial process have been completed, the judge submits the case to the jury, if the trial is one by judge and jury. If it is a trial by judge alone, the judge performs the role of judge and jury: he or she finds the facts and then applies the law to them. In a trial by judge and jury, the more usual situation, the submission of the case to the jury is a significant and complex judicial task. It is variously referred to as "charging," or "instructing," or "summing up the case to," the jury. In many jurisdictions, before the submission of the case to the jury, the judge is authorized, either at his or her own instance or on a motion by the defense, if the interests of justice so dictate, to direct the jury to return a verdict of not guilty in favor of the defendant. This is referred to as a *directed verdict*. By law, this extraordinary power can be exercised only if the entire evidence adduced in court is too weak and unconvincing to justify, beyond a reasonable doubt, that the defendant is guilty of the charges presented in the indictment. Thus, the law recognizes that, in such an eventuality, it would be a travesty or miscarriage of justice to permit the case to go to the jury.

The judge's instructions to the jury are a matter of much legal complexity. Some key aspects of this phase of the trial process are as follows. First, they generally involve guidance in matters of law. Second, in some jurisdictions, the judge is required to consider proposed instructions from the prosecution and the defense, though the final instructions given to the jury are entirely within the judge's discretion. Third, and most complex, the instructions must be crafted in simple and clear terms, and legal propositions must be explained in language intelligible to lay persons and others not trained in the law. If the instructions are too complicated and obscure, they may provide grounds for appeal. Fourth, in the federal system and in some states' jurisdictions, the judge is permitted to comment on the evidence when the instructions are given to the jury. The instructions to the jury must not fail to address two tenets of immense legal significance: (i) the presumption of innocence and (ii) the burden and standard of proof in a criminal case.

Jury Deliberations

After the case has been submitted to the jury, it retires from the courtroom to the jury room, where it will deliberate on its verdict. A foreperson, who is usually elected by the members of the panel, presides over the deliberations. The deliberations are conducted in secret and are confidential, even though it is not uncommon in the American criminal justice system for a juror, after the verdict, to discuss openly some aspect or aspects of the deliberations without judicial sanction. The practice in jurisdictions varies on the issue of whether members of the jury, during the trial or particularly during deliberations, should be sequestered. In some states, sequestration is often ordered in high-profile and sensational cases. Otherwise, the practice is usually a matter of judicial discretion. In addition to the issue of jury sequestration is the concept of jury nullification. Jury nullification occurs when the jury decides a case contrary to the weight of the evidence adduced in court. The common perception here is that the jury's verdict was based either on some strong reservation about the morality or wisdom of the specific law under which the defendant had been charged or on some law-enforcement impropriety in the investigation of the case. Two recent cases concerning which this phenomenon was alleged to have played a part in the juries' verdicts were the first Menendez brothers' trial and the O. J. Simpson trial. Jury nullification is problematic in that it is difficult to prove.

Verdict

After its deliberations the jury returns to the courtroom to announce its verdict. Technically, the *verdict* is the pronouncement of guilt or innocence. Usually, it is either "guilty" or "not guilty"; however, in some states, it may be "not guilty by reason of insanity." In both the federal and most state jurisdictions, the jury's vote for conviction or acquittal must be unanimous. If unanimity is lacking, the result is a "hung jury" and consequentially a mistrial. The judge determines the length of time a jury must deliberate before it is declared "hung." If a jury is dismissed on the grounds that it cannot reach a verdict, the law permits the defendant to be retried before another jury. (In this instance, the defendant is not subject to double jeopardy since, at law, no prior verdict was reached.) Regarding the requirement that a jury's verdict be unanimous, the U.S. Supreme Court has held that state laws requiring only majority verdicts are valid and constitutional. Related to the Court's endorsement of majority jury verdicts is the number of members comprising a jury. The Court has decided that a state law providing for a six-member jury in all criminal cases, except for those involving the death penalty, is valid but that the verdict must be unanimous. However, the Court did not approve a state law providing for a five-member jury on the grounds that it would inhibit effective jury discussion, impair the accuracy of fact-finding, and make it unlikely for the panel to reflect a fair and representative cross-section of the community. After the jury announces its verdict, the defendant is entitled to have the jury polled—that is, its members should indicate in open court how they voted individually or collectively.

PART THREE: POSTTRIAL PROCESS

Sentencing

After a guilty verdict comes a very important phase of the posttrial process—*sentencing*. Technically, sentencing in the American criminal justice system is the formal pronouncement of judgment by the court or the judge on the defendant after conviction in a criminal prosecution, imposing the punishment to be inflicted as prescribed by law. As a rule, sentencing occurs after the guilty verdict in order to allow time for presentencing reports to be submitted. Also, a sentence may involve a jury recommendation. (For example, Florida and Alabama allow jury inputs in death-penalty cases.) Five key facets of sentencing as a logical imperative of the United States criminal justice system are as follows. First, in most states, the sentencing power is exercised by the judge alone; in a few states, however, the convicted person is granted the right to elect whether to be sentenced by the judge or the jury after a jury trial. If the offense of which the accused has been convicted carries the death penalty, states normally grant a twelve-member jury the prerogative to impose the death penalty. Second, some states and the federal government require judges to follow legislative guidelines in sentencing. This requirement has severely restricted judicial discretion, a key feature of indeterminate sentencing. In other jurisdictions, sentencing remains discretionary in the absence of legislative guidelines. Third, in states where it is the prerogative of the jury to impose the sentence if the defendant so elects, juries usually decide simultaneously both the ultimate question of guilt or innocence and the particular sentence to be imposed in the event of a guilty verdict. Fourth, and by contrast, in some state jurisdictions these two major functions are performed during separate phases in what is technically called a *bifurcation procedure*. According to the procedure, after the accused has been found guilty, the evidence on the penalty to be imposed is presented to the jury by both the prosecution and the defense. The strict and technical rules of admissibility of evidence are considerably relaxed at this stage in order to allow evidence not adduced at trial to be considered—for example, the defendant's prior record or disposition to violence. The jury then deliberates on the evidence to determine an appropriate sentence.

Fifth, and finally, if there has not been a trial per se but the defendant has agreed to a plea bargain, the sentence is imposed by a judge. Generally, most judges adhere to the sentence agreed on by both the prosecutor and the defense attorney or by the accused himself. In legal theory, even though the judge has the prerogative to sentence, the actual sentence imposed is usually a product of several major influences. One is a state's legislative prescription concerning either a fixed or a maximum and minimum penalty for the crime in question. A second major influence is the provisions of the parole law in states permitting determinate sentencing. In those states, their parole boards' decisions are a factor in the length of a convicted person's term of imprisonment. A third major influence is that in practically all states the governor has the prerogative to pardon a convicted person or to commute a sentence.

Appeal

After the sentence has been imposed on a convicted person, there is usually a legally prescribed period of time within which he or she may file an *appeal* against both conviction and sentence to a court exercising appellate jurisdiction. According to constitutional law, there is no right of appeal. Instead, such a right is usually granted by statute law or rules of procedure. Essentially, in an appeal in a criminal case, the defendant or other party requests that a court with appellate jurisdiction rule on or review a decision that has been rendered by a trial court or administrative agency. Obviously, the appellate jurisdiction of a court is usually invoked by the party who was adversely affected by the trial court's or agency's decision. The appeal usually begins when the party which lost the case in the trial court—the "appellant"—files a notice of appeal, usually a month or two after the decision of the trial court. A few months later, the appellant files the trial court's record in the appellate court. The record, often bulky, consists of the papers filed in the trial court along with a transcript of the trial testimony. Next, the appellant and the opposing party, the "appellee," file briefs that set out their respective arguments and submissions. The briefs are usually followed by short oral presentations to the judges. Finally, the judges decide the case and issue a written opinion. In making the final disposition of the case, an appellate court may (i) affirm or uphold the decision of the lower court; (ii) modify the decision—that is, change it in part but not totally reverse it; (iii) reverse or set aside the decision; (iv) reverse the decision and remand it to the lower court for conducting a new trial to enter a proper judgment; or (v) remand all or part of the decision to the lower court without reversing it but with instructions for conducting a new trial as in (iv).

In some states, decisions in capital cases can be appealed directly from the trial court to the state supreme court, bypassing the states' courts of appeals. In legal theory, any criminal case in the United States may be appealed as far as the U.S. Supreme Court. However, in such an appeal the case must involve issues of federal or constitutional law. Practically, such a right may be constrained by the Court's own guideline for accepting petitions for appeals: its Rule of Four requires the votes of no fewer than four justices for a case to qualify for hearing and determination as to its merits (Wasby, 1989).

Habeas Corpus

One unique feature of the American criminal justice system is its utilization of the *writ of habeas corpus* as a postappellate device for challenging the legality of prolonged incarceration of convicted persons after the appellate process has been exhausted. When, for example, a prisoner has served a substantial portion of his or her term of imprisonment and has exhausted all the remedies available on appeal, the prisoner can file a writ of habeas corpus, alleging that his or her continuing incarceration is unconstitutional and therefore invalid. *Habeas corpus* is a Latin term which means "you have the body." Hence, in its technical, legal sense, habeas corpus is a writ directed to any person detaining or having custody of another person and commanding the former (usually a sheriff or a prison warden) to produce the body of the other person in court and to justify his or her detention and why it should be continued (Peltason, 1988). Originally, under English common law the writ of habeas corpus, designated a writ of high prerogative, was an order from the court to the warden of a prison having custody of the person concerning whom the writ was issued to produce the person in court at a specified time in order to justify the legality of the person's detention. As already noted, the contemporary value of habeas corpus as a legal device for challenging the lawfulness of restrictions on the right to liberty is more extensive—hence its well-known epithet "the Great Writ of Liberty."

Since there is a tendency to confuse the appeal process with that of the writ of habeas corpus, the chapter concludes with a comparison between the two. A criminal appeal by a convicted person is a direct attack upon the conviction and is therefore part of a criminal proceeding. The rationale behind the appeal is to reverse, or overturn, the conviction. It is filed only after the conviction—and must be filed within a certain period of time; otherwise the right to appeal is extinguished. Even though the accused has been convicted, he or she may be granted bail, pending appeal. The appeal is usually predicated on errors of law made during the course of a trial. All issues of appeal must emanate from the record of the original trial.

The writ of habeas corpus is a collateral attack: it is a separate case from the criminal conviction. It is a civil, not a criminal, proceeding. The writ is designed to secure the release of the applicant from prison. It may be filed at any time a person's liberty is restricted without legal justification by a public officer, either before or after conviction. At the time of filing, the applicant must be serving a term of imprisonment or must be detained illegally. The writ must be premised on the infringement of a constitutional right, usually during the trial. The right to file the writ is never extinguished. During the hearing, new testimony may be presented.

REFERENCES

Adler, F., Mueller, G., & Laufer, W. (2006). *Criminal justice: An introduction* (4th ed.). New York: McGraw-Hill.

Albanese, J. S. (2005). *Criminal justice* (3rd ed.). New York: Allyn and Bacon.

Anderson, P. R., & Newman, D. J. (1998). *Introduction to criminal justice* (5th ed.). New York: McGraw-Hill.

Bohm, R. M., & Haley, K. N. (2005). *Introduction to criminal justice* (4th ed.). New York: McGraw-Hill.

del Carmen, R. V. (1995). *Criminal procedure: Law and practice* (3rd ed.). Belmont, CA: Wadsworth.

del Carmen, R. V. (2001). *Criminal procedure: Law and practice* (5th ed.). Belmont, CA: West/Wadsworth.

Fagin, J. A. (2005). *Criminal justice.* New York: Allyn and Bacon.

Fattah, E. A. (1986). *From crime policy to victim policy: Reorienting the justice system.* New York: St. Martin's Press.

Fuller, J. R. (2006). *Criminal justice: Mainstream and crosscurrents.* Upper Saddle River, NJ: Prentice Hall.

Peltason, J. W. (1988). *Understanding the Constitution.* New York: Holt, Rinehart and Winston.

Regoli, R. M., & Hewitt, J. D. (1996). *Criminal justice.* Upper Saddle River, NJ: Prentice Hall.

Reid, S. (1996). *Criminal justice* (4th ed.). Chicago: Brown and Benchmark.

Tobolowsky, P. M. (2000). *Understanding victomology.* Cincinnati, OH: Anderson.

Wasby, S. L. (1989). *The Supreme Court in the federal judicial system* (3rd ed.). Chicago: Nelson-Hall.

Cases Cited

Ballew v. Georgia, 435 U.S. 223 (1978)

Berger v. United States, 295 U.S. 78 (1935)

Boykin v. Alabama, 395 U.S. 238 (1969)

Brady v. United States, 397 U.S. 742 (1970)

Burah v. Louisiana, 441 U.S. 130 (1979)

Johnson v. Louisiana, 406 U.S. 356 (1972)

Podaca v. Oregon, 406 U.S. 404 (1972)

Riverside v. McLaughlin, 111 S. Ct. 1601 (1991)

Taylor v. Louisiana, 419 U.S. 522 (1975)

United States v. Salemo, 481 U.S. 739.(1987)

Williams v. Florida, 399 U.S. 78 (1970)

CHAPTER 3

Probable Cause

Focal Points

- Definition of Probable Cause
- Who Determines Probable Cause?
- Factors Invalidating Arrests and Searches
- Sources of Probable Cause
- Measures Warranting Probable Cause
- Advantages of an Arrest Warrant
- How Is Probable Cause Established?
    General Guidelines
    The Officer's Own Knowledge of Facts and Circumstances
    Information Given by Informants
    Informant Involved in Criminal Activity
    Informant Not Involved in Criminal Activity
    Information Reinforced with Corroboration
- Probable Cause and Other Standards of Proof Differentiated
- Probable Cause and Reasonable Suspicion Differentiated
- Reviewability of Findings of Probable Cause and Reasonable Suspicion

Introduction

During the discovery procedure at a high-profile trial, a judge granted a public defender's motion to suppress key evidence over a prosecutor's objection on the grounds that the evidence was illegally obtained (pursuant to the Fourth Amendment) by a rookie police officer. With the motion, the charges were subsequently dropped and the suspect was set free, since the state's entire case was built upon the police officer's seizure of the evidence.

When the prosecutor later questioned the arresting officer and asked him about the legality of the arrest and the seizure of the evidence, the patrol officer conceded that the actions were not performed in textbook fashion since he acted only on a hunch and nothing more when he entered the suspect's apartment and discovered incriminating evidence. The prosecutor chastised the officer and reminded him of the use of probable cause when making searches-and-seizures. The prosecutor also lectured the officer on the exclusionary rule and the suppression of evidence.

The news that the case had been dismissed ignited public outcry and harsh criticism from some community residents who had always believed the police department typically targeted racial minorities for crime and relied on a lesser degree of certainty to arrest and bring them to justice. To the minority population, justice and vindication had finally occurred because a falsely accused suspect had been exonerated and set free. The minority group felt that in light of this news the general public would now believe its past claims of disparate treatment, such as racial profiling and selective law enforcement by police and other justice officials. For others, concerns mounted over the implications of what had been revealed during the discovery phase of the trial. Concerned citizens pondered whether police officers routinely made arrests and seized property on a hunch and operated in a manner outside the realm of the law. In fact, some citizens demanded that the courts consider reopening cases that had been previously tried in the jurisdiction.

This chapter deals with a key concept in American criminal justice—the concept of probable cause. The chapter is divided into ten parts. Part One provides several definitions of probable cause. Part Two discusses who determines probable cause. Part Three presents the factors which invalidate arrests and searches. Part Four explains the sources of probable cause. Part Five addresses measures warranting probable cause. Part Six presents the advantages of an arrest warrant. Part Seven discusses how probable cause is established. Part Eight differentiates between probable cause and other standards of proof. Part Nine discusses probable cause and reasonable suspicion. Part Ten addresses the question: Are the findings of probable cause and reasonable suspicion judicially reviewable?

Part One: Definition of Probable Cause

The concept of probable cause in American criminal justice originates from the Fourth Amendment to the United States Constitution, which requires that a warrant shall not be issued except upon a finding of probable cause. Legally, therefore, the validity of an arrest warrant or a search warrant is premised upon a finding of probable cause. Likewise, the validity, at law, of a warrantless arrest or a warrantless search-and-seizure depends upon a finding of probable cause. What, then, is probable cause? The concept has been variously defined. In one sense, probable cause is a reasonable ground to suspect that a person has committed or is committing a crime or that a place contains specific items connected with a crime (Black, 1999). In another sense, in the context of arrest warrants, it constitutes a set of facts and circumstances leading to the reasonable belief that the suspect has committed a crime (Reid, 1996). In the context of a search warrant, it constitutes a set of facts and circumstances leading to the reasonable belief that the items sought are located in a particular place (Reid, 1996). There have also been strictly judicial definitions of the term. The most frequently cited judicial definition is the one given by the United States Supreme Court. It defines probable cause as follows:

[It is] more than bare suspicion; it exists when the facts and circumstances within the officers' knowledge and of which they had reasonably trustworthy information are sufficient in themselves to warrant a man of reasonable caution in the belief that an offense has been or is being committed.

Commenting on this definition, Hall (1992) notes:

[It] measures probable cause by the test of reasonableness, a necessarily subjective standard that falls between mere suspicion and certainty. Facts and circumstances leading to an arrest or seizure must be sufficient to persuade a reasonable person that an illegal act has been or is being committed. Always the test involves the consideration of a particular suspicion and a specific set of facts. Hunches or generalized suspicions are not reasonable grounds for concluding that probable cause exists.

Despite the judicial trend toward defining probable cause by referring to the anthropomorphic conception of justice, namely, the "reasonable man" or the "man of reasonable caution" or the "ordinarily prudent and cautious man," the concept is not intended to include a person trained or skilled in the law. The reference is simply to the average man on the street who, under the same circumstances, would believe that the person being arrested had committed the offense in question or that the items to be seized would be found in a particular place. However, the approach of the courts has been to factor into the probable-cause equation the investigative experience of the police officer. Hence, in

United States v. Ortiz, the Court ruled that "officers are entitled to draw reasonable inferences from these facts in light of their knowledge of the area and their prior experience with aliens and smugglers." Concerning the definition of probable cause, one problematic issue is the constant tension between so-called legal definitions and so-called practical definitions. Examples have already been given of some of the legal definitions. One key practical definition of probable cause is that it exists when it is more likely than not that the suspect committed an offense or that the items sought can be found in a certain place (del Carmen, 2001). In this sense, the concept is considered equivalent to a certainty of 50 percent. Even in this practical sense, the perception is that most American courts would probably be satisfied with a certainty of less than 50 percent as constituting probable cause. The United States Supreme Court, in *Illinois v. Gates*, made the authoritative statement on this issue:

> Probable cause is a fluid concept—turning on the assessment of probabilities in particular factual contexts—not readily, or even used fully, reduced to a neat set of legal rules.... While an effort to fix some general, numerically precise degree of certainty corresponding to "probable cause" may not be helpful, it is clear that "only the probability, and not a prima facie showing of criminal activity, is the standard of probable cause."

Part Two: Who Determines Probable Cause?

After defining probable cause for understanding the law on the subject in American criminal procedure, the next logical inquiry is: Who determines probable cause? The question is uncomplicated. In an arrest executed as a result of a warrant, probable cause is predetermined by the magistrate issuing the warrant. Likewise, when a search-and-seizure is carried out in pursuance of a warrant, probable cause is predetermined by the magistrate issuing the warrant. However, when an arrest is effected without a warrant, probable cause is a matter of the judgment of the police officer effecting the arrest. The police officer's judgment also applies to probable cause when a search-and-seizure is effected without a warrant.

When probable cause is predetermined judicially, the finding of the judicial officer, usually a magistrate (as already noted), is reviewable by the trial court or an appellate court if the case has been appealed. In warrantless arrests and searches, to sustain the legality of the arrest or search, the police officer must establish probable cause with much care and caution. Specifically, he or she must refer to the supporting facts and circumstances that allegedly establish probable cause. For example, if a police officer arrests a person seen coming out of a building at midnight, the police officer must be able to articulate (if asked to do so later in court) what factors led him or her to make the arrest—such as the suspect's furtive behavior, the suspect's nervousness when being questioned, the suspect's possession of what appear to be stolen items, and the suspect's prior criminal record (del Carmen, 2001).

PART THREE: FACTORS INVALIDATING ARRESTS AND SEARCHES

If a police officer fails to show probable cause in support of a warrantless arrest or search-and-seizure, the legality of such an action is highly questionable and the action will therefore be declared invalid by a reviewing court. That probable cause is subsequently established will not make the action valid or legal. The standard judicial response to evidence gathered as a result of an illegal arrest or search is to exclude it on the grounds that it was illegally obtained. In short, the courts view such law-enforcement actions with great disfavor. In effect, probable cause, in the context of a warrantless arrest and a warrantless search-and-seizure, is a prerequisite for the validity or legality of such law-enforcement measures. For example, when a police officer arrests a suspicious-looking person and a body search reveals that the person had several vials of cocaine in his or her pocket, the evidence obtained cannot be used in court because there was no probable cause to make the arrest (del Carmen, 2001).

There are a few other observations of collateral interest on the concept of probable cause. First, the supporting affidavit for the issue of an arrest warrant must itself show probable cause because what is not embodied in the affidavit cannot legally be used to establish that standard of proof. Second, if there was no initial probable cause for a warrantless arrest or search-and-seizure, it is impermissible to utilize evidence that comes subsequently into the possession of the officer to establish probable cause. The new evidence cannot reverse the initial illegality. Third, the officer's presence during the commission of the crime is not a condition for establishing probable cause. Despite these observations, there has been a strong judicial aversion, on the part of the U.S. Supreme Court, to technical interpretations in the context of probable cause. Indeed, the Court has emphasized that, in establishing probable cause, technical interpretations of the sufficiency of complaints and supporting affidavits are to be avoided. Instead, the approach should be one of applying common sense.

Part Four: Sources of Probable Cause

What are the sources of probable cause? The question is important because probable cause is a core requirement of the legality of law-enforcement action in American criminal justice and therefore its sources must be regarded as fundamental. In essence, they provide the raw materials of the legal regime governing police investigation of crime as a continuing phenomenon in American society. The starting point in this inquiry is that the magistrate or other judicial officer empowered to determine the merit or otherwise of an application for the issue of an arrest warrant may consider any kind of evidence, irrespective of its source. The only requirement is that the information be trustworthy and reliable. In this regard, two points are worthy of note. First, hearsay evidence and prior criminal record, which are, as a rule, inadmissible in criminal proceedings, can properly form the basis of probable cause. Second, there is an infinite variety of sources from which probable cause may be derived, notably, police radio bulletins, tips from "good citizen" informers, victims' reports, anonymous tips, "habitual" informers who may have contact with the criminal underworld. In order to guide judicial officers, the U.S. Supreme Court has required a new test to determine what should be used in establishing probable cause. It is called the "totality of the circumstances" test. According to the requirement, in deciding whether to issue a search warrant, a judicial officer should evaluate all of the available information—that is, examine the "whole picture"—and then make a judgment, based on the circumstances outlined in the affidavit for a search warrant, whether or not there is a good probability that what the police are looking for will be found where they say it is located. This requirement is the existing law.

Part Five:
Measures Warranting Probable Cause

The measures warranting probable cause are fourfold. The first is an arrest warrant. The second is a warrantless arrest. The third is a search-and-seizure executed in pursuance of a warrant. The fourth is a warrantless search-and-seizure. In this context, an arrest, in the technical sense, is a form of seizure—but that of a person as distinct from that of property. Despite our analysis in the foregoing paragraphs, the notion of probable cause varies contextually in respect to an arrest and a search-and-seizure. In an arrest, the inquiry concerning the existence of probable cause focuses on whether an offense was committed and whether the suspect did, in fact, commit it. However, in a search-and-seizure, the inquiry focuses on whether the items of property targeted for seizure have a nexus with criminal activity and can be found in the place to be searched. Logically, therefore, what constitutes probable cause in an arrest may not amount to probable cause in a search-and-seizure.

On the basis of the foregoing analysis, three key points should be emphasized. First, for the issue of a warrant for an arrest or a search-and-seizure, there exists a judicial predetermination of probable cause based on the complaint and affidavit presented by the police officer. Second, in a warrantless arrest or warrantless search-and-seizure, the predetermination of probable cause is a matter for an on-the-spot decision by the police officer. Both determinations and findings are subject to judicial review. In an arrest or search-and-seizure without a warrant, the finding of probable cause may be reviewed during the trial, and if probable cause is found not to exist, the evidence obtained will not be admissible in court. Third, in the context of a judicial predetermination of probable cause, a challenge by the defendant is legally sustainable only upon a showing of clear and convincing evidence. In the context of a police officer's predetermination of probable cause, the judgment of the police officer is also judicially reviewable following a motion made before or during the trial for suppression of evidence. Such a judicial determination by the trial court is, in turn, reviewable at the appellate level.

Part Six: Advantages of an Arrest Warrant

What, then, are the advantages of securing an arrest warrant as the initial law-enforcement measure in combating crime? Briefly, the advantages are twofold. First, obtaining an arrest warrant both logically and legally implies that the issue of the arrest warrant was predicated upon a judicial finding of probable cause. Obviously, this presumption is rebuttable, meaning that its validity can be challenged. However, as already noted, only clear and convincing evidence can contradict such a presumption. The second advantage is that an arrest warrant can operate as a valid defense in any civil lawsuit for compensation brought by the suspect or accused, alleging violation of his or her constitutional rights by the police officer. According to the law, if the arrest was executed by the police officer in pursuance of a warrant of arrest, generally he bears no liability. However, if the warrant is seriously defective (for example, if it is unsigned), liability may ensue.

PART SEVEN: HOW IS PROBABLE CAUSE ESTABLISHED?

General Guidelines

There are three distinct modes of establishing probable cause as a preliminary step in determining criminal responsibility under the American criminal justice system. These are (i) the police officer's own knowledge of the particular facts and circumstances, (ii) information given by reliable third persons, i.e., informants, and (iii) information reinforced by corroboration. When a police officer applies for the issue of an arrest or search-and-seizure warrant, probable cause is established, generally in most jurisdictions through an affidavit, though in some states the affidavit may be supplemented by oral testimony. When the police officer acts without the authorization of a warrant, probable cause is established through oral testimony during the course of the trial. Occasionally, the officer may present oral testimony before the judge in addition to the affidavit. As to whether such additional evidence should be factored into the probable-cause equation, there are two main judicial approaches. It is factored by some courts, but not by others. In order to guide judicial and law-enforcement officials, the Court, in *United States v. Harris*, ruled that a suspect's reputation for criminal activity may be considered as probable cause. In the original case, the officer's affidavit submitted to the magistrate to support a request for a search warrant stated "that the suspect had a reputation with me for over four years in being a trafficker of nontaxpaid distilled spirits, and over this period I have received numerous information from all types of persons as to his activities." The affidavit further stated that another officer had located illicit whiskey in an abandoned house under the suspect's control and that an informant had purchased illegal whiskey from the suspect (del Carmen, 2001). The proposition of law to be deduced from that decision is that though a suspect's reputation for criminal activity is not by itself an indication of probable cause, when information of that nature is considered along with factual statements about the suspect's activities, their cumulative effect may well provide a valid basis for an inference of probable cause.

The Officer's Own Knowledge of Facts and Circumstances

What are the factors that a police officer may legitimately take into account in working out the probable-cause calculus? Mainly, they include the prior criminal record of the suspect, the suspect's flight from the scene of the crime when approached by the officer, admissions by the suspect, the presence of incriminatory evidence, the unusual time of day, the resemblance of the suspect to the description of the perpetrator, the failure by the suspect to answer questions satisfactorily, physical clues (for example, fingerprints, footprints linked to a particular person), the suspect's presence in a high-crime area, and the suspect's reputation for criminal activity (del Carmen, 2001). Any combination, or even one, of these factors may be sufficient to establish probable cause, depending upon the circumstances.

Information Given by Informants

We noted earlier in the chapter that probable cause may be established by information provided by an informant. An informant is one who gives information to law-enforcement officials about a crime or planned criminal activity (Reid, 1996). Otherwise referred to as an informer, such a person's identity remains undisclosed, and the information the person provides is also confidential (Black, 1990). In the context of this definition, a key distinction should be made between (i) an informant involved in criminal activity and (ii) an informant not involved in criminal activity.

Informant Involved in Criminal Activity

Regarding the determination of probable cause on the basis of information about a crime supplied to the police by an informant involved in criminality, the U.S. Supreme Court formulated a two-pronged test in the case *Aguilar v. Texas*. The major presumption, from the judicial perspective, is that such an informant must be treated as a person with low credibility. Hence, information derived from such a source must be examined with much circumspection. The test is based on reliability. It focuses, first, on the reliability of the informant and, second, on the reliability of the informant's information. The first part of the test, the reliability of the informant, requires that the affidavit set out the underlying circumstances by which a neutral and detached magistrate may find the informant to be reliable—for example, "Affiant [a person who makes or subscribes to an affidavit] receives information this morning from a trustworthy informant who has supplied information to the police during the past five years and whose information has proved reliable, resulting in numerous drug convictions."

The second part of the test, the reliability of the informant's information, requires that the affidavit set out the underlying circumstances by which a neutral and detached magistrate can find that the informant's information is in fact itself reliable and not the product of mere rumor or suspicion—for example, "My informant told me that he personally saw Henry Banks, a former convict, sell heroin worth $500 to a buyer named Skippy Smith, at ten o'clock last night in Bank's apartment, located at 1300 Shady Lane, Apartment 10, and that Banks has sold and continues to sell drugs from this location." The Court restated this two-pronged test in a subsequent case, *Spinelli v. United States*, where the evidence which formed the legal basis of the defendant's conviction was obtained by a warrant issued by a magistrate authorizing the search of Spinelli's apartment. To fully understand the nature and scope of the *Aguilar* test, it is necessary to highlight the four key factual allegations deposed to in the affidavit as the basis for the application for the search warrant. First, the FBI had kept watch of Spinelli's movements for five days during August 1965 and four times during that period had seen Spinelli crossing one of two bridges leading from Illinois into St. Louis, Missouri, between 11 a.m. and 12:25 p.m. Second, an FBI check with the telephone company had revealed that an apartment house near a parking lot that Spinelli frequented had two telephones listed under the name of Grace P. Hagan. Third, Spinelli had been known by federal law-enforcement agents and local police as a "bookmaker, an associate of bookmakers, a gambler and an associate of gamblers." Fourth, the FBI "had been informed by a confidential informant that William Spinelli [was] operating a handbook and accepting wagers and disseminating wagering information by means of the telephones" listed under the name of Grace P. Hagan.

As already noted, predicated upon the foregoing facts, Spinelli was convicted. He appealed his conviction, contending that the factual allegations deposed to in the affidavit did not, at law, establish probable cause to justify the issue of a search warrant. The Court found merit in his contention and overturned the conviction on clear and specific grounds. First, the first and second allegations reflected apparently innocent activity and data in that "Spinelli's travels to and from the apartment building and his entry into a particular apartment on one occasion could hardly be taken as bespeaking gambling activity; and there is nothing unusual about an apartment containing two separate telephones." The Court further noted that the main allegation was "a bald and illuminating assertion of suspicion that is entitled to no weight in appraising the magistrate's decision." In addition, the Court indicated that the fourth allegation must be measured against the two-pronged *Aguilar* test. Applying the test, the Court reached the conclusion that the affidavit failed to satisfy the two requirements of the test in that both the reliability of the informant and that of the informant's information had not been established.

One analytical difficulty which the courts faced in interpreting the two-pronged test was whether it was conjunctive or disjunctive. There was a clear

judicial misconception that the two parts of the test were separate and independent of each other (that is, disjunctive) until the matter was resolved by
the United States Supreme Court in *Illinois v. Gates.* In that case, the Court
criticized the separate and independent interpretation as too rigid and replaced
the *Aguilar* test by the "totality of the circumstances" test. Therefore, the existing law on establishing probable cause is that if a neutral and detached magistrate determines that, based on an informant's information and all other
available facts, there is probable cause to believe that an arrest or a search is
justified, the warrant may be issued. Regarding the informant's identity, a police officer has no constitutional duty to disclose the identity of an informant
either to the judicial officer from whom the warrant is sought or to the trial
judge. However, when the informant's identity is relevant to the ultimate question of guilt or innocence, the state is under a legal obligation to reveal his or
her identity. Failure to do so will result in the dismissal of the case.

Informant Not Involved in Criminal Activity

Regarding the determination of probable cause on the basis of information
about a crime supplied to the police by informants not engaged or involved
in criminal conduct, judicial officials recognize the primacy accorded to the
credibility of such informants. From this presumption of reliability flow two
judicial attitudes. First, information about a crime stemming from a victim
of a crime or a witness to a crime is presumed to be reliable. In fact, many
courts have ruled accordingly. For example, if a woman tells an officer that
she has personally witnessed a particular individual selling narcotics in the adjoining apartment, gives a detailed description of the alleged seller, and describes the way sales are made, there is probable cause to obtain a warrant or,
under exigent circumstances, to make a warrantless arrest. Second, there is a
presumption of reliability when the information about a crime is supplied by
another police officer. It is safe to assume that the courts will attach a very
high degree of reliability to such information, as is illustrated by the attitude
of the U. S. Supreme Court in *United States v. Ventresca*, where the Court
stated: "Observations of fellow officers of the government engaged in a common investigation are plainly a reliable basis for a warrant applied for by one
of their number."

Two decisions of the U. S. Supreme Court are instructive in putting these
judicial attitudes in their problematic context. The first is that of *Segro v.
United States.* In that case, the Court held that there was no probable cause to
search for illegally sold alcohol in a hotel where the affidavit claimed that a
purchase of beer had occurred more than three weeks earlier. The second is

that of *United States v. Leon*. In that case, an informant claimed that he had witnessed a drug sale at the suspect's residence approximately five months earlier and had observed a shoe box belonging to the suspect that contained a large amount of cash. The Court took the view that this was stale information that could not ground a finding of probable cause. However, a legally open question remains concerning how much time should elapse between an informant's observation and the issuing of a warrant before the doctrine of "stale" information fails to establish probable cause.

Information Reinforced with Corroboration

When a police officer discovers or perceives some deficiency in the information available to the officer or supplied to the officer by another officer, he or she is at liberty to conduct his or her own investigation in order to verify the available information and thus remedy the observed deficiency. This method of establishing probable cause is also referred to as information reinforced with corroboration. For example, suppose an informant tells a police officer that X is selling drugs and that sales are usually made at night in the apartment of X's girlfriend. That information alone would not establish probable cause. The case *Draper v. United States* illustrates this aspect of probable cause. In that case, a narcotics agent received information that the petitioner had gone to Chicago to bring three ounces of heroine back to Denver by train. The informant also gave a detailed description of Draper. Given this information, police officers set up surveillance of trains coming from Chicago on the mornings of September 8 and 9, the dates the informant had indicated. On seeing a man who fit the informant's description, the police moved in and made the arrest. Heroin and a syringe were seized in a search incidental to the arrest. During trial, Draper sought exclusion of the evidence, claiming that the information given to the police had failed to establish probable cause. Ultimately, the U.S. Supreme Court disagreed, stating that information received from an informant that is corroborated by an officer may be sufficient to establish probable cause for an arrest, even though some information was hearsay and would not otherwise have been admissible in a criminal trial.

PART EIGHT: PROBABLE CAUSE AND OTHER STANDARDS OF PROOF DIFFERENTIATED

In American criminal justice, there are other levels or standards of proof besides probable cause. Since it is not the focus of this chapter to examine their applications within the American criminal justice system, it is sufficient merely to highlight them and to differentiate them from probable cause.

The first is absolute certainty, which, in comparison with probable cause, imports a certainty of 100 percent. The second is guilt beyond a reasonable doubt, which, in comparison with probable cause, imports a certainty of 95 percent. The third is clear and convincing evidence, which, in comparison with probable cause, imports a certainty of 80 percent. The fourth is preponderance of the evidence, which, in comparison with probable cause, imports a certainty of more than 50 percent. The fifth is reasonable suspicion, which, in comparison with probable cause, imports a certainty of 30 percent. The sixth is suspicion, which, in comparison with probable cause, imports a certainty of not more than 10 percent. The last is reasonable doubt, which, in comparison with probable cause, imports a certainty of not more than 5 percent. It may be recalled that, as a standard of proof, the certainty attributed to probable cause is 50 percent.

PART NINE: PROBABLE CAUSE AND REASONABLE SUSPICION DIFFERENTIATED

One complex and problematic aspect of the themes discussed in this chapter is the frequent confusion that arises between the concept of probable cause and that of reasonable suspicion in the sphere of American criminal justice. Therefore, it is necessary to articulate, however briefly, the distinction between them. What is reasonable suspicion? According to Black (1990), reasonable suspicion is the "quantum of knowledge sufficient to induce an ordinarily prudent and cautious man under circumstances to believe criminality is at hand. It must be based on specific and articulable facts, which, taken together with rational inferences from those facts, reasonably warrants intrusion." In the recent case *Alabama v. White*, the United States Supreme Court defined reasonable suspicion in these terms:

> Reasonable suspicion is a less demanding standard than probable cause not only in the sense that reasonable suspicion can be established with information that is different in quality or content than that required to establish probable cause, but where in the sense that reasonable suspicion can arise from information that is less reliable than that required to show probable cause.

Regarding the existing state of the law, the clear judicial position, as reflected in relevant decisions of the United States Supreme Court, is that no precise articulation of the concepts of reasonable suspicion and probable cause is possible. The Court, in Ornelas et al. v. United States, left no doubt concerning this perspective of the law:

> They are commonsense, non-technical conceptions that deal with judicial and practical considerations of everyday life on which reasonable and prudent men, not legal technicians, act.... They are instead fluid concepts that take their substantive content from the particular contexts in which the standard being assessed is ... correlative to what must be proved.

PART TEN: REVIEWABILITY OF FINDINGS OF PROBABLE CAUSE AND REASONABLE SUSPICION

It is logical to conclude this chapter, from the perspective of American criminal procedures, by addressing the question of whether there is any judicial control, at the appellate level, of the findings of probable cause and reasonable suspicion. The inquiry can also be put this way: Are the findings of probable cause and reasonable suspicion final or appealable? Unequivocally, the answer is that they are not final. They are appealable. Concerning probable cause, it has already been noted that regardless of whether a predetermination was made by a judicial officer in respect to an arrest or a search-and-seizure or a predetermination was made by a police officer while executing a warrantless arrest or search, the finding of probable cause is judicially reviewable, at both the trial-court and appellate levels. The same applies to reasonable suspicion. Such a finding is reviewable at both trial and appellate levels. But the review is limited to clear errors of law and fact. In effect, the legal challenge must target questionable conclusions of fact and misleading conclusions of law. Unless the inferences of fact and law are palpably wrong, due weight must be given to the inferences drawn by the trial judge or the police officer.

REFERENCES

Black, H. C. (1990). Black's law dictionary with pronunciations (4th ed.). St. Paul, MN: West.

Black, H. C. (1999). Black's law dictionary with pronunciations (5th ed.). St. Paul, MN: West.

del Carmen, R. V. (2001). Criminal procedure: Law and practice (5th ed.). Belmont, CA: West/Wadsworth.

Hall, K. L. (1992). The Oxford companion to the Supreme Court of the United States New York: Oxford University Press.

Reid, S. T. (1996). Criminal justice. (4th ed.). Chicago: Brown and Benchmark.

Cases Cited

Aguilar v. Texas, 378 U.S. 108 (1964)

Alabama v. White, 496 U.S. 325 (1990)

Draper v. United States, 358 U.S. 307 (1959)

Illinois v. Gates, 462 U.S. 213 (1983)

Ornelas et al. v. United States, 517 U.S. 690 (1996)

Segro v. United States, 420 U.S. 377 (1975)

Spinelli v. United States, 393 U.S. 410 (1969)

United States v. Harris, 964 F.2d 1234 (1992)

United States v. Leon, 468 U.S. 897 (1984)

United States v. Ortiz, 422 U.S. 891 (1975)

United States v. Ventresca, 380 U.S. 102 (1965)

CHAPTER 4

The Exclusionary Rule

Focal Points

- The Fourth Amendment and the Exclusionary Rule
- Exclusionary Rule Defined
- The History of the Exclusionary Rule
- The Federal Court Level
- Fruit of the Poisonous Tree Doctrine
- Silver Platter Doctrine
- The State Court Level
- When Can the Exclusionary Rule Be Invoked?
- Exceptions to the Exclusionary Rule
    Good Faith
    Error Was Made by a Judge
    Error Was Made by a Court Employee
    Police Erroneously Believed That the Information Given to a Magistrate Was Correct
    Police Reasonably Believed That the Person Who Gave Authority to Enter Premises Had Authority to Give Consent
    Police Action Was Based on a Law That Was Later Declared Invalid or Unconstitutional
    Inevitable Discovery
    Purged Taint
    Independent Source
    Plain View Doctrine
    Searches Incidental to a Lawful Arrest
    Searches with Consent
- Advantages and Disadvantages of the Exclusionary Rule
    Advantages
    Disadvantages

- Alternatives to the Exclusionary Rule
- The Erosion of the Fourth Amendment and the Future of the Exclusionary Rule
- Some Pertinent Cases

Introduction

When crimes are committed, offenders often perpetrate them in a manner likely to ensure that they are not apprehended and brought to justice. In fact, they use the most efficient and effective methods of which they are capable to succeed in committing their crime (Messner & Rosenfeld, 2001). Sometimes, however, in their quest to bring criminal suspects to justice, police officers may purposefully or inadvertently circumvent the law on searches, seizures, and arrests. When such behavior occurs, police officers operate in a manner above the law or beyond the scope of their authority (Gaines, Kaune, & Miller, 2001; Schmalleger, 2001). The general rule in these circumstances is that police officers are not allowed to benefit from their misconduct. Therefore, courts have decided that any illegally obtained evidence collected by police will not be admitted to gain a criminal conviction. The message that the courts have routinely sent to police has been crystal clear: police are not above the law. Over the years, courts have ruled that police must work to ensure suspects' constitutional rights and civil liberties and that they must be careful not to infringe upon them. Because of these rulings, police officers quickly learn that they are held to standards of behavior defined by the U.S. Constitution, state constitutions, and statutes (Klotter, 2002). They must function within guidelines prescribed by law.

Chapter 4 is divided into seven parts. Part One presents the Fourth Amendment and the exclusionary rule (ER). Part Two provides a definition of the ER. Part Three gives a brief history of the ER and includes salient cases to show how it emerged—first on the federal-court level and then on the state-court level. Part Four provides exceptions to the ER and discusses several cases decided by the United States Supreme Court. Part Five lists some advantages and disadvantages of the ER. Because of the controversy over the exclusionary rule, Part Six presents alternatives to the rule and what the future holds for the ER. Part Seven closes the chapter with a summary of cases pertinent to the development of the ER.

Part One: The Fourth Amendment and the Exclusionary Rule

The Fourth Amendment to the Constitution states:

> The right of the people to be secure in their persons, houses, papers, and effects, against unreasonable searches and seizures, shall not be violated, and no Warrants shall issue but upon probable cause, supported by oath or affirmation, and particularly describing the place to be searched, and the persons or things to be seized.

The Fourth Amendment does not state that police officers are not allowed to search suspects and seize articles of evidence. The Amendment prohibits only those searches and seizures that are deemed unreasonable. In other words, it protects people from unreasonable searches and seizures in places where they have a reasonable expectation of privacy. At the same time, it allows warrants to be issued only upon a finding of probable cause. The United States Supreme Court has ruled that reasonableness within the meaning of the Fourth Amendment is determined by probable cause. Probable cause must first be established by the police officer at the crime scene and later supported by a neutral and detached magistrate. After his or her own determination of probable cause, the magistrate then issues a warrant for a search or an arrest to be made (Wallace & Roberson, 2001). For example, if a police officer completes and submits an affidavit to a magistrate to procure a warrant, it may be issued if the magistrate finds probable cause in the affidavit. If the magistrate does not, he or she will not grant the officer a warrant to effect a search or seizure. Establishing probable cause is a constitutional safeguard to protect citizens from police harassment.

Exclusionary Rule

The exclusionary rule is not based on the Constitution but is made by judges and designed by the courts to control police misconduct and to deter violations of constitutional rights (Moskovitz, 2000). The Constitution does not offer a remedy for what courts should do when an unreasonable search-and-seizure has occurred. However, since courts proactively refuse to accept evidence obtained illegally, they are relieved from participating in such illegal conduct. The ER goes hand in hand with the Fourth Amendment prohibiting unreasonable searches and seizures. In fact, the rule is used to enforce the

Amendment. The rule requires that police function within the parameters of the law or risk having crime-scene evidence suppressed by a court having jurisdiction over the case (Scheb & Scheb, 1999; Friedland, 1994). The ER does not apply to private individuals who violate the law (*Burdeau v. McDowell*). It does, however, apply to private citizens who act under the color of the law (*People v. Zelinski*). The ER affects the day-to-day operations of law enforcement; hence, every officer should be intimately familiar with the rule: the success of a criminal prosecution depends on it. It is a controversial rule in criminal procedures that has created many debates among criminal-justice practitioners as well as scholars. Indeed, since the ER is not based on the Constitution but is made by judges, it can be overturned or invalidated by the U.S. Supreme Court.

Part Two: Exclusionary Rule Defined

The *exclusionary rule* states that any evidence (physical or testimonial) obtained by the government in violation of the Fourth Amendment's guarantee against unreasonable searches and seizures is not admissible in a criminal prosecution to prove a suspect's guilt. Anderson and Newman (1993) define the ER as the prohibition of improperly obtained evidence, whether from an improper search or an improper interrogation. del Carmen (2001) contends that items excluded under the rule include contraband, fruits of the crime (stolen goods), instruments of the crime (weapons and tools), and mere evidence (shoes, clothes, etc). While the ER applies only to the Fourth Amendment, its reach may extend to other amendments. For example, the Fifth Amendment protects criminal suspects against self-incrimination, as established in *Miranda v. Arizona*. As a result, before suspects can be questioned by police officers, they must be warned of their right to remain silent unless they choose to waive that right. If they choose to give up that right, they must do so voluntarily and intelligently. They must understand the consequences of such a waiver. Experts argue that the Fourth Amendment extends to the Fifth and Sixth Amendments. For example, the courts may suppress testimonial evidence taken from suspect X if he or she was interrogated before having been Mirandized. The courts will view the behavior by officer Y as a violation of X's constitutional right. The Sixth Amendment affords criminal defendants the right to counsel to represent their legal interests, as established in *Gideon v. Wainwright*. If officers apprehend suspect X, fail to provide the suspect with an attorney, and interrogate X until he or she confesses to the crime, the testimony will not be admitted in court because it constitutes an illegal seizure within the meaning of the Fourth Amendment and will therefore be suppressed under the ER.

Part Three: The History of the Exclusionary Rule

The Federal Court Level

Prior to 1914, federal and state law-enforcement officers engaged in questionable practices in collecting evidence to build cases against criminal suspects. In fact, some experts argue that during this period such behavior was a standing practice since no one enforced the requirements of the Constitution for gathering evidence. It was common for officers to conduct searches without a warrant (Schmalleger, 2001). However, in *Weeks v. United States* such practices were challenged on the federal level. In this case, Freemont Weeks was suspected of using U.S. mail to sell lottery tickets, a federal crime. Without a search warrant, federal officers entered Weeks's home and confiscated articles of incriminating evidence, as well as many of his personal possessions, including clothes, papers, books, and even candy. Before trial, Weeks's attorney demanded that the items be returned and suppressed from being entered in the criminal trial because they had been illegally obtained, in violation of the Fourth Amendment. A judge agreed with the defense in part and ordered that some items be returned. However, Weeks was convicted in a federal court on the basis of the items that were admissible. Weeks was subsequently sentenced to prison. On appeal, the U.S. Supreme Court granted certiorari and heard the case. The issue before the Court was whether federal agents violated Weeks's Fourth Amendment right by entering his home without a search warrant. The Court agreed, ruling that if some items were illegally seized, the others were also improperly seized. The Court overturned Weeks's conviction.

The importance of *Weeks* is that it formed the basis for the ER. As a result, if federal agents obtained evidence in an illegal manner, it cannot be used in a federal trial to convict the criminally accused. The rule acts as a mechanism to control the behavior of officers who, intentionally or unintentionally, violate the rights of criminal suspects by not securing warrants to make searches or arrests. However, the Court's ruling in *Weeks* applied only to federal officers, since it was federal agents who were involved in the illegal seizure. Therefore, questionable practices continued unabated on the state level since *Weeks* was a federal case.

Another federal case where the ER was applied is *Silverthorne Lumber Co. v. United States*. In 1918, Frederick Silverthorne and his sons operated a lumber company and were accused of avoiding payment of federal taxes. When asked to turn over the company's books to federal investigators, the Silverthornes refused, asserting their Fifth Amendment right to avoid self-incrimination. Shortly afterward, federal agents, without a search warrant, went to the lumber company and took possession of the books. The attorney for the lumber company argued in court that the books be returned on the grounds that they were the products of an illegal seizure, in violation of the Fourth Amendment and *Weeks*. A federal judge agreed and ordered that the books be returned to the Silverthornes. At trial, the Silverthornes thought that they would be acquitted since the prosecution no longer had the incriminating evidence to convict them. However, in a surprising move, the prosecution introduced photographic copies of the incriminating evidence. The Silverthornes were convicted in federal court and appealed. The U.S. Supreme Court granted certiorari and heard the case. The Court ruled that just as illegally seized evidence cannot be used in a trial, neither can evidence be used which derives from an illegal seizure. The Silverthornes' conviction was overturned and a new legal principle emerged called the *fruit of the poisonous tree* doctrine. Essentially, the doctrine holds that any illegally acquired evidence cannot be used to obtain a criminal conviction. del Carmen (2001) argues that the doctrine provides that once the primary evidence is shown to have been unlawfully obtained, any secondary or derivative evidence from it is also inadmissible in court. For example, if officer X illegally enters the home of suspect Y without a warrant and finds stolen property, the unlawful entry is the poisonous tree and the stolen items are the fruit. If officer X tries to use the items in court, they will not be admitted because they are tainted by officer X's illegal behavior. The fruit of the poisonous tree doctrine has far-reaching implications on law-enforcement practices.

Another concept that emerged from *Weeks* is the *silver platter* doctrine. As stated earlier, when *Weeks* was decided, it prohibited only federal agents from engaging in illegal searches and seizures. The ruling did not apply to state law-enforcement officers. As a result, state officers assisted federal agents by illegally obtaining evidence against criminal suspects and turning it over to the agents. This practice was appropriately referred to as the silver platter doctrine. When the evidence was challenged in federal court, federal agents argued that they did not collect the evidence themselves but that the evidence was given to them by state officers. For example, officer X (a federal agent) has several friends who are state officers. X indicates to the friends that he or she has a hunch where stolen weapons used in a bank robbery are being hidden. So without a search warrant, X's friends (the state officers) retrieve the weapons and give them to officer X, who uses them to gain a criminal conviction in federal court. The evidence is admissible since *Weeks* did not apply to state officers. This practice survived until the U.S. Supreme Court ruled it unconstitutional in *Elkins v. United States*. In *Elkins*, the Court argued that the Fourth Amendment prohibited the use of illegally obtained evidence in federal prosecutions, whether obtained by federal or state officers. This ruling signaled the end of the silver platter doctrine. Yet the ER did not affect law-enforcement practices on the state level or in state courts—as was indicated in *Wolf v. Colorado*. In *Wolf*, the U.S. Supreme Court held that state courts were not constitutionally required to exclude illegally obtained evidence. However, in *Rochin v. California*, the Court argued that when searches are "shocking" to the conscience, the evidence seized must be excluded under the due process clause. In *Rochin*, officers witnessed Rochin ingest drugs and therefore had his stomach pumped to retrieve the evidence to use against him. Because *Rochin* applied only to cases that were deemed shocking, no uniform standard existed. There was no consistent standard to determine when illegal searches warranted exclusion. Consequently, the ER was left to the discretion of the states: some followed *Rochin* and others did not. *Rochin* essentially amounted to a small modification of *Wolf*. However, *Wolf* was soon overturned by *Mapp*. In leaving behind *Wolf* and adopting *Mapp*, the U.S. Supreme Court sought to control police conduct and offer greater Fourth Amendment protection at the state level (del Carmen, 2001).

The State Court Level

Though *Weeks* was decided in 1914, the ER did not apply to the state level until 1961—in the case of *Mapp v. Ohio*. In *Mapp*, Dolree Mapp was suspected of harboring a fugitive wanted in connection with several bombings. When police arrived at Mapp's house and announced their purpose, she refused to let them enter. She asked if they had a warrant and they replied no. They said that they could leave and return with one and she told them to do so. They left and returned with what they said was a warrant. She opened her door and grabbed what appeared to be a warrant and placed it in her bra. They retrieved the paper from her and engaged in an extensive search of the property. During the search, they discovered pornographic materials, possession of which was a violation of Ohio law. At trial, the prosecution was asked to produce the warrant, but it could not do so. Nevertheless, Mapp was subsequently convicted of possession of pornographic materials. Mapp appealed to the U.S. Supreme Court. The Court granted certiorari and heard the case.

It argued that both state and federal law-enforcement officers must be held to the same standard. After *Mapp*, the exclusionary rule applied to the state level.

When Can the Exclusionary Rule Be Invoked?

In general, the ER is invoked during the discovery period of the preliminary hearing in both federal and state courts. At this time, the defense usually makes motions to suppress evidence believed to have been collected in violation of the Fourth Amendment. If the defense is successful, the judge will exclude the items because they are protected. If the defense is not successful, the evidence will be admitted into trial. Nevertheless, the defense may reenter the motion later. If denied again, the defense may appeal the decision of the court if the defendant is found guilty by a judge or a jury. In these scenarios, if the police had a search warrant at the time of the search, del Carmen (1991) argues, probable cause is presumed to exist. Therefore, the burden of proof is on the defense to establish with clear and convincing evidence that probable cause did not exist at the time the warrant was issued. If searches are made without a warrant, the state must show either that probable cause did exist or that the search was an exception to the warrant.

The ER is invoked only by the person whose Fourth Amendment rights have been violated. The question emerges: Who or what is protected under the amendment? For example, does protection extend to people or places? The rule extends only to those whose reasonable expectation of privacy has been breached by law-enforcement officers. In *Minnesota v. Olson*, the U.S. Supreme Court extended protection against warrantless searches to overnight guests residing in the home of another. The Court argued that overnight guests have a reasonable expectation of privacy. The capacity to claim the protection of the Fourth Amendment, said the Court, depends upon whether the person who makes that claim has a legitimate expectation of privacy in the place to be searched. However, in *Minnesota v. Carter*, the Court ruled that for a defendant to be entitled to Fourth Amendment protection, it must be demonstrated that he or she has an expectation of privacy in the place searched and that the expectation is reasonable. In *Carter*, the Court argued that the defendants, who were on a short-term visit and who, together with the lessee, "used the apartment for a business purpose to package drugs," had no legitimate expectation of privacy in the apartment. Therefore, when a police officer looked in an apartment window through a gap in the closed blinds and observed the defendants and the apartment lessee bagging cocaine, the officer did not violate the defendants' legitimate expectation of privacy. The Court also added that the extent to which the Amendment protects people depends on where those people are.

Part Four: Exceptions to the Exclusionary Rule

Prior to the 1960s, the U.S. Supreme Court rarely intervened in the operations of the criminal justice system. However, under the leadership of Chief Justice Earl Warren, the hands-off approach changed. The "Warren court" (1953–1969), as it was referred to, advocated civil rights and civil liberties of criminal defendants, sometimes to the detriment of law-enforcement officers. In fact, the Court was criticized for being too judicially active and for engaging in social engineering. The Court decided many landmark cases that favored the personal rights and freedoms of citizens rather than promoting the legitimate concerns of police officers. Some of the cases include *Mapp v. Ohio*, *Miranda v. Arizona*, *Escobedo v. Illinois*, and *Gideon v. Wainwright*. These cases changed the operations of the criminal justice system because most of the cases marked the first time that the Court prescribed procedures to be followed in encounters police have with citizens. However, as the composition of the Court changed from liberal to conservative in the Burger and Rehnquist courts (from 1970 to the present), many cases previously heard by the Court were interpreted differently. For example, while the Court has not eliminated the ER, modifications have been made to the rule. Since its inception, the judiciary has never agreed on the ER. The rule has been debated on the grounds of whether the courts had the right to create this remedy. More specifically, it has been hotly contested whether the rule really serves the intended purpose of protecting the constitutional right to privacy and whether it actually deters police misconduct. Because of the controversy surrounding the rule, instead of throwing it out "lock, stock, and barrel," the Court has made exceptions to the rule. These modifications include good faith; inevitable discovery; purged taint; independent source; the plain view doctrine; searches incidental to a lawful arrest; and consent. Supporters of these exceptions argue that they were designed to promote public order by not allowing suspects to escape criminal prosecution based on a technicality. Critics charge that such modifications and exceptions to the ER have only served to erode the Fourth Amendment. Supporters counter that they have rewarded police officers facing the challenge of bringing offenders to justice.

Good Faith

The *good faith* exception allows the admissibility of evidence obtained by police when there was a mistake made at the time the evidence was seized. The exception is contingent upon whether the officer intentionally made the error.

Put differently, police officers can argue the good faith exception to prevent evidence from being suppressed during the discovery period of the preliminary hearing if they can establish that they were honest, reasonable, and well-intentioned at the time the evidence was collected. According to del Carmen (2001), the exception may apply when (1) an error was made by a judge; (2) an error was made by a court employee; (3) police erroneously believed that the information given to a magistrate was correct; (4) police reasonably believed that the person who gave authority to enter premises had authority to give consent; and (5) police action was based on a law that was later declared invalid or unconstitutional.

Error Was Made by a Judge

In *Massachusetts v. Sheppard*, the suspect was wanted on suspicion of murder. Police went to Sheppard's home and searched for items described in a warrant (the clothing of the victim and a blunt instrument). Sheppard was convicted of first-degree murder after evidence was found. On appeal, the defense argued that the warrant was invalid because it had been altered from a warrant specifically drawn for a search of a controlled substance to a general search warrant. Detectives had told the magistrate that the affidavit needed additional work. Nevertheless, the magistrate found probable cause and issued the warrant. He also told the detectives that he would make changes to the document. The U.S. Supreme Court ruled that evidence obtained by a search is admissible in court when the officer conducting the search objectively and reasonably relied on a search warrant subsequently declared invalid. In this case, the Court reasoned that the items were admissible and should not have been excluded from trial because the officer had acted in good faith. The Court also noted that the ER was in place to prevent police misconduct and not to punish judges who committed errors. Similarly, in *United States v. Leon*, police officers completed an affidavit, based on the testimony of an informant, in which they asked to search the defendant's car and three residences. They had several deputy prosecutors and a judge review the affidavit for a probable-cause determination. The judge agreed that there was probable cause. But the defense objected to the warrant, calling it invalid since the reliability of the informant had not been established. The trial court agreed and suppressed the evidence, having found that no probable cause existed and that the government's information was stale. The U.S. Supreme Court decided that the Fourth Amendment's ER should not be applied to bar the prosecution from using evidence obtained by officers acting in reasonable reliance on a search warrant that was issued by a detached and neutral magistrate but that was ultimately found invalid because it lacked probable cause. The Court thus reversed the trial court's ruling, holding 1) that there were objectively reasonable grounds for the police officers' mistaken belief that the warrants had authorized the search and 2) that the evidence was therefore admissible because the judge, not the police, had made the mistake and the ER does not apply to judges.

Error Was Made by a Court Employee

In *Arizona v. Evans*, Evans was stopped for a minor traffic violation. It was discovered he had an outstanding arrest warrant. He was asked to step out of his car, and a search by police revealed he was in possession of marijuana. He was subsequently arrested and convicted. Evans moved to suppress the evidence under the ER, contending that the warrant had been dismissed seventeen days before the arrest but had not been entered into the computer because of a court employee's error. In *Evans*, the U.S. Supreme Court ruled that the ER does not require suppression of evidence seized in violation of the Fourth Amendment when the erroneous information resulted from clerical errors of court employees. Evans had no evidence that court employees were inclined to ignore or subvert the Fourth Amendment or that lawlessness by court employees required the extreme court action of excluding the evidence.

Police Erroneously Believed That the Information Given to a Magistrate Was Correct

In *Maryland v. Garrison*, police obtained a warrant to search one location but mistakenly entered the wrong apartment, found drugs, and arrested Garrison. Garrison asked for suppression of the evidence under the ER, citing that no warrant existed for police to make a search of his apartment. The U.S. Supreme Court held that the validity of a warrant must be judged in light of the information available to officers when the warrant is sought.

Police Reasonably Believed That the Person Who Gave Authority to Enter Premises Had Authority to Give Consent

In *Illinois v. Rodriguez*, police entered the home of Fischer to inquire about a potential suspect. Fischer gave police permission to enter. He unlocked the door with a key. Upon entrance, officers observed a man in possession of drugs and quickly arrested him. Police arrested and charged Rodriguez with possession of illegal drugs, citing that they were in plain view when police entered the apartment. Rodriguez sought suppression of evidence under the exclusionary rule since police lacked a warrant to conduct a search. In this case, the U.S. Supreme Court ruled that consent given by someone who the police reasonably and honestly believed had authority to give consent is valid. Therefore, any incriminating evidence seized is admissible in court to gain a criminal conviction.

Police Action Was Based on a Law That Was Later Declared Invalid or Unconstitutional

In *Illinois v. Krull*, police arrested Krull without a warrant at a garage shop and found stolen vehicles in his possession. At the time of the arrest, a warrantless entry was valid under Illinois state law. However, the next day, a federal court declared the statute unconstitutional in violation of the Fourth Amendment. Krull moved for suppression of the evidence under the ER, citing that police officers lacked a warrant. The U.S. Supreme Court held that evidence obtained by the police in accordance with a state law later declared unconstitutional is admissible in court as part of the good faith exception to the exclusionary rule.

Inevitable Discovery

The *inevitable discovery* exception can be used when police officers can show that they would have inevitably discovered the object of their search by lawful means, regardless of their illegal behavior. Consequently, no warrant is needed to justify the search or intrusion. del Carmen (1991) contends that the inevitable discovery exception relates to the fruit of the poisonous tree doctrine. It is typically restricted to cases where the evidence is a body or an abandoned weapon. This exception was first used in *Nix v. Williams*. In *Nix*, evidence discovered by police officers as they were interrogating a suspect who had been told by his attorney not to speak to officers was considered admissible. While Nix argued that the police violated his Fifth and Sixth Amendment rights and that therefore the evidence should have been suppressed, the U.S. Supreme Court ruled that no violation occurred since police had already been dispatched to the area where the body was placed and would have inevitably discovered the body through legitimately lawful efforts.

Purged Taint

The *purged taint* exception also stems from the fruit of the poisonous tree doctrine whereby the police engage in illegal behavior. Under this exception, the free-will behavior of the suspect removes the "taint" attached to evidence illegally seized by the police. This exception applies when the defendant's subsequent voluntary act dissipates the "taint" of the initial illegality. In *Wong Sun v. United States*, police broke into Wong Sun's house and illegally obtained a confession from him, but he refused to sign a statement. Police released him and left his home. Wong Sun later went to the police station and signed the confession. In *Wong Sun*, the U.S. Supreme Court held that a defendant's intervening act of free will is sufficient to break the causal chain between tainted evidence and illegal police conduct; thus, the evidence, otherwise illegally obtained, becomes admissible.

Independent Source

The *independent source* exception can be used if police officers can establish that evidence was obtained from an independent source not connected with the illegal search or seizure. While the ER applies to police officers, it does not extend to other citizens. Therefore, if citizens provide officers with evidence to be used against criminal suspects, the rule cannot be invoked because the Fourth Amendment does not prohibit searches made by private citizens. In *United States v. Crews*, the U.S. Supreme Court ruled that illegally obtained evidence is admissible if the police can prove that it was obtained from an independent source not connected to the illegal search or seizure.

Plain View Doctrine

The *plain view* doctrine holds that police officers do not need a warrant to seize items within their eyesight or open to public inspection (Schmalleger, 2001). Plain view applies to emergency situations, such as crimes in progress, fires, and accidents. For example, police officers responding to any of these situations may discover incriminating evidence and are justified in seizing it and making a valid arrest without a warrant. The plain view doctrine was first invoked in *Harris v. United States*. A police officer conducting inventory of an impounded vehicle had discovered evidence of a robbery. In *Harris*, the U.S. Supreme Court ruled that "objects falling in the plain view of an officer who has a right to be in the position to have that view are subject to seizure and may be introduced in evidence" in gaining a criminal conviction.

In *United States v. Irizarry*, agents had arrested a number of men in a motel room in Isla Verde, Puerto Rico. Officers had a valid arrest warrant. While effecting the arrest, some quantities of plainly visible drugs were seized from the room. An agent, looking through a window into the room prior to the arrest, had seen one of the defendants with a gun. After the arrest, no gun was found on the suspects, but another officer noticed a bathroom ceiling panel out of place. He concluded that the weapon had been hidden there. Upon inspection, a substantial quantity of cocaine and various firearms were found hidden in the ceiling. The evidence was used against the defendants, who were subsequently convicted. On appeal, the U.S. Supreme Court held that the weapons and drugs that had been admitted as evidence constituted a violation of the defendants' Fourth Amendment rights because the evidence found above the ceiling was not plainly visible to the agents standing in the room. Therefore, a warrant was needed. Surprisingly, the only action that police had to take after they had noticed the ceiling had been altered was to obtain a warrant. They had already established probable cause to believe that weapons or drugs were hidden. With a warrant, any evidence discovered would have been admissible. Similarly, in *Arizona v. Hicks*, *Irizarry* was reaffirmed. In *Hicks*, officers responded to a shooting in an apartment building. A bullet had been fired in a second-floor apartment and had gone through the floor, injuring a man in the apartment below. The quarters of James Hicks were found in considerable disarray when investigating officers entered. As officers looked for the person who might have fired the weapon, they discovered and confiscated a number of guns and a stocking mask—of the kind that might be used in robberies. In one corner, officers noticed two expensive stereo sets. One of the officers, suspecting that the sets were stolen, went over to the equipment and was able to read the serial number on one of the components where it rested. However, the serial numbers of some of the components were not clearly visible, and the investigating officer moved those components in order to read their numbers. When he called the numbers into headquarters, he was told that the equipment had been stolen. The stereo components were seized, and Hicks was arrested. He was subsequently convicted of armed robbery based on the evidence seized. On appeal, the U.S. Supreme Court ruled that the officer's behavior had become illegal when he moved the stereo equipment to record the serial numbers. The Court also held that persons have a "reasonable expectation to privacy." Hence, officers lacking a search warrant should act more like guests than inquisitors.

The Fourth Amendment protection against unreasonable searches and seizures does not apply to items in plain view; it applies only to places where people have a reasonable expectation of privacy. Again, items in open view do not enjoy protection. For example, if police make a routine traffic stop and notice a weapon, drugs, or drug paraphernalia on the seat of the vehicle, the items will be confiscated and an arrest will be made. However, the plain view exception can only be used as a defense when the officer is legally in the place where the traffic stop is made and is not engaging in an illegal search or a fishing expedition. The sighting of the item (or the items) must be inadvertent, or the evidence must have been immediately apparent to the officer making the seizure. Under the plain view doctrine, the police officer cannot remove items to obtain a better view. Nevertheless, in *Horton v. California*, the U. S. Supreme Court retreated from this position. In *Horton*, a warrant was issued authorizing the search of Terry Brice Horton's home for stolen jewelry. The affidavit, completed by the officer who requested the warrant, alluded to an Uzi submachine gun and a stun gun purportedly used in the jewelry robbery. It did not request that those weapons be listed on the search warrant. Officers searched the defendant's home but did not find the stolen jewelry. They did, however, seize a number of weapons, among them an Uzi, two stun guns, and a .38 caliber revolver. Horton was convicted of robbery in a trial in which the seized weapons were admitted as evidence. He appealed his conviction, claiming that officers had reason to believe that the weapons were in his home at the time of the search and were therefore not seized inadvertently. His conviction was overturned by the Court. *Horton* signals that inadvertence is no longer considered a necessary condition to ensure the legality of a seizure which occurs when evidence other than that listed in a search warrant is discovered.

Searches Incidental to a Lawful Arrest

A *search incidental to a lawful arrest* is a common practice in policing. Officers are legally authorized to briefly stop suspects and pat their outer garments to ensure their own protection (see *Terry v. Ohio*). In addition, before suspects are taken into custody, they are generally searched. Searches can be made with or without a warrant. Officers typically search suspects not only to ensure their own safety but also to check for contraband, such as drugs. After performing such searches, officers confiscate evidence to be used in a criminal conviction. These searches do not require that an officer have a warrant; rather, they are viewed as part of the arrest. To effect a valid arrest, an officer needs either probable cause that a crime was committed to make a legal stop or a reasonable suspicion to justify a *Terry* stop. If a weapon or drugs are discovered, an arrest will be made and the suspect will be taken into custody. When arrests are made in a person's house, officers are legally allowed to search the person's area of immediate control to prevent the destruction of evidence and to prevent injury from a weapon that the suspect could quickly access. The area of immediate control is generally referred to as "the wing span" of the suspect.

In *Chimel v. California*, police arrived at Chimel's home with an arrest warrant but not a search warrant. Even though Chimel refused their request to "look around," the officers searched the entire three-bedroom house for nearly an hour. They searched bedrooms, attics, and other places. They eventually found stolen coins. Chimel was convicted of the burglary of a coin shop based on evidence gathered at the scene of his arrest—his home. He appealed, arguing that the coins should have been suppressed because the search was illegal. The U.S. Supreme Court agreed, ruling that the search was unreasonable under the Fourth Amendment. In so ruling, the Court established guidelines regarding the extent of a search incident to a lawful arrest. In *Chimel*, the Court held that police may legally search any area within the suspect's immediate control to confiscate any weapons or evidence that the suspect could destroy. According to the Court, there was no justification

> for routinely searching rooms other than that in which the arrest occurs or, for that matter, for searching through all desk drawers or other closed or concealed areas in that room itself. Such searches, in the absence of well recognized exceptions, may be made only under the authority of a search warrant.

The Court thus ruled that the search was invalid because it had gone beyond the area of the police's immediate control. Though the police argued that the search was made incidental to an arrest, the Court disagreed because the officers were never in jeopardy: Chimel had voluntarily complied with the arrest. The arrest had been made and Chimel had posed no threat, yet the officers had searched his home. The *Chimel* decision was reiterated in *United States v. Robinson*. In *Robinson*, the U.S. Supreme Court ruled that searches incidental to an arrest are valid for two reasons. First, officers must find and confiscate any weapons a suspect may be carrying. Second, officers must protect any evidence on the suspect's person from being destroyed. However, the Court held that officers must not use a search or an arrest as an opportunity to go on a fishing expedition.

Searches with Consent

A *search with consent* typically takes place when an officer does not have a warrant but gains permission from the suspect to conduct a search of his or her home, person, or belongings. After consent is given, anything an officer finds can be confiscated and used against the suspect. The suspect cannot move to suppress evidence under the ER if he or she agrees to a search that later reveals incriminating evidence. The U.S. Supreme Court has ruled that consent must be voluntary and free from coercion and threats of physical violence made by a law-enforcement officer. Forced consent would invalidate the search and require that incriminating evidence be inadmissible in a criminal trial. For consent to be "voluntary," it must be given on the basis of free will. Consent must also be given in an intelligent manner: the suspect must be aware of the consequences of what the search may reveal.

Schneckcloth v. Bustamonte established the standard of searches made with consent. In *Schneckcloth*, after being asked to submit to a search, the defendant told officers to "go ahead" and search his car. Officers found a packet of stolen checks in the trunk of the car. When Schneckcloth moved to suppress the evidence, contending that the search was invalid because officers did not have a warrant, the U.S. Supreme Court disagreed, ruling that the evidence was valid because Schneckcloth had voluntarily consented to the search. As indicated above, despite the Fourth Amendment's prohibition against unreasonable searches and seizures, the exceptions to the ER have given police officers freedom to gather evidence in a manner that runs counter to the Amendment. Some scholars argue that the exceptions have essentially weakened citizens' reasonable expectation of privacy and have thus eroded the Fourth Amendment.

PART FIVE: ADVANTAGES AND DISADVANTAGES OF THE EXCLUSIONARY RULE

Advantages

While the ER is not based on the Constitution, it has provided legal procedures that guide the day-to-day behavior of police officers. The rule has made police officers and prosecutors more careful about how evidence is collected and about how affidavits must be completed—that is, as specifically as possible or in a manner as matter of fact as possible. Some experts even argue that the rule has improved the quality of justice dispensed by the system. For example, when evidence has been collected in a proper manner, it enhances the strength of the state's case and increases the likelihood that criminal suspects will be convicted on solid evidence presented to a judge or a jury which will determine the guilt or innocence of the defendant (del Carmen, 2001). Officers are keenly aware that if they violate the rights of criminal suspects, they run the risk of having evidence suppressed and the case dismissed. The rule has also been the main reason why the justice system has invested resources in ongoing police training. For example, officer training does not end after recruits graduate from their respective training academies. Training continues, and when technology is developed to enhance the performance of officers, they must continue to train to become recertified. Because of this requirement, experts argue that the ER has improved the quality of justice a defendant receives in the criminal justice system. Several other advantages of the ER are as follows: it reduces the likelihood of appeals; it ensures sound police work; it promotes better police/prosecutor communication; it fosters continuous police training to improve effectiveness and professionalism; it reassures the public that police are guided by procedural safeguards; it makes officers more accountable for their actions; and it protects the constitutional right to privacy (del Carmen, 2001).

Disadvantages

While the rule has a number of disadvantages, perhaps the biggest is that suspects could be released because of a police technicality. Officers disdain the rule because criminals do not hold to any rules and flee the crime scene by any means necessary. However, police officers are restricted by the U.S. Constitution, states' constitutions, and statutes which have created a body of policies governing how they must discharge their duty. Officers are aware that an error on a warrant could invalidate an arrest or a drug seizure, which could mean that the suspect will go free. Police generally feel that the ER protects criminal offenders and paralyzes law-enforcement efforts. The rule means that police officers will have to work harder and smarter when bringing criminal suspects to justice. Several disadvantages of the ER are as follows: it allows criminals to go free on a technicality; it negates crime-control efforts; it subjects the community to continued criminal behavior; it does not punish police officers who engage in illegal conduct; it is not based on the Constitution; it may not deter police misconduct; and it makes the public lose respect for the criminal justice system and the legal process (del Carmen, 2001).

Part Six: Alternatives to the Exclusionary Rule

Though the ER was created to control police misconduct, removing it does not necessarily mean that there will be an abundance of civil rights violations committed by police. Indeed, there are several alternatives that can be used to control police. First, internal departmental discipline can be used, backed up by police review boards. Second, tort actions can be filed by people who have been falsely arrested or who have had their privacy invaded by police. Such tort actions are usually available under state statutory or common law. Third,

Section 1983 claims can be used to make police accountable to the public. These claims are filed against officers acting under color of state law who violate a person's Fourth Amendment rights. Officers found guilty are subject to damages and other remedies under this civil rights statute in federal court. Fourth, the illegal behavior of federal officers can be brought to court under the *Bivens* doctrine. Despite such remedies, police have several defenses that they can invoke, such as acting in good faith (see *Pierson v. Ray*). In addition, federal officers are entitled to the qualified-immunity defense based on an objectively reasonable belief that a warrantless search later determined to violate the Fourth Amendment was supported by probable cause or exigent circumstances (see *Anderson v. Creighton*). Another defense that could enable officers to prevent offenders from receiving justice is that the perception by judges and juries of persons subject to illegal arrests and searches and seizures is often negative. Such persons are seen as people of disreputable character and judges and juries are therefore often unsympathetic toward their plight.

The Erosion of the Fourth Amendment and the Future of the Exclusionary Rule

While the Fourth Amendment protection against unreasonable searches and seizures is deemed fundamental, courts have given police officers much leeway, as shown by the number of exceptions made to the ER that have allowed illegally seized evidence to be used in court to win criminal convictions. As a result, some supporters of the rule (who are also critics of the exceptions) argue that new technological developments in law enforcement will continue to challenge the United States' commitment to the Fourth Amendment. For example, does electronic surveillance, such as wiretapping and other forms of eavesdropping, infringe upon one's reasonable expectation of privacy (see *Katz v. United States* and *Berger v. New York*)? Recently, challenges have come from the use of helicopters and high-tech devices, such as infrared sensors, supersensitive microphones, and miniature radio transmitters. The question may emerge: Which concern is more important to citizens, their own right to be free from unreasonable governmental intrusion or the possible danger of allowing presumed criminal offenders to be set free? The exceptions made to the ER suggest to critics that the latter is true. For this reason, some argue that the Fourth Amendment has been seriously compromised. Nevertheless, it is doubtful that the ER will ever be totally eliminated because abolishing it would open the floodgates of police misconduct and other criminal behaviors that were commonplace before its creation. Stated bluntly, if the ER goes, so goes the Fourth Amendment, along with every citizen's reasonable expectation of privacy. So when officers are in doubt about the legality of their behavior, they should procure a search warrant, and in cases where officers are in hot pursuit of offenders or faced with exigent circumstances, they should explore the idea of phoning in for a search warrant. Either of these efforts would negate motions made by defendants to suppress evidence. As a result, evidence would be used against the suspect to gain a criminal conviction and the Fourth Amendment would be at least momentarily preserved.

PART SEVEN: SOME PERTINENT CASES

Arizona v. Evans
115 S. Ct. 1185 (1995)

Evans was arrested by Phoenix police during a routine traffic stop when a patrol car's computer indicated that there was an outstanding misdemeanor warrant for his arrest. A subsequent search of Evans's car revealed a bag of marijuana, and he was charged with possession. Evans moved to suppress the marijuana as the fruit of an unlawful arrest, since the misdemeanor warrant had been quashed before the arrest. The trial court granted the motion, but the court of appeals reversed it on the grounds that the exclusionary rule's purpose would not be served by excluding evidence obtained because of an error by employees not directly associated with the arresting officers or their police department. In reversing the appeals court's decision, the Arizona Supreme Court rejected the distinction between clerical errors committed by law-enforcement personnel and similar mistakes by court employees and predicted the exclusionary rule's application would serve to improve the efficiency of criminal justice system record keepers. The case was appealed to the U.S. Supreme Court. In essence, the Court decided that the "good faith" exception to the exclusionary rule applies to evidence seized incidental to an arrest resulting from an inaccurate computer record indicating there was an outstanding arrest warrant for the suspect, regardless of whether police or court personnel were responsible for the record's continued presence in the police computer.

Arizona v. Hicks
107 S. Ct. 1149 (1987)

A bullet fired through the floor of Hicks's apartment injured a man on the floor below. Police entered the apartment to search for the shooter, for other victims, and for weapons, and seized three weapons and discovered a stocking-cap mask. While in the apartment, one of the policeman noticed two sets of expensive stereo components and, suspecting that they had been stolen, read and recorded their serial numbers. In doing so, he moved some of them, including a turntable, and phoned in the numbers to headquarters. Upon learning that the turntable had been stolen in an armed robbery, he seized it immediately. Hicks was subsequently indicted for the robbery, but the state trial court granted his motion to suppress the evidence that had been seized, and the Arizona Court of Appeals affirmed. In this case, the court also cited *Mincey v. Arizona*, stating that a warrantless search must be "strictly circumscribed by the exigencies which justify its initiation." The Court of Appeals held that the policeman's obtaining the serial numbers violated the Fourth Amendment because it was unrelated to the shooting, the exigent circumstances that justified the initial entry and search. Thus, both state courts rejected the contention that the policeman's actions were justified under the plain view doctrine. Although the mere recording of serial numbers does not constitute a "seizure," moving a stereo found in plain view in order to obtain its serial number comes within the Fourth Amendment as a "search" independent of actions that justified exigent entry into the dwelling.

Berger v. New York
388 U.S. 41 (1967)

Berger was indicted and convicted of conspiracy to bribe the chairman of the New York State Liquor Authority based upon evidence obtained by eavesdropping. An order pursuant to statute 813-a of the New York Code of Criminal Procedures permitting the installation of a recording device in an attorney's office for a period of sixty days had been issued by a justice of the state supreme court after he had been advised of recorded interviews between a complainant and first, an authority employee and later, the attorney in question. Section 813-a authorizes the issuance of an "ex parte order for eavesdropping" upon "oath or affirmation of a district attorney, or of the attorney general or of an officer above the rank of sergeant of any police department. The oath must state that there is reasonable ground to believe that evidence of a crime may be thus obtained, and particularly describing the person or persons whose communications … are to be overheard or recorded and the purpose thereof." The order must specify the duration of the eavesdropping, which may not exceed two months, unless extended. A second order, also for a sixty-day period, was issued, permitting an installation elsewhere. After two weeks of eavesdropping a conspiracy was uncovered, in which the petitioner was a "go-between." The New York courts sustained the status against constitutional challenge. The case was appealed to the U.S. Supreme Court. The Court ruled that conversations could not be seized under the Fourth Amendment. The Court held unconstitutional on its face a state eavesdropping statute under which judges were authorized to issue warrants permitting police officers to trespass on private premises to install listening devices. Under the statute, the warrants were to be issued upon a showing of reasonable grounds that evidence of a crime may be thus obtained; in addition, the warrants were to specifically describe the person to be overheard or recorded.

Chimel v. California
395 U.S. 752 (1969)

A warrant for the arrest of the petitioner was issued for the burglary of a coin shop. The officers identified themselves and were allowed entrance into the house by the petitioner's wife, where they waited for the accused man to come home. Upon the petitioner's arrival, the officers showed the arrest warrant to the accused and asked permission to "look around." The petitioner refused the request, and the officers told the petitioner that a search could be conducted on "the basis of lawful arrest" and carried out the search. The officers searched the entire house, including the attic, the garage, a small workshop, and so forth, and found various items which were admitted as evidence in the arrest, over the defendant's objection that they were admitted unconstitutionally. In *Chimel*, the U.S. Supreme Court held that a search incident to a lawful arrest in a home must be limited to "the area into which an arrestee might reach in order to grab a weapon or other evidentiary items."

Elkins v. United States
364 U.S. 206 (1960)

The petitioners were indicted in the District Court of Oregon, pursuant to 47 U.S.C. 501, 605 and 18 U.S.C. 371, for intercepting and divulging telephone communications and for conspiracy to do so. Before trial, the petitioners made a motion to suppress as evidence several tape and wire recordings and a recording machine which had originally been seized by state law-enforcement officers in the home of petitioner Clark; they had been seized under circumstances which two Oregon courts had found had rendered the search-and-seizure unlawful. At the hearing on the motion, the district judge assumed, without deciding, that the articles had been obtained as the result of an unreasonable search-and-seizure, but the judge denied the motion to suppress the items seized because there was no evidence that any "agent of the

United States had any knowledge or information or suspicion of any kind that this search was being contemplated or was eventually made by the State officers until they read about it in the newspapers." At trial, the articles in question were admitted as evidence against the petitioners and they were convicted. They appealed. The Court of Appeals for the Ninth Circuit affirmed the convictions, reasoning that it was unnecessary to determine whether the original state search-and-seizure had been lawful because federal officers had not participated. "Hence the unlawfulness of the State search and seizure, if indeed they were unlawful, did not entitle defendants to an order of the District Court suppressing the property seized." The case was appealed to the United States Supreme Court. The Court ruled that the silver platter doctrine, which permitted evidence obtained by state officers during a search conducted by federal officers, would violate the defendant's immunity from unreasonable searches and seizures under the Fourth Amendment and that therefore evidence permitted by the doctrine is inadmissible over the defendant's timely objection in a federal criminal trial, even when federal officers did not participate in the search-and-seizure.

Horton v. California
110 S. Ct. 2301 (1990)

A police officer investigating an armed robbery determined that there was probable cause to search the suspect's home for the property stolen in the robbery and for the weapons used by the robber. However, the warrant issued for the search of the suspect's home only authorized a search for the suspect's stolen property. The officer searched the suspect's home pursuant to the warrant but found no stolen property. In the course of the search, the officer discovered the robbery weapons in plain view and seized the weapons and several other items. The officer testified that while he was searching for the stolen property, he was interested in finding other evidence connecting the accused to the crime. The suspect was subsequently convicted and appealed to the U.S. Supreme Court. In the case, the Court held that evidence does not need to be inadvertently discovered in order to be covered by the plain view doctrine.

Illinois v. Krull
107 S. Ct. 1160 (1987)

A 1981 Illinois statute required licensed sellers of motor vehicles and vehicular parts to permit state officials to inspect certain records. In 1981, pursuant to the statute, a police detective entered the respondent's automobile wrecking yard and asked to see records of vehicle purchases. He was told that the records could not be located but was given a list of approximately five purchases. After receiving permission to look at the cars in the yard, the detective determined that three were stolen and that a fourth had its identification number removed. He then seized the cars, and the respondent was arrested and charged with various crimes. The state trial court granted the respondent's motion to suppress the evidence seized from the yard, agreeing with a federal-court ruling, issued by the day after the search, that the state statute violated the Fourth amendment because it permitted officers unbridled discretion in their warrantless searches. The Illinois State Supreme Court affirmed, rejecting the petitioner's argument that the seized evidence was admissible because the detective had acted in good-faith reliance on the statute in making the search. The defendant was convicted and appealed. The U.S. Supreme Court granted certiorari. In this case, the Court held that the "good faith" exception to the exclusionary rule applies to searches conducted by police officers acting in objectively reasonable reliance upon a statute authorizing warrantless administrative searches, even though the statute was later found to violate the Fourth Amendment.

Illinois v. Rodriguez
110 S. Ct. 2793 (1990)

Rodriguez was arrested in his apartment and charged with possession of illegal drugs, which the police had observed in plain view and seized. The officers did not have an arrest or search warrant but gained entry into the apartment with the assistance of Gail Fischer. She claimed that the apartment was "our[s]" and that she had clothes and furniture there, then unlocked the door with a key, and gave the officers permission to enter. The trial court granted the respondent's motion to suppress the seized evidence, holding that at the time Fischer consented to the entry, she did not have common authority because she had moved out of the apartment. The court also rejected the state's contention that, even if Fischer did not have common authority, there was no Fourth Amendment violation if the police reasonably believed at the time of their entry that she possessed the authority to consent. The Appellate Court of Illinois affirmed. The case was appealed to the U.S. Supreme Court. In *Rodriguez*, the Court held that a consent search was valid when consent was obtained from a third party if the police, at the time of the entry, reasonably believed that the party possessed common authority over the premises even though, in fact, it did not have such authority.

Katz v. United States
389 U.S. 347 (1967)

Charles Katz used a public phone booth in Los Angeles to place bets in Miami and Boston. Unknown to Katz, FBI agents affixed a listening device to the outside wall of the telephone booth he regularly used and activated it each time he entered. Katz was convicted under an indictment charging him with transmitting waging information by telephone across state lines in violation of 18 U.S.C. 1084. At trial, FBI agents introduced the conversations that they recorded of Katz which revealed that he was transmitting waging information. The trial court allowed the evidence, reasoning that no violation of the Fourth Amendment had occurred since there had been no physical trespass into the phone booth. Katz was subsequently convicted and sentenced to prison. He challenged his conviction in the Ninth Circuit Court of Appeals on the grounds that the wiretap infringed on his reasonable expectation of privacy. The appeals court affirmed the conviction, holding that there was no Fourth Amendment violation since there was "no physical entrance into the area occupied by petitioner." The case was appealed to the U.S. Supreme Court. In *Katz*, the Court disagreed with the Court of Appeals, ruling that once it is recognized that the Fourth Amendment protects people and not simply areas against unreasonable searches and seizures, it becomes clear that the reach of the Amendment cannot turn upon the presence or absence of a physical intrusion into any given enclosure. Even though the surveillance had been authorized by a magistrate, the Court ruled it invalid.

Mapp v. Ohio
81 S. Ct. 1684 (1961)

On May 23, 1957, police officers responding to a tip that a bombing suspect was hiding at the home of Dolree Mapp, visited her residence. The officers were also told that gambling materials were being concealed at the residence. After arriving, the officers demanded entrance, but after Mapp phoned her lawyer, she refused to allow the officers entry without a search warrant. The police left but returned three hours later with additional officers. The officers forced their way into Mapp's home. She demanded to see a warrant, and one of the officers waved what he claimed was the warrant. She grabbed the paper and placed it inside of her bra. After a struggle during which the officer retrieved the warrant, Mapp was handcuffed and arrested. The police then proceeded to search the entire dwelling. Officers did not find gambling materials or the suspect who was wanted in connection with a bombing. However, Mapp was convicted in a state court of possessing pornographic materials in violation of an Ohio law. Her conviction was obtained on the basis of evidence taken by police after they had entered her boarding house without a search warrant and while they were looking for gambling materials. At her trial, no search warrant was presented as evidence. She appealed her conviction, and the U.S. Supreme Court granted certiorari. In *Mapp*, the Court overturned the conviction, holding that the exclusionary rule applies to the states through the due process clause of the Fourteenth Amendment.

Massachusetts v. Sheppard
104 S. Ct. 3424 (1984)

Based on evidence gathered in the investigation of a homicide in the Rox-bury section of Boston, a police detective drafted an affidavit to support an application for an arrest warrant and a search warrant authorizing the search of the respondent's residence. The affidavit stated that the police wished to search for specific items, such as the clothes of the victim and a blunt instrument that might have been used on the victim. The affidavit was reviewed and approved by the district attorney. Because it was Sunday, the local court was closed and the police had difficulty finding a warrant application form. The detective finally found a warrant form previously used in another district to search for controlled substances. After making some changes to the form, the detective presented it and the affidavit to the judge at his residence, inform-ing him that the warrant form might need to be changed further. After con-cluding that the affidavit established probable cause to search the respondent's residence and after telling the detective that the necessary changes in the war-rant form would be made, the judge made some changes but did not change the substantive portion, which still authorized a search for controlled sub-stances; nor did he alter the form to incorporate the affidavit. The judge then signed the warrant and returned it and the affidavit to the detective, inform-ing him that the warrant was of sufficient authority in form and content to carry out the requested search. The ensuing search of the respondent's resi-dence by the detective and other police officers was limited to the items listed in the affidavit, and several incriminating pieces of evidence were discovered. Thereafter, the respondent was charged with first-degree murder. At a pretrial suppression hearing, the trial judge ruled that although the warrant was de-fective under the Fourth Amendment since it did not describe the specific items to be seized, the incriminating evidence could be admitted in trial since the police had acted in good faith in executing what they reasonably believed was a valid warrant. At the subsequent trial, Sheppard was convicted. The case was appealed and the Massachusetts Supreme Court held that the evidence should have been suppressed. The case was appealed to the U.S. Supreme Court. The Court ruled that the exclusionary rule should not be applied to evidence during the execution of a defective search warrant when the officers acted in objectively reasonable reliance on a warrant issued by a detached and neutral magistrate.

Minnesota v. Olson
110 S. Ct. 1684 (1990)

Police suspected Olson of being the driver of the getaway car used in a robbery-murder. After recovering the murder weapon and arresting the suspected murderer, they surrounded the home of two women with whom they believed Olson had been staying. When police telephoned the home and told one of the women that Olson should come out, a male voice was heard saying, "Tell them I left." Without seeking permission and with weapons drawn, they entered the home, found Olson hiding in a closet, and arrested him. Shortly thereafter, he made an inculpatory statement, which the trial court refused to suppress. He was convicted of murder, armed robbery, and assault. The conviction was appealed and the Minnesota Supreme Court reversed it, ruling that Olson had a sufficient interest in the women's home to challenge the legality of his warrantless arrest, that the arrest was illegal because there were no exigent circumstances to justify warrantless entry, and that his statement was tainted and should have been suppressed. The case was appealed to the United States Supreme Court. The Court granted certiorari and ruled that *Olson* established that overnight guests in a house have an expectation of privacy protected by the Fourth Amendment.

Miranda v. Arizona
86 S. Ct. 1602 (1966)

Ernesto Miranda, who had less than a ninth-grade education, was arrested at his home in Phoenix on March 13, 1963. He was taken into custody for suspicion in a kidnapping and rape case. The victim was an eighteen-year-old woman. At the police lineup, Miranda was identified by the victim. He was later interrogated for two hours. After the interrogation, the police collected a written confession signed by Miranda, which was used as evidence in trial. He was subsequently found guilty and sentenced to twenty to thirty years on each count. Miranda appealed the case and the U.S. Supreme Court granted review. In *Miranda*, the Court ruled that protection against self-incrimination is available outside of criminal-court proceedings and therefore applies to police interrogations of persons "in custody." Prior to custodial interrogation, the following warnings must be given: (1) You have the right to remain silent; (2) anything you say can be used in a court of law against you; (3) you have the right to have an attorney with you during the interrogation; (4) if you are unable to hire an attorney, one will be provided for you without cost during questioning.

Nix v. Williams
104 S. Ct. 2501 (1984)

Following the disappearance of a ten-year-old girl in Des Moines, Iowa, the respondent was arrested and arraigned in Davenport, Iowa. The police informed the respondent's counsel that they would drive the respondent back to Des Moines without questioning him. But during the trip one of the officers began a conversation with the respondent that ultimately resulted in his making incriminating statements and directing the officers to the child's body. A systematic search of the area that was being conducted with the help of two hundred volunteers and that had been started before the respondent made the incriminating statements was terminated when the respondent guided police to the body. Before trial in an Iowa state court for first-degree murder, the court denied the respondent's motion to suppress the evidence consisting of the first of his illegally obtained statements made during the automobile ride. The respondent was convicted, and the Iowa Supreme Court affirmed the conviction. But later habeas corpus proceedings in federal court ultimately resulted in the court's holding that the police had obtained the respondent's incriminating statements through interrogations in violation of his Sixth Amendment right to counsel. The case was appealed to the U.S. Supreme Court. In essence, the Court reasoned that the body of the murder victim, which was found after the defendant was illegally interrogated, was admissible on the grounds that it would have been discovered even if no violation of a constitutional right had occurred. Prosecutors must show inevitable discovery by preponderance of evidence and need not show absence of bad faith in originally securing the evidence.

Schneckcloth v. Bustamonte
93 S. Ct. 2041 (1973)

During the course of a consent search of a car that had been stopped by officers for traffic violations, evidence was discovered that was used to convict the respondent of possessing stolen checks. In a habeas corpus proceeding, the court of appeals reversed the district court, holding that the prosecution had failed to prove that consent to the search had been made with the understanding that it could be freely withheld. The court held that when the subject of a search is not in custody and the state would justify a search on the basis of his or her consent, the Fourth and the Fourteenth Amendments require the state to demonstrate that the consent was in fact voluntary. Voluntariness is to be determined from the totality of the surrounding circumstances. While knowledge of a right to refuse consent is a factor to be taken into account, the state need not prove that the one giving permission to search knew that he or she had a right to withhold his or her consent. In *Schneckcloth*, the U.S. Supreme Court held that the advisement of Fourth Amendment rights is not a prerequisite to a consent search in a noncustodial situation. The standard for the evaluation of consent is voluntariness as determined from all the circumstances.

United States v. Leon
104 S. Ct. 3405 (1984)

Acting on the basis of information from a confidential informant, officers of the Burbank, California Police Department initiated a drug trafficking investigation involving surveillance of the respondent's activities. Based on an affidavit summarizing the police officers' observations, officer Rombach prepared an application for a warrant to search three residences and the respondent's automobiles for an extensive list of items. The application was reviewed by several deputy district attorneys, and a search warrant valid on its face was issued by a state-court judge. Ensuing searches produced large quantities of drugs and other evidence. The respondent was arrested and indicted for federal drug offenses. The defense filed motions to suppress the evidence seized pursuant to the warrant. After an evidentiary hearing, the district court granted the motion in part, concluding that the affidavit was insufficient to establish probable cause. Although recognizing that officer Rombach had acted in good faith, the court rejected the government's suggestion that the Fourth Amendment exclusionary rule should not apply when evidence is seized in reasonable, good faith reliance on a search warrant. Leon was subsequently convicted. He appealed and the court of appeals affirmed, refusing the government's invitation to recognize a good-faith exception to the ER. The government petitioned the U.S. Supreme Court for certiorari, asking whether a good-faith exception to the exclusionary rule should be recognized. The Court granted review and held that *Leon* established that evidence seized under a warrant valid on its face and executed in good faith should only be suppressed in the unusual case in which exclusion will further the purposes of the exclusionary rule.

Weeks v. United States
34 S. CT. 341 (1914)

Weeks was arrested by a San Francisco law-enforcement officer. During the apprehension, the arresting officer performed a search of Weeks's business, although he did not have a search warrant. The search turned up evidence of violation of federal law whereby U.S. mail was used to send lottery tickets. The police also searched Weeks's home, likewise without a warrant, and located other papers that proved to be of no importance to the case. Encouraged by the results of the search of Weeks's business, a United States marshal, together with a local police officer and a federal postal inspector, searched Weeks's residence for the third time (again without a warrant) and seized some letters and documents in order to retrieve the papers. Weeks's attorney petitioned to have the illegally seized evidence excluded from the trial. In *Weeks*, the U.S. Supreme Court ruled that in a federal prosecution the Fourth Amendment barred the use of evidence secured through an illegal search-and-seizure by federal officers.

Wolf v. Colorado
69 S. Ct. 1359 (1949)

In 1949, a deputy sheriff seized a physician's appointment book without a warrant, interrogated patients whose names were listed in the book, and obtained the evidence needed to charge Wolf with performing illegal abortions. Wolf was subsequently convicted. The case was appealed to the United States Supreme Court. Wolf challenged the use of the evidence, arguing that it had been seized illegally. The Court rejected Wolf's contention, even though it held that the Fourth Amendment protected individuals against state as well as federal action. Indeed, the Court came short of extending the exclusionary rule to the states. Essentially, the Court agreed that the Fourth Amendment also applied to the states, but it neutralized this interpretation by continuing to sanction the admission of evidence that had been illegally obtained by the states. The Court ruled that *Wolf* prohibited unreasonable searches and seizures by the states but that if the evidence was trustworthy, it was admissible regardless of how it was obtained. *Wolf* established that the Fourth Amendment applied to the states, but the majority of the states declined to take steps to enforce this constitutional protection, which they could have done by banning the use of illegally seized evidence in court.

Wong Sun v. United States
83 S. Ct. 407 (1963)

Federal agents, acting on a tip and without a warrant, broke down the door of James Wah Toy's dwelling and arrested him. They searched his home for narcotics but found none. After an interrogation, Toy told police that Johnny Yee was selling narcotics. Yee was arrested, and narcotics were taken from his home. Yee, in turn, implicated Wong Sun. Federal agents visited Wong Sun's home and arrested him. The officers searched his home but did not find any narcotics. He was later released. After several days, he was again visited by federal agents, who interrogated him. They took his statement, but he refused to sign it and the agents left. Later, Wong Sun thought about the interrogation and went to the station to sign the statement he had given several days earlier. He was subsequently arrested, charged with, and convicted of violating federal narcotics laws. Wong Sun appealed his conviction, arguing that his statement should have been suppressed because before he gave it, federal agents had committed several illegal acts against him and his associates. Therefore, the statement was the fruit of the poisonous tree. In this case, the U.S. Supreme Court agreed that federal agents' behavior nullified some evidence against Wong Sun and his associates. However, the Court held that when Wong Sun freely returned to visit the agents and admit to the accuracy of his previous statement, his action removed the taint of the agents' illegal behavior and made the evidence admissible.

REFERENCES

Anderson, P. R., & Newman, D. J. (1993). *Introduction to criminal justice* (5th ed.). New York: McGraw-Hill.

del Carmen, R. V. (1991). *Civil liabilities in American policing: A text for law enforcement personnel.* Englewood Cliffs, NJ: Brady/Prentice Hall.

del Carmen, R. V. (2001). *Criminal procedure: Law and practice.* Stamford, CT: Wadsworth/Thomson Learning.

Friedland, S. I. (1994). *Evidence problems and materials.* Charlottesville, VA: Michie.

Gaines, L., Kaune, M., & Miller, R. (2001). *Criminal justice: In action*. Belmont, CA: Wadsworth/Thomson Learning.

Kappeler, V. (1993). *Critical issues in police civil liability*. Prospect Heights, IL: Waveland.

Klotter, J.C. (2002). *Legal guide for police: Constitutional issues* (6th ed.). Cincinnati, OH: Anderson.

Messner, S. F., & Rosenfeld, R. (2001). *Crime and the American dream* (3rd ed.). Stamford, CT: Wadsworth/Thomson Learning.

Moskovitz, M. (2000). *Cases and problems in criminal procedure: The police* (3rd ed.). New York: Lexis.

Scheb, J., & Scheb, J. (1999). *Criminal law and procedure* (3rd ed.). New York: West/Wadsworth.

Schmalleger, F. (2001). *Criminal justice today: An introductory text for the 21st century* (6th ed.). Upper Saddle River, NJ: Prentice Hall.

Wallace, H., & Roberson, C. (2001). *Principles of criminal law* (2nd ed.). Needham Heights, MA: Allyn and Bacon.

Cases Cited

Anderson v. Creighton, 483 U.S. 635 (1987)

Arizona v. Evans, 115 S. Ct. 1185 (1995)

Arizona v. Hicks, 107 S. Ct. 1149 (1987)

Berger v. New York, 388 U.S. 41 (1967)

Burdeau v. McDowell, 256 U.S. 465 (1921)

Chimel v. California, 395 U.S. 752 (1969)

Elkins v. United States, 364 U.S. 206 (1960)

Escobedo v. Illinois, 378 U.S. 478 (1964)

Gideon v. Wainwright, 372 U.S. 335 (1963)

Harris v. United States, 390 U.S. 234 (1968)

Horton v. California, 110 S. Ct. 2301 (1990)

Illinois v. Krull, 107 S. Ct. 1160 (1987)

Illinois v. Rodriguez, 110 S. Ct. 2793 (1990)

Katz v. United States, 389 U.S. 347 (1967)

Mapp v. Ohio, 81 S. Ct. 1684 (1961)

Maryland v. Garrison, 107 S. Ct. 1013 (1987)

Massachusetts v. Sheppard, 104 S. Ct. 3424 (1984)

Minnesota v. Olson, 110 S. Ct. 1684 (1990)

Minnesota v. Carter, 119 S. Ct. 469 (1998)

Miranda v. Arizona, 86 S. Ct. 1602 (1966)

Nix v. Williams, 104 S. Ct. 2501 (1984)

People v. Zelinski, Cal. 3d 357 (1979)

Pierson v. Ray, 386 U.S. 547 (1967)

Rochin v. California, 72 S. Ct. 205 (1952)

Schneckcloth v. Bustamonte, 93 S. Ct. 2041 (1973)

Silverthorne Lumber Co. v. United States, 251 U.S. 385 (1920)

Terry v. Ohio, 88 S. Ct. 1868 (1968)

United States v. Crews, 100 S. Ct. 1244 (1980)

United States v. Irizarry, 673 F 2d 554, 556–67 (1st Cir. 1982)

United States v. Leon, 104 S. Ct. 3405 (1984)

United States v. Janis, 96 S. Ct. 3021 (1976)

United States v. Robinson, 94 S. Ct. 467 (1973)

Weeks v. United States, 34 S. CT. 341 (1914)

Wolf v. Colorado, 69 S. Ct. 1359 (1949)

Wong Sun v. United States, 83 S. Ct. 407 (1963)

CHAPTER 5

STOP AND FRISK

FOCAL POINTS

- Legal Basis for Detention
    - What Constitutes Reasonable Suspicion?
- Reasonable Suspicion Defined
    - Who Determines Reasonable Suspicion?
    - Factors Precipitating Reasonable Suspicion
    - Appearance of the Suspect
    - Actions of the Suspect
    - Area in Which the Suspect Is Observed
- Measures Warranting Reasonable Suspicion
    - Stop and Frisk
        - A Stop
        - A Frisk
    - Leading Cases on Stop and Frisk
- Stop and Frisk Exceptions
    - Investigatory Automobile Stops
    - Automobile Stops Based on Anonymous Tips
    - Automobile Stops Based on Pretexts
    - Can Police Require Drivers and Passengers to Exit Their Vehicles?
    - Use of Drug Courier Profiles
    - Racial Profiling in Stop and Frisk
- Factors Invalidating a Stop and Frisk
- Some Pertinent Cases

INTRODUCTION

When police officers are led to believe that a person is acting in an unusual manner, such action alone may be sufficient to justify a stop and frisk or a field interrogation. During the course of routine patrol, officers typically have encounters that are normal and some that are unusual in light of the circumstances. For example, officers often encounter people who quickly become suspects based on their actions, their responses to questions, or even the way they are dressed. Any suspicious actions by a person may indicate to an officer that crime is afoot. Similarly, if a person is dressed in a manner that suggests he or she is secreting a weapon, drugs, or stolen goods, the officer may conclude that a crime is about to occur or has already been committed. When an officer has reasonable suspicion, he or she is justified in stopping the suspect to investigate the matter or engage in investigatory detention (Scheb & Scheb, 1999). Sometimes what an officer retrieves from a stop and frisk can necessitate that an arrest be made (del Carmen, 1991b). Moreover, Weston and Wells (1976) argue that when police officers reasonably believe that a suspect is armed with a weapon, they should have the power to frisk him or her to retrieve the weapon. An officer may want to frisk a suspect or a suspicious-looking or suspicious-acting person for self-protection and for the safety of others near the scene where the stop was made. If a weapon is found, along with any other contraband, the officer is justified in arresting the suspect.

Chapter 5 is divided into several sections. Part One presents the legal basis for detention and defines what constitutes reasonable suspicion. Part Two defines *reasonable suspicion* and indicates the officials who determine reasonable suspicion. It also lists factors that precipitate reasonable suspicion. Part Three addresses measures warranting reasonable suspicion and essential elements in stop and frisk procedures. It also presents leading cases in stop and frisk based on reasonable suspicion. Part Four offers several exceptions to stops and frisks. Part Five addresses factors that invalidate a stop and frisk. Part Six provides some pertinent cases involving reasonable suspicion and stop and frisk.

PART ONE: LEGAL BASIS FOR DETENTION

A *detention* is an intrusion, though minimal, on a citizen's liberty. Therefore, officers must justify any detention. The U.S. Supreme Court has ruled that any detention must be based on reasonableness or reasonable suspicion (Peoples, 2003). Essentially, the responding police officer must believe that a person has committed, is committing, or is about to commit a crime. However, the detention should only be brief enough to settle the officer's suspicion. For example, in *Dunaway v. New York*, the U.S. Supreme Court held that detentions must be as brief as possible unless the police officer's suspicion about a crime is confirmed. Put plainly, temporary detention should either dispel or confirm an officer's suspicion about the commission of crime. While detention is supposed to be brief, the Court has shown less concern with a time limit and more concern with the purpose of the stop and the reasonableness of the time it takes police officers to obtain any additional information they require. Specifically, the Court observes the totality of the circumstances to determine whether police officers acted in a reasonable manner or whether they infringed upon the suspect's Fourth Amendment rights (Scheb & Scheb, 1999). Cases such as *Florida v. Royer*, *United States v. Sharpe*, and *State v. Merklein* are instructive in this regard.

In *Florida v. Royer*, the U.S. Supreme Court ruled that police had acted in an unreasonable manner when they detained a suspect in a room at the police station and brought his luggage to him fifteen minutes later. In *United States v. Sharpe*, the U.S. Supreme Court ruled that although detention must be brief in stop and frisk situations, the time span must be evaluated in light of the totality of the circumstances. In *State v. Merklein*, a Florida court of appeals stated that it was reasonable for officers to detain a suspect for twenty to forty minutes while waiting for available officers, witnesses, and the victim of a robbery to arrive at the scene. In *State v. Werner*, a Washington district court held that police are acting reasonably if they are diligently investigating to confirm or dispel the suspicions that led to a stop. After stopping a suspect, the officer may conduct a *pat down* of the suspect's outer clothing. This is not the same as a search, which enjoys more protection under the Fourth Amendment, but is conducted to protect the safety of the officer and any bystander by ensuring that the suspect is unarmed. Because a pat down is not a search, it is referred to as a "frisk." The U.S. Supreme Court ruled in *Minnesota v. Dickerson* that any items that plainly feel like contraband can be retrieved by police officers.

What Constitutes Reasonable Suspicion?

Reasonable suspicion is a very important concept not only in criminal justice in general but also in law enforcement in particular, since it is a concept that law-enforcement officers put into practice every day in the United States. Therefore, the U.S. Supreme Court has had to define what constitutes reasonable suspicion (Gaines & Miller, 2004). In *United States v. Cortez*, the U.S. Supreme Court held that a trained officer develops reasonable suspicion that a person is, or is about to be, engaged in criminal activity from the officer's objective observations and from inferences and deductions (Scheb & Scheb, 1999). Essentially, the Court defined reasonable suspicion as a technical matter that police officers learn after having been trained as law-enforcement professionals. While *Cortez* has been viewed as difficult to interpret, the U.S. Supreme Court in *United States v. Sokolow*, ruled that reasonable suspicion was more than "inchoate and unparticularized suspicion" or a "hunch" but that reasonable suspicion should be based on the totality of the circumstances.

PART TWO: REASONABLE SUSPICION DEFINED

In ordinary and plain language, the term *suspicion* carries several related meanings—including "the act of suspecting," "the state of being suspected," "imagination generally of something ill," "distrust," "mistrust," "doubt," "the apprehension of something without proof or with only slight evidence," or "a belief or opinion based upon facts or circumstances which do not amount to proof" (Black, 1979). But in the context of American criminal procedure, when the term *suspicion* is qualified by the adjective *reasonable* it takes on an entirely technical meaning. One key definition of *reasonable suspicion*—which fits the requirements of the Fourth Amendment—is that quantum of knowledge which will induce an ordinarily prudent and cautious person to justify a police officer in stopping a person in the belief that criminal activity is at hand. "It [reasonable suspicion] must be based on specific and articulable facts, which, taken reasonably, warrant intrusion" (Black, 1979).

As a concept applicable to law enforcement, reasonable suspicion has not been free from definitional problems. As was noted in Chapter 3, the U.S. Supreme Court has taken a forthright approach to the problem of defining standards of proof in American criminal procedure. The Court has emphasized the futility of attempting to define both *reasonable suspicion* and *probable cause* with any degree of mathematical certainty. It has characterized them as "fluid concepts." For example, the Court observed in *Alabama v. White*:

> Reasonable suspicion is a less demanding standard than probable cause not only in the sense that reasonable suspicion can be established with information that is different in quality and content than that required to establish probable cause, but also in the sense that it is less reliable than that required to show probable cause.

Reasonable suspicion is therefore viewed as the amount of information sufficient to induce a prudent and cautious person under circumstances to believe criminal activity is at hand (Black, 1979). By including the "totality of the circumstances" in its formulation of reasonable suspicion, the U.S. Supreme Court has given officers leeway in conducting stops and frisks. However, determining reasonable suspicion must be based on specific facts that can be articulated in court (Stuckey, Roberson, & Wallace, 2004). Peoples (2003) suggests that officers must state the relevant factors in their report that supported the legality of the stop and possible frisk, as well as any evidence that was subsequently seized as a result of the detention.

Who Determines Reasonable Suspicion?

Who, indeed, determines reasonable suspicion? The answer is uncomplicated in that it is not a judicial determination. Initially, it is a subjective law-enforcement decision made by a police officer who, during the temporary detention of a suspect, must establish, on the basis of his or her experience, observations, and essential awareness of a person's liberties protected by the Fourth Amendment, whether there is reasonable suspicion that criminal activity is afoot. The Fourth Amendment liberty implicated here is a person's freedom from unreasonable searches and seizures. It is clear, therefore, that determining reasonable suspicion must originate from the police officer in exercise of his or her right to stop and frisk a suspect as an initiatory step in investigating a suspected crime. In other words, in American criminal procedure, determining reasonable suspicion, as a proper standard of proof for police actions, is a law-enforcement judgment call. There are several factors that can assist an officer in his or her determination of suspicion.

Factors Precipitating Reasonable Suspicion

While several factors influence police officers in establishing reasonable suspicion, the most important include the following: (a) the appearance of the suspect, (b) the actions of the suspect, and (c) the area where the suspect is observed.

Appearance of the Suspect

While establishing reasonable suspicion, officers typically consider whether the suspect is under the influence of alcohol or another mind-altering substance, such as cocaine or amphetamines (Gaines & Miller, 2004). They also consider whether the suspect fits the description given by the victim or the witness of the crime. In addition, police officers must determine if the detained suspect fits the description of a wanted fugitive. They may also stop individuals they observe casing houses, stores, banks, or any other establishment. Others who may be stopped include people who appear to be injured or mentally ill. People who park in unusual places or work at unusual hours often give police officers reasonable suspicion to believe that crime is afoot (Peoples, 2003). However, police must be cautious in relying solely on race or ethnicity as part of a profile. Such behavior could be the same as racial profiling and raise legal questions related to due process and equal protection under the law.

Actions of the Suspect

While a police officer is determining reasonable suspicion, his or her curiosity may be piqued by suspects who flee from law enforcement or someone else. Indeed, suspects who flee a crime scene draw quick attention from an officer. Police suspicion increases when people appear to be concealing a weapon or contraband. When suspects are accosted by police officers and the suspects discard contraband, reasonable suspicion is generated. Reasonable suspicion may increase when officers witness two people engaging in an exchange. Reasonable suspicion is also established when a suspect changes his or her driving patterns immediately after a police car gets behind the suspect's vehicle (Peoples, 2003).

Area in Which the Suspect Is Observed

Areas known for criminal activity typically receive more law-enforcement attention. High-crime areas attract the most police attention. Therefore, officers may establish reasonable suspicion because of the types of crime committed in an area. For example, in high-crime areas where drug sales are common, officers may suspect that if people are discovered in such places, they will either sell or purchase drugs. Such suspicion is especially likely if outsiders frequent these areas. Out-of-town license plates may arouse the attention of police officers who work in drug-infested communities.

While this list of factors that may justify a brief detention is not meant to be exhaustive, it includes some of the factors that an officer may have to articulate to a judge and jury to justify a stop and frisk. If the officer fails to show how he or she acted in a reasonable manner, any evidence derived from the seizure will probably be inadmissible in court to gain a criminal conviction. Nevertheless, the U.S. Supreme Court ruled in *Illinois v. Wardlow* that under certain circumstances the mere prospect that a suspect poses a flight risk may be sufficient to justify reasonable suspicion. However, in *Florida v. J. L.*, the

Court ruled that an anonymous telephone tip that a person was carrying a handgun is not sufficient evidence to justify a detention or a pat down for a weapon when independent corroboration is wanting. Despite the ruling in *Florida v. J. L.*, a California appeals court held in *People v. Coulombe* that multiple tips given to police that a suspect possessed a handgun were sufficient to justify the detention and pat down of the suspect.

PART THREE: MEASURES WARRANTING REASONABLE SUSPICION

Consistent with the foregoing discussion, it is settled law that reasonable suspicion is the recognized standard of proof for assessing the legality of the law-enforcement measure succinctly referred to in American criminal law as "stop and frisk." What precisely, then, is a *stop and frisk*? To put the question in another way: Can the police stop, question, and search a person who is behaving suspiciously? The answer is in the affirmative. Procedurally, therefore, a *stop and frisk* is the measure by which police officers suspicious of an individual run their hands lightly over the suspect's outer garments to determine if the person is carrying a concealed weapon. Also called a "pat down" or a "threshold inquiry," a stop and frisk is intended to preclude any activity that could be considered a violation of Fourth Amendment rights (Black, 1979). The legal principle governing a stop and frisk is that a police officer has the right to stop and pat down a person suspected of contemplating the commission of a crime. This principle was established in the landmark case *Terry v. Ohio*. As a matter of law, therefore, reasonable suspicion is the test by reference to which the legality of a stop and frisk is measured. Reasonable suspicion is more than a police officer's hunch, but it is also less than probable cause. But what really constitutes a stop and/or a frisk within the meaning of the U.S. Constitution?

Stop and Frisk

Though the concepts *stop* and *frisk* are often used together, they constitute two separate procedures with different requirements. In fact, just because a stop takes place, a frisk need not automatically follow. The officer's suspicion could be removed after a brief stop.

A Stop

As stated earlier, a stop is not an arrest within the meaning of the Constitution. However, since it represents an intrusion, it enjoys some degree of protection under the Fourth Amendment. Hence, a stop requires reasonable suspicion instead of probable cause that a person has committed or is about to commit a felony. Figure 5.1 indicates the degree of certainty that an officer must establish before stopping and arresting a suspect. The figure also shows the scope of a search allowed during a stop and frisk, the scope of a search allowed during an arrest, the purposes of the two procedures, and whether the officer needs a warrant to engage in either procedure. When an officer executes a stop, he or she typically asks the suspect's name, address, and an explanation of his or her actions (del Carmen, 1991b, 2004). The officer derives reasonable suspicion by considering the totality of the circumstances and by relying on his or her policing experience. Therefore, a stop is justified only to prevent criminal activity. Figure 5.1 also contrasts the requirements for conducting a stop and frisk with those for making an arrest. In order for the practice of stop and frisk to be legal and for the evidence derived from it to be admissible in a criminal court, a police officer involved in a stop and frisk must first establish reasonable suspicion. Afterward, he or she can engage in the procedure but must be aware that it is very limited in scope and not intrusive. In fact, the officer is allowed only to conduct a brief pat down of a suspect's outer garments. Its purpose is to prevent criminal activity and to serve as a method of protection if the officer believes that a suspect is armed and dangerous or is about to engage in committing a crime. Because the limited pat down permissible in a stop and frisk is not a search within the meaning of the Fourth Amendment, the procedure does not require an officer to procure a warrant. An arrest is quite different. Because it is an intrusive procedure, it requires that an officer performing it have probable cause. The scope of the search covers the full body of the suspect. Unlike a stop and frisk, the purpose of an arrest is to take a person into custody to answer charges of crimes pending against him or her. Arrests can be made with or without a warrant, depending on certain exceptions.

Figure 5.1.: Stop and Frisk versus Arrest

	STOP AND FRISK	ARREST
Degree of Certainty	Reasonable suspicion	Probable cause
Scope	Limited to a pat down	Full body search allowed
Purpose	To prevent criminal activity or to ensure an officer's safety	To take persons into custody
Warrant	Not needed	May or may not be needed

Source: del Carmen, R. V. (1991b). *Criminal procedure: Law and practice* (p. 109). Pacific Grove, CA: Brooks Cole.

A Frisk

A *frisk* is a pat down of a suspect only to discover a weapon. The scope of a frisk is more limited than that of a full search. It is conducted when the officer wishes to dispel fear that a criminal suspect is armed and poses a threat to the officer's safety or the safety of others. A frisk does not automatically follow a stop (del Carmen, 1991a). When deciding to conduct a frisk, the officer should consider the totality of the circumstances that led to the stop. The officer must also remember that a frisk is not a search and, therefore, is limited to a pat down for weapons to eliminate the threat of danger. The officer cannot use a frisk as an opportunity to go on a "fishing expedition" and engage in a full-scale search. However, if the officer pats the suspect's outer garments and feels a weapon, the officer can effect an arrest and then search the suspect for other articles of evidence. For example, if an officer stops and frisks a suspect and he or she touches an illegal weapon, the officer may confiscate it and place the suspect under arrest. Once arrested, the suspect may be subjected to a full-scale search and if contraband is found, it may be used to make a case against the suspect (del Carmen, 1991a). One might ask: From what source or sources did police officers derive the right to conduct stop and frisk procedures?

Leading Cases on Stop and Frisk

Terry v. Ohio
392 U.S. 1 (1968)

At 2:30 p.m. on October 31, 1963, the attention of Cleveland police detective Martin McFadden (a policeman for thirty-nine years) was drawn to the activities of two men, Richard Chilton and John Terry, who were conversing at the intersection of two downtown thoroughfares. Periodically, one of the men would separate from the other, walk southwest along one of the streets, pause for a moment to peer into a particular store window, walk a short distance further, and then turn around and head back to the corner, pausing once again to peer into the same window. The two men would then confer briefly before the second man would stroll down the street and peer into the same store window. Detective McFadden observed Chilton and Terry repeat this reconnaissance ritual roughly a dozen times until a third man appeared, spoke with them briefly, and departed down one of the streets. Chilton and Terry resumed their pacing, peering, and conferring for another ten minutes, after which they departed together, following the path taken earlier by the third man. At this point, the police detective was thoroughly convinced that Chilton and Terry were "casing a job, a stick up." He followed them, and when they stopped to converse with the third man who had met them earlier on the street corner, he decided to intervene. Detective McFadden approached the three men, identified himself as a police officer, and asked for their names. When the men "mumbled something" in response to his inquiry, McFadden spun Terry around so that he was facing the other two men, patted down the outside of his clothing, and felt what he believed was a pistol. A more thorough search found that it was a .38 caliber revolver, and a frisk of the other two men revealed a revolver in Chilton's overcoat pocket. All three of the suspects were taken to the police station, where Chilton and Terry were formally charged with carrying concealed weapons.

In *Terry*, the prosecution argued that the guns were "seized" in a "search incidental to a lawful arrest." The defense countered that Detective McFadden lacked probable cause to make an arrest and that, therefore, the guns obtained must be suppressed as evidence since the search and seizure were illegal within the meaning of the Fourth Amendment. The trial court in Ohio recognized that Officer McFadden's search was not made incidental to a lawful arrest because no arrest had been made before the search. Instead, the court saw the case as one of stop and frisk. Hence, the court ruled that Detective McFadden's method of obtaining the guns was lawful. In fact, the court stated that McFadden had a duty to investigate suspicious activity and to protect himself by frisking for weapons. As a result, Chilton and Terry were sentenced to one to three years in the state penitentiary. Two appellate courts in Ohio upheld Terry's conviction, and the U.S. Supreme Court granted certiorari (Inciardi, 1987). In *Terry*, the Court ruled that Detective McFadden had reasonable grounds to believe that the "suspects" were armed and dangerous, that swift measures were necessary for the protection of himself and others, and that his frisk was appropriate since it was limited to a patting down of the outer clothing until he felt weapons (Inciardi, 1987). *Terry* established policing procedures that would guide all stop and frisk encounters. They are often referred to as "Terry stops." In the Court's opinion, Chief Justice Earl Warren stated that five conditions must be met to justify a stop and frisk action: first, when a police officer observes unusual conduct which leads the officer to reasonably conclude, in light of his or her experience, that criminal activity may be afoot; second, that the person with whom he or she is dealing may be armed and dangerous; third, when in the course of investigating this conduct, the officer identifies himself or herself as a police officer; fourth, when the officer makes a reasonable inquiry; and fifth, when nothing in the initial stages of the encounter serves to dispel the officer's reasonable fear for the safety of himself or herself or for the safety of others. Chief Justice Warren also stated that the scope of the frisk must be a limited search of the outer clothing in an effort to discover weapons and that the search must be limited by the circumstances of the particular encounter (Inciardi, 1987, p. 229). The *Terry* ruling essentially established that police officers do not have the authority to stop, search, and interrogate just any person he or she sees on the street; rather, the officer must have reasonable grounds for doing so.

Adam v. Williams
407 U.S. 143 (1972)

While patrolling in a high-crime area, a police officer was approached by an informant who had provided him with reliable information in the past. The informant pointed at a car and told the officer that the driver was in possession of drugs and a handgun. The informant also told the officer that the weapon and the drugs could be found in the driver's waistband. After receiving this information, the officer went over to the vehicle, tapped on the window, and asked the driver to roll the window down. The driver lowered the window, and the officer reached into the car and retrieved the handgun (which was not visible from the officer's view outside of the car) from the driver's waistband, where the informant had said it would be located. The officer asked the driver to get out of the car and effected an arrest. The driver was also searched incident to a lawful arrest. The search revealed that the driver was in possession of heroin (as the informant had suggested). The officer proceeded to search the vehicle and discovered other contraband. The respondent was charged with possession of a handgun and drugs. At trial, Adam filed a motion to suppress the handgun and drugs on the grounds that the officer did not have probable cause to stop or search him. The court refused the motion and he was subsequently convicted. Adam appealed the case and the U.S. Supreme Court granted review. In *Adam*, the Court held that a police officer making a reasonable investigatory stop may conduct a limited protective search for concealed weapons when he or she has reason to believe that the suspect is armed and dangerous. In this case, the information provided by the informant in the past had proven reliable enough to justify the actions of the officer: first, stopping the petitioner and then seizing the weapon for the officer's own protection. Both actions provided the officer with reasonable grounds for the search incidental to the arrest that followed.

United States v. Cortez
449 U.S. 411 (1981)

From footprints found over a period of time, officers concluded that groups of illegal immigrants were walking over a well-defined path from the Mexican border to a highway where they would be picked up by a motor vehicle. A similar set of footprints was found in each group; therefore, officers further concluded, one person was acting as a guide to these groups. On the basis of the time of day when the tracks were found, officers determined that the crossings occurred on nights during the weekend, when the weather was clear. Because the tracks approached the highway and then turned to the east, the officers finally concluded that the vehicle would approach from the east and then return in the same direction. On the basis of these conclusions and because a particular Sunday was the first clear night in three days, officers set up surveillance of the highway. Of the fifteen to twenty vehicles that passed the officers during their surveillance, only two matched the type they were looking for. As one truck passed, the officers obtained a partial license plate number. When the same vehicle passed them again, heading east, they pursued and stopped it. Cortez was driving the truck, and a man wearing shoes with soles matching those found in the desert was a passenger. The officers told Cortez they were conducting an immigration check, and they searched the truck. In the back of the truck were six illegal immigrants. Cortez and his companions were arrested, charged with, and convicted of transporting illegal aliens. In *Cortez*, the U.S. Supreme Court stated that the totality of the circumstances must be taken into account and that the officers must have a particularized objective basis for suspecting that the individual stopped is engaged in criminal activity.

United States v. Sokolow
490 U.S. 1 (1989)

Sokolow purchased two round-trip tickets for a flight from Honolulu to Miami under an assumed name. He paid for the tickets from a roll of $20 bills that appeared to contain about $4,000. He appeared nervous during the transaction. Neither he nor his companion checked their luggage. Additional investigation revealed that Sokolow had scheduled a return flight for three days later. On the basis of these facts, which fit a "drug courier profile" (developed by the Drug Enforcement Administration [DEA]), officers stopped the pair and took them into the DEA office at the airport, where their luggage was examined by a narcotics-detection dog. The examination revealed the presence of narcotics in one of Sokolow's bags. Sokolow was arrested and a search warrant was obtained for the bag. No narcotics were found in the bag, but documents indicating involvement in drug trafficking were discovered. Upon a second search by the narcotics-detection dog, narcotics were detected in another of Sokolow's bags. Sokolow was released until a search warrant was obtained the next morning. A search of the bag revealed 1,063 grams of cocaine. Sokolow was again arrested and charged with possession of cocaine with intent to distribute it. In this case, the U.S. Supreme Court held that a "drug courier profile" is valid under the Fourth Amendment because the facts in their totality created reasonable suspicion for officers to stop Sokolow and make a subsequent search of his luggage.

Minnesota v. Dickerson
508 U.S. 366 (1993)

On the evening of November 9, 1989, two Minneapolis police officers were patrolling an area on the city's north side in a marked squad car. At about 8:15 p.m., one of the officers observed the respondent leaving a twelve-unit apartment building on Morgan Avenue North. The officer, having previously responded to complaints of drug sales in the building's hallways and having executed several search warrants on the premises, considered the building a notorious "crack house." According to testimony credited by the trial court, the respondent began walking toward the police, but upon spotting the squad car and making eye contact with one of the officers, he halted abruptly and began walking in the opposite direction. His suspicion aroused, this officer watched as the respondent turned and entered an alley on the other side of the apartment building. Because of the respondent's seemingly evasive actions and because he had just left a building known for cocaine traffic, the officers decided to stop the respondent and investigate further. The officers pulled their squad car into the alley and ordered the respondent to stop and submit to a pat down. The frisk revealed no weapons, but the officer conducting the frisk did take an interest in a small lump in the respondent's nylon jacket. The officer later testified: "As I pat searched the front of his body, I felt a lump, a small lump, in the front pocket. I examined it with my fingers and it slid and it felt to be a lump of crack cocaine in cellophane." The officer then reached into the respondent's pocket and retrieved a small plastic bag containing one-fifth of a gram of crack cocaine. The respondent was arrested and charged in Hennepin County District Court with possession of a controlled substance. Before trial, the respondent moved to suppress the cocaine. The trial court first concluded that the officers were justified under *Terry* in stopping the respondent to investigate whether he might be engaged in criminal activity. The court further found that the officers were justified in frisking the respondent to ensure that he was not carrying a weapon. The U.S. Supreme Court, in an opinion by Justice Byron White in which all the justices concurred on the rule but not on its application to the facts of this case, held that an officer may seize nonthreatening contraband detected during a protective pat down under *Terry v. Ohio* only if, by the object's contour or mass, its identity is immediately apparent. Six justices agreed that the actions of the officer in "squeezing, sliding and otherwise manipulating the contents of the defendant's pocket" to identify a lump of crack cocaine that weighed one-fifth of a gram went beyond what was permissible.

Alabama v. White

496 U.S. 325 (1990)

A policeman received an anonymous phone call stating White would be leaving a certain apartment at a certain time, driving a certain car, and going to a certain motel. The caller also said that White would be carrying cocaine in a brown attaché case. The policeman went to the apartment house, saw White leave the apartment house (carrying nothing), get into the described car, and drive towards the designated motel. The policeman then stopped the car, and the stop led to a consent search that revealed cocaine in the car. The U.S. Supreme Court upheld the stop. While the anonymous tip alone would not have been sufficient (since neither the reliability of the informant nor the basis of knowledge had been shown), the policeman's corroboration of details was sufficient to supply the necessary showing. Comparing this case with *Illinois v. Gates*, the Court acknowledged that the tip in *Dickerson* was not as detailed as it had been in *Gates* and the corroboration was not as complete. The Court, in an opinion by Justice White for six justices, held that a modified version of the "totality of the circumstances" test in *Gates* could be used to establish reasonable suspicion. Both the content of information possessed by police and its degree of reliability are considered in determining "totality of the circumstances."

Illinois v. Wardlow
528 U.S. 119 (2000)

Narcotics officers were caravanning to make arrests in an area known for heavy narcotics trafficking. One officer noticed Wardlow standing next to a building and holding an opaque bag. Wardlow looked toward the officers and fled quickly; the officers followed him. When the officer stopped Wardlow, another officer conducted a Terry pat down on the basis of his experience that weapons were commonly found in the area of the narcotics trafficking. The officer found a handgun and arrested Wardlow. The U.S. Supreme Court argued that Wardlow's presence in a high-crime area, combined with his unprovoked flight after seeing police officers, gives officers sufficient grounds to investigate whether criminal activity is afoot.

United States v. Hensley
469 U.S. 221 (1985)

Hensley was wanted for questioning about an armed robbery in St. Bernard, Ohio. The police issued a "wanted" flyer to other police departments in the area. Knowing of the flyer and after inquiring, without success, about the existence of an arrest warrant, officers in Covington, Kentucky, stopped the automobile that Hensley was driving. Firearms were found in the car and Hensley was arrested. Hensley was ultimately convicted of being a convicted felon in possession of a handgun. He appealed the conviction, claiming that the stop was illegal because there was no probable cause and that therefore the evidence should have been suppressed from trial. The U.S. Supreme Court, in a unanimous decision as written by Justice Sandra Day O'Connor, held that police officers may make an investigative stop in objective reliance on a "wanted flyer" issued by another police department, as long as the flyer was issued on the basis of reasonable suspicion that the wanted person had committed an offense.

Florida v. J. L

529 U.S. 266 (1999)

Police responded to an anonymous tip that a young black male was standing at a particular bus stop wearing a plaid shirt and carrying a gun. When officers observed a person matching that description standing at the bus stop with two other persons, they frisked J. L. and found a pistol. The two other persons were also frisked, but nothing was found. Before the frisks, the officers had not seen a gun and therefore had had no reason to suspect any of the three of illegal conduct. In *J. L.*, the U.S. Supreme Court ruled that "an anonymous tip that a person is carrying a gun is [not], without more, sufficient to justify a police officer's stop and frisk of that person." In this case, the anonymous tip alone did not amount to reasonable suspicion.

United States v. Aruizu

534 U.S. 266 (2001)

The U.S. Border Patrol operated a checkpoint in an isolated area of Arizona. A limited number of roads circumvented the checkpoint and were routinely used by smugglers to avoid it. As a result, sensors were placed along these roads to detect vehicular traffic. When one of the sensors indicated traffic, an officer responded. While following the vehicle for several miles, the officer observed several indicators of suspicious behavior: (1) the time of day when the vehicle was on the road coincided with that of the shift change for roving patrols in the area; (2) the roads taken by the vehicle were remote and not well-suited for the vehicle type; (3) the vehicle slowed suddenly when the driver, Aruizu, first observed the officer (presumably through his rear-view mirror); (4) Aruizu did not look at the officer when the officer's vehicle passed him; (5) children in the vehicle waved mechanically at the passing officer as if they were being instructed; and (6) the vehicle made turns that allowed it to completely avoid the checkpoint. On the basis of these observations, the officer stopped the vehicle. After obtaining consent from Aruizu, who was driving the vehicle, the officer searched the vehicle and found drugs. The court of appeals ruled in favor of suppressing the evidence from the search on the basis of an analysis of what it determined to be ten factors related to the stop. Each of the factors was examined individually and seven were held to be lacking sufficient grounds for reasonable suspicion. Because the majority of these factors were not found sufficient to support reasonable suspicion, the court of appeals ruled the search unconstitutional. The U.S. Supreme Court ruled that "in making reasonable suspicion determinations," reviewing courts must look at the totality of the circumstances of each case to see whether the determining officer has a particularized and objective basis for suspecting legal wrongdoings.

Part Four: Stop and Frisk Exceptions

Terry v. Ohio essentially represents an exception to the rules of search and seizure (Bartollas, 1988). The Terry rule allows a pat down for weapons, but not a full-scale search of the body. If a weapon is found, the person can be arrested and a full-scale search can be conducted incidental to the arrest. While *Terry* specifies how people are supposed to be treated during encounters with police, automobile drivers may enjoy less protection, especially during investigatory automobile stops, automobile stops based on anonymous tips, and automobile stops based on pretext.

Investigatory Automobile Stops

An *investigatory automobile stop* is considered a seizure within the meaning of the Fourth Amendment. In fact, a court has stated: "[T]he police do not have an unrestricted right to stop people, either pedestrians or drivers. The 'good faith' of the police is not enough, nor is an inarticulate hunch. They must have an articulable suspicion of wrongdoing, done, or in prospect" (*United States v. Montgomery*). When officers lawfully stop a vehicle, they can make observations that could change their original "articulable" suspicion to the establishing of probable cause to believe that the vehicle contains contraband—a belief which justifies a full search of the vehicle. When contraband is discovered, officers can effect an arrest. After the driver of a vehicle has been arrested, officers can conduct a search of the passenger compartment of the vehicle (del Carmen, 1991b, 2004). Moreover, the scope of the search can include the entire vehicle and can comprise the contents of any container found near the passenger compartment, as long as the container is viewed by the officer as a place where the suspect may be able to hide a weapon or articles of evidence connected with the crime he or she is believed to have committed (del Carmen, 1991b, 2004). Experts argue that lower federal and state courts have routinely allowed the stop and frisk doctrine to apply to stops of vehicles as well as persons (Scheb & Scheb, 1999). They argue that the Terry rule implies that the addition of vehicles is rational. Just as police officers treat persons on the street, they must be sure that reasonable suspicion exists before they stop motorists.

When police officers stop a vehicle, they must ask the suspect to present his or her license and vehicle registration. Officers also typically check the license plate to confirm the suspect's identification. In addition, the officer may ask questions of the suspect and verify the suspect's explanations with the station house to discover if he or she has any outstanding warrants (Scheb & Scheb, 1999). In *Michigan v. Long*, the U.S. Supreme Court held that when police officers stop a vehicle based on reasonable suspicion, they have the right to search the passenger compartment for weapons, provided that they have reason to believe (on the basis of specific and articulable factors together with rational inferences) that a suspect is dangerous. However, the search must be limited in scope: it cannot be conducted beyond the area where the suspect can access a weapon that could be hidden. del Carmen (1991b) argues that warrantless searches may not be allowed if a vehicle is not "mobile." Such cases may not come under the automobile exception since officers have time to procure a search warrant without fear that the vehicle will be gone. However, the U.S. Supreme Court has not given a definitive ruling on this issue. Therefore, police would do well to get a search warrant.

In cases where vehicles are impounded, officers can search the car for inventory purposes without ever obtaining a search warrant. If they find evidence of a crime or other contraband, it can be used against a suspect to gain a criminal conviction. Any challenge to suppress the evidence from admission into trial will probably be denied since officers will claim that the evidence was inadvertently discovered. They can also claim that the vehicle was inventoried to protect the owner's personal effects. The U.S. Supreme Court has considered many circumstances in which police can have reasonable suspicion. These circumstances include: (1) the officer's knowledge, expertise, and experience on the force; (2) the physical appearance of the suspect as fitting the description of the person wanted for having committed the crime; (3) the description of the suspect's vehicle; or (4) the place where the suspect or vehicle was seen. Moreover, the suspect's behavior and gestures or any attempts at flight have also been considered (Scheb & Scheb, 1999).

Automobile Stops Based on Anonymous Tips

Appellate courts have had to address the issue of whether a police officer's reasonable suspicion can be established on the basis of anonymous tips. In *Alabama v. White*, the U.S. Supreme Court held that an anonymous tip corroborated by independent police work can help an officer establish reasonable suspicion that necessitates an investigatory stop of a vehicle. Since the decision in *White*, state courts have had to address the same issue. A number of them have followed a strict interpretation of the Court's decision: they are disinclined to allow police to conduct investigatory stops when independent corroboration does not exist and anonymous sources lack credibility (see *State v. Hjelmstad*). Nevertheless, many other state courts allow information provided by an anonymous source to warrant an investigatory stop if the information is verified by sufficient independent evidence of criminal activity (see *People v. George*).

Automobile Stops Based on Pretexts

Stopping a motor vehicle based on the pretext that it has committed a minor traffic infraction is another tactic that police may use to conduct an investigatory stop and search (Scheb & Scheb, 1999). While once criticized, making a stop based on a pretext appears to be a legal law-enforcement practice. For example, in *United States v. Smith*, the U.S. Supreme Court held that the appropriate standard was whether a reasonable officer would have stopped the vehicle if he or she did not have an additional invalid purpose. Many state courts have followed the ruling in *Smith*. Yet in *Alejandre v. State*, the Nevada Supreme Court ruled that when police stopped a vehicle for crossing a fog line twice by "about a tire width," the stop was merely a pretext for a search for possible drugs. The court argued that such a minor traffic violation would not have caused a reasonable officer to stop the defendant's vehicle. However, in *Whren v. United States*, the U.S. Supreme Court held that an officer's motives in stopping a vehicle are irrelevant as long as he or she has an objective basis for the stop. The Court went on to say that as long as the police officer has probable cause to believe that a minor traffic violation has occurred, there is no violation of the Fourth Amendment. The complete impact of *Whren* is unknown.

Can Police Require Drivers and Passengers to Exit Their Vehicles?

Police officers routinely stop vehicles and request that the driver exit the vehicle. In some cases, officers may also request that passengers exit the vehicle (Scheb & Scheb, 1999). Such a practice can only be justified when an officer believes that his or her life is in jeopardy because a driver or passenger could be hiding a weapon within a compartment of a vehicle. The U.S. Supreme Court in *Maryland v. Wilson* reaffirmed this position: the Court held that when drivers and passengers are required to exit their automobiles, police often discover contraband or observe behavior indicating intoxication. In *Wilson*, after passengers had been ordered out of a vehicle, one of them dropped a quantity of crack cocaine onto the ground. The evidence was admitted into court to gain a criminal conviction.

Use of Drug Courier Profiles

Using drug courier profiles has become a controversial law-enforcement practice because it tends to treat people of color and other minorities in a biased fashion. In preparing and using this kind of profile, police typically consider such behavioral factors as paying cash for an airline ticket, spending short periods of time in major cities, not checking luggage, and showing a nervous demeanor. Police often use these profiles to identify and detain suspected drug couriers. The U.S. Supreme Court has upheld the use of a drug courier profile, along with other factors that create reasonable suspicion that criminal activity is occurring. In *United States v. Sokolow*, the U.S. Supreme Court argued that as long as a police officer considered the "totality of the circumstances," an investigatory stop of an airline passenger was reasonable. However, in *City of St. Paul v. Uber*, a Minnesota appeals court reversed the conviction of a defendant whose vehicle had been stopped because his behavior was consistent with the police profile of a person looking for prostitutes. In *Uber*, the court reasoned that the police had conducted the stop without a particular suspicion. While applying *Sokolow*, the court stated that "the observable facts taken together do not approach the composite bundle available to the DEA in *Sokolow*" but that *Uber* is tantamount to a random stop.

Racial Profiling in Stop and Frisk

An issue that has come to the attention of the broader society, as well as the law-enforcement community, is that of racial profiling, or "driving while black." When cases involving this issue emerge, suspects contend that they were unfairly targeted for a stop and frisk, or even arrested, only because of their race or ethnicity. Legal experts contend that this practice is unconstitutional since it fails to meet the standards established in *Terry* and violates the Fourteenth Amendment's equal-protection clause. In brief, *Terry* requires suspicious behavior for a police officer to initiate a stop and the feeling of danger for an officer to effect a pat down; the equal-protection clause requires that every person in the United States be treated equally. Nevertheless, in their research Maclin (1998) and Gaines and Miller (2004) conclude that in cities around the country, police agencies appear to engage in racial discrimination against African-American and Latino motorists. In fact, racial profiling is reported to be commonplace in states such as New Jersey, New York, and Maryland. For example, class-action lawsuits have been filed in these states, contending that police officers disproportionately stopped African-Americans and other minorities without reasonable suspicion or probable cause and searched their vehicles. An investigation revealed that local police officers were using racial profiling in deciding which vehicles to stop (Gaines & Miller, 2004).

Recently, New York settled a class-action lawsuit brought by the Center for Constitutional Rights on behalf of young black and Latino men, alleging that police officers engaged in racial profiling by unjustly stopping and frisking them. The settlement required that New York pay damages and that its law-enforcement officers use a form detailing their reasons for stopping and frisking motorists. Moreover, four times a year the forms are to be tabulated and released so that watchdog groups can look for evidence of racial profiling ("City Agrees to Change," 2003). Nevertheless, police officers have been given leeway to consider the "totality of the circumstances" in determining reasonable suspicion. To some officers, race and ethnicity should be factors included in their determination of suspicion. While this practice may seem legal, it was rejected in *Whren v. United States*. In *Whren*, the U.S. Supreme Court ruled that the subjective intentions of police officers, including any motives stemming from racial stereotyping or bias, are irrelevant under the Fourth Amendment. The Court went on to say that as long as there is objective probable cause regarding a traffic violation, any other reasons for the stop of a moving vehicle will not be considered (Gaines & Miller, 2004). The *Whren* decision allows police to stop a suspect who violates a traffic law. At that point, the decision to stop the motorist is constitutional even if the "real" reason for the stop is the motorist's race.

Part Five: Factors Invalidating a Stop and Frisk

A stop and frisk is illegal when an officer is unable to establish that reasonable suspicion existed at the time when he or she stopped and frisked the suspect. That reasonable suspicion is subsequently established cannot validate the previous action. Evidence obtained by an illegal stop and frisk is inadmissible in court. An officer's mere suspicion or hunch that a crime is afoot cannot suffice to validate a stop and frisk. In addition, the frisk itself must not be more than a superficial search. If it is too intrusive, it will violate the suspect's Fourth Amendment protection against unreasonable searches and seizures. A frisk of the suspect's inner clothing will also constitute a Fourth Amendment infringement. Another factor invalidating a frisk concerns its duration: if a frisk lasts for a long period of time, it may amount to an arrest, thereby requiring probable cause as justification for this type of search. The stop and frisk may also turn out to be illegal if the officer fails to identify himself or herself as a law-enforcement official. Other factors which may invalidate a stop and frisk depend on the particular facts and circumstances of each case. The categories of invalidating factors cannot be regarded as exhaustive. However, the legal limits of a stop and frisk may be summed up thus: "[A]n investigative detention must be temporary and last no longer than necessary to effectuate the purpose of the stop ... [and] the investigative methods employed should be the least intrusive means reasonably available to verify or dispel the officer's suspicion in a short period of time. It follows, therefore, that if an officer detains a person longer than is necessary, the investigating detention is transformed into a full seizure or arrest justifiable only on grounds of probable cause" (Sheb & Sheb, 1999, p. 419).

Part Six: Some Pertinent Cases

Maryland v. Wilson
519 U.S. 408 (1997)

A passenger was ordered out of the car in which he was sitting after an officer observed that he was sweating and acting extremely nervous. As Wilson exited the vehicle, a quantity of crack cocaine fell to the ground and he was placed under arrest. In holding that officers are entitled to order passengers out of a car as a matter of course, the majority of the U.S. Supreme Court recognized that when a traffic stop occurs, "[t]here is probable cause to believe that the driver has committed a minor vehicular offense, but there is no such reason to stop or detain the passengers." By noting the absence of any objective justification to detain passengers in cars stopped for traffic violations, however, the Court obviously did not mean to imply that passengers are routinely subjected to illegal seizures. The Court, in a 7-2 decision written by Chief Justice William Rehnquist, held that police officers may routinely order passengers out of vehicles that are legally stopped. No showing of suspicion or probable cause regarding the passenger's activities is necessary. The Court did not address the issue of whether a passenger could be detained or searched once he or she was out of the vehicle.

Pennsylvania v. Bruder
488 U.S. 9 (1988)

After being stopped by a police officer, the respondent Bruder was given several sobriety tests and, in answer to questions, stated that he had been drinking. He failed the tests and was then arrested and given Miranda warnings. At his trial, his statements and conduct before the arrest were admitted into evidence, and he was convicted of driving while under the influence of alcohol. The Pennsylvania Superior Court reversed the conviction on the grounds that the roadside questioning had been conducted by custodial interrogation and should have been suppressed for lack of Miranda warnings. The U.S. Supreme Court, in a per curiam opinion by the seven justices, held that no Miranda warnings are required during a routine traffic stop because the motorist's freedom of action is not curtailed to a degree associated with formal arrest.

Michigan v. Chesternut
486 U.S. 567 (1988)

Police officers in a patrol car saw Chesternut observe the patrol car nearing his corner and then begin to run. The officers followed Chesternut around the corner "to see where he was going" and then drove alongside him. Chesternut discarded several packets. The officers stopped, picked up the packets, and saw that they contained illegal narcotics. They then arrested Chesternut and he was convicted. Chesternut challenged the legality of the arrest. The U.S. Supreme Court held that no "seizure" of Chesternut had occurred before the arrest. In fact, the Court, in a unanimous opinion written by Justice Harry Blackmun, held that the facts of this case which supported an "investigatory pursuit" of a suspect during which officers drove alongside the suspect but did not stop him did not amount to a seizure within the meaning of the Fourth Amendment because it would not have communicated to a reasonable person that he or she was not at liberty to ignore the police presence and go about his or her business.

Hayes v. Florida
470 U.S. 811 (1985)

While Hayes was wanted on suspicion in a burglary and rape committed in Punta Gorda, Florida, the police, without a warrant, went to Hayes's home to obtain his fingerprints. When police arrived at his home, they indicated that they wanted him to come to the station house. Hayes told the officers that he had no interest in accompanying them. At this point, one of the officers told him that if he did not come, he would be placed under arrest. Hayes told the officers that he would rather accompany them than be arrested. He was taken to the station house and fingerprinted. When police were able to match his prints with those found at the crime scene, he was arrested. During the trial, Hayes moved to suppress the fingerprints as evidence, but his request was denied and he was subsequently convicted. On appeal, the Florida District Court of Appeals affirmed, holding that the police could, without the petitioner's consent or probable cause to arrest, transport the petitioner to the station house and take his fingerprints on the basis of reasonable suspicion that he was involved in committing a crime. The U.S. Supreme Court, in an opinion written by Justice White for five justices, held that police action, without probable cause, a warrant, or consent, cannot transport a suspect to the police station for fingerprinting. Brief detention in the field, based on reasonable suspicion for the purpose of fingerprinting, may be permissible under the Fourth Amendment.

United States v. Sharpe
470 U.S. 675 (1985)

On the morning of June 9, 1978, Agent Cooke of the Drug Enforcement Administration (DEA) was on patrol in an unmarked vehicle on a costal road near Sunset Beach, North Carolina, an area under surveillance for suspected drug trafficking. At approximately 6:30 a.m., Cooke noticed a blue pickup truck with an attached camper shell traveling on the highway in tandem with a blue Pontiac Bonneville. The respondent Savage was driving the pickup and the respondent Sharpe was driving the Pontiac. The Pontiac also carried a passenger, Davis—the charges against whom were later dropped. Observing that the truck was riding low in the rear and that the camper shell did not bounce or sway appreciably when the truck drove over bumps or around curves, Agent Cooke concluded that it was heavily loaded. A quilted material covered the rear and side windows of the camper shell. Cooke's suspicions were sufficiently aroused to follow the two vehicles for approximately twenty miles as they proceeded south into South Carolina. He then decided to make an "investigative stop" and radioed the State Highway Patrol for assistance. Officer Thrasher, driving a marked patrol car, responded to the call. Almost immediately after Thrasher caught up with the procession, the Pontiac and the pickup turned off the highway and onto a campground road. Cooke and Thrasher followed the two vehicles as the latter drove along the road at fifty-five to sixty miles an hour, exceeding the speed limit of thirty-five miles an hour. The road eventually looped back to the highway, onto which Savage and Sharpe turned and continued to drive south. At this point, all four vehicles were in the middle lane of the three right-hand lanes of the highway. Agent Cooke asked Officer Thrasher to signal both vehicles to stop. Thrasher pulled alongside the Pontiac, which was in the lead, turned on his flashing light, and motioned for the driver of the Pontiac to stop. As Sharpe moved the Pontiac into the right lane, the pickup truck cut between the Pontiac and Thrasher's patrol car, nearly hitting the patrol car, and continued down the highway. Thrasher pursued the truck while Cooke pulled up behind the Pontiac. Cooke approached the Pontiac and identified himself. He requested identification, and Sharpe produced a Georgia driver's license bearing the name of Raymond J. Pavlovich. Cooke then attempted to radio Thrasher to determine whether he had been successful in stopping the pickup truck, but he was unable to make contact for several minutes, apparently because Thrasher was not in his patrol car. Cooke radioed the local police for assistance, and two officers from the Myrtle Beach Police Department arrived about ten minutes later. Asking the two officers to "maintain the situation," Cooke left to join Thrasher. Meanwhile, Thrasher had stopped the pickup truck about one-half mile down the road. After stopping the truck, Thrasher approached it with his revolver drawn, ordered the driver, Savage, to get out and assume a "spread eagled" position against the side of the truck, and patted him down. Thrasher then holstered his gun and asked Savage for his driver's license and the truck's vehicle registration. Savage produced his own Florida driver's license and a bill of sale for the truck bearing the name of Pavlovich. In response to questions from Thrasher concerning the ownership of the truck, Savage said that the truck belonged to a friend and that he was taking it to have its shock absorbers repaired. When Thrasher told Savage that he would be held until the arrival of Cooke, whom Thrasher identified as a DEA agent, Savage became nervous, said that he wanted to leave, and requested the return of his driver's license. Thrasher replied that Savage was not free to leave at that time. Agent Cooke arrived at the scene approximately fifteen minutes after the truck had been stopped. Thrasher gave Cooke Savage's license and the bill of sale for the truck. Cooke noted that the bill of sale bore the same name as the one on Sharpe's license. Cooke identified himself to Savage as a DEA agent and said that he thought the truck was loaded with marijuana. Cooke twice sought permission to search the camper, but Savage declined to give it, explaining that he was not the owner of the truck. Cooke then stepped on the rear of the truck and, since it did not sink any lower, his suspicion was confirmed that the truck was probably overloaded. He put his nose against the rear window, which was covered from the inside, and reported that he could smell marijuana. Without seeking Savage's permission, Cooke removed the keys from the ignition, opened the rear of the camper shell, and observed a large number of burlap-wrapped bales resembling the bales of marijuana that Cooke had seen in previous investigations. Agent Cooke then placed Savage under arrest and left him with Thrasher. Cooke returned to the Pontiac and arrested Sharpe and Davis. Approximately thirty to forty minutes had elapsed between the time Cooke stopped the Pontiac and the time he returned to arrest Sharpe and Davis. Cooke assembled the various parties and vehicles and led them to the Myrtle Beach police station. That evening, DEA agents took the truck to the Federal Building in Charleston, South Carolina. Several days later, Cooke supervised the unloading of the truck, which contained forty-three bales weighing a total of 2,629 pounds. Acting without a search warrant, Cooke had eight randomly selected bales opened and sampled. Chemical tests showed that the samples were marijuana. Sharpe and Savage were charged with possession of a controlled substance with intent to distribute. The United States District Court for the District of South Carolina denied the respondents' motion to suppress the contraband and the respondents were convicted. The U.S. Supreme Court, in an opinion written by Chief Justice Warren Burger for six justices, held that the Fourth Amendment imposes no rigid time limitations on investigatory detentions. Given the circumstances of the case, the investigation was conducted in a diligent and reasonable manner and a thirty-to-forty-minute stop was not unreasonable.

New Jersey v. T. L. O.
469 U.S. 325 (1985)

A teacher at a New Jersey high school discovered Ms. T. L. O., a fourteen-year-old freshman, and her companion smoking cigarettes in a school lavatory, in violation of a school rule. The two girls were taken to an office where they were questioned by a vice-principal. When T. L. O. denied smoking and claimed that she was not a smoker, the vice-principal demanded to see her purse. Upon opening it, he observed cigarettes and the rolling papers typically associated with marijuana use. He then searched the purse thoroughly and found marijuana, a pipe, plastic bags, a substantial amount of money, an index card listing students who owed T. L .O. money, and two letters that implicated T. L. O. in marijuana dealings. The police were called and delinquency charges were brought against Ms. T. L. O. in juvenile court. The court denied T. L. O.'s motion to suppress the evidence found in her purse on Fourth Amendment grounds, declared the search to be a reasonable one, and adjudicated T. L. O. to be delinquent. T. L. O. appealed the decision. The decision was reversed by the New Jersey Supreme Court. However, the Reagan administration appealed to the U.S. Supreme Court on behalf of the state of New Jersey. The U.S. Supreme Court, in an opinion written by Justice White, relevant parts of which were signed by eight justices, held that the Fourth Amendment applies to searches by public-school officials. These searches are judged on reasonableness under all the circumstances and do not require probable cause if school officials believe that a student is currently violating, or has violated, a school regulation or the law.

Michigan v. Long
463 U.S. 1032 (1983)

Officers observed an automobile traveling erratically and at a high rate of speed. When the automobile swerved into a ditch, the officers stopped to investigate. They were met at the rear of the car by Long, who "appeared to be under the influence of something" and did not respond to a request to produce his license. Upon a second request, Long did produce his license. After a second request to see his registration, Long began walking toward the rear door of the vehicle. The officers followed him and noticed a large hunting knife on the floorboard of the vehicle. They then stopped Long and frisked him. No other weapons were found. One of the officers shined his flashlight into the car and discovered marijuana. Long was then arrested. The officers then opened the unlocked trunk and discovered approximately seventy-five pounds of marijuana. Long was charged with and then convicted of possession of marijuana. The U.S. Supreme Court, in an opinion written by Justice O'Connor for five justices, held that a protective search of the passenger compartment of a vehicle is permissible when the vehicle has been stopped on reasonable suspicion and the officer reasonably believes the occupants are dangerous and may gain immediate access to weapons inside the vehicle. That officers intended to release the suspect is immaterial.

United States v. Place
462 U.S. 696 (1983)

Raymond Place's behavior aroused the suspicions of law-enforcement officers as Place waited in line at Miami International Airport to purchase a ticket to New York's LaGuardia Airport. DEA agents at New York's LaGuardia Airport received a tip from police officers at Miami Airport that Place had given them inaccurate information about his home address, which suggested that he might be carrying drugs. When Place landed at LaGuardia, the agents approached Place and asked him to consent to a search of his luggage, but he refused. The agents took his luggage to Kennedy Airport, where they subjected it to a "canine sniff test" ninety minutes later. After the dog alerted the agents of a suspicious substance, they opened the luggage and found cocaine. Place challenged the seizure of the luggage. The U.S. Supreme Court, in an opinion written by Justice O'Connor for six justices, held that the Fourth Amendment was not violated by a temporary detention of personal luggage based on reasonable suspicion for the purpose of allowing a dog trained in narcotics detection to sniff it. The Court found that a ninety-minute detention in this case was unreasonable and therefore invalidated the search.

Brown v. Texas
443 U.S. 47 (1979)

Two Texas law-enforcement officers in a patrol car observed the defendant (Ed Brown) and another man in an alley, walking in opposite directions. The officers believed that the two men had been together or were about to meet when their police vehicle approached them. The officers did not detain the unnamed man, but they stopped Ed Brown and asked for identification because, according to the officers, he "looked suspicious" and had not been seen in the area before. The officers later testified that he had not been acting suspiciously and that they had not thought he might have a weapon. The stop had been conducted because the officers wanted to know who he was. But Brown refused to identify himself to the officers. He was then arrested under a Texas criminal law which required a person to identify himself or herself properly and accurately when requested to do so by police officers. Brown's conviction was appealed to the U.S. Supreme Court on the basis of whether the Texas statute was valid. In *Brown*, the Court applied a three-pronged test to determine if a brief seizure of a person was reasonable. The Court weighed: (1) the gravity of the public concerns served by the seizure; (2) the degree to which the seizure advances the public interests; and (3) the severity of the interference with individual liberty. The Court, in a unanimous opinion written by Chief Justice Burger, held that the Texas law was invalid insofar as it allowed officers to require a person to identify himself or herself when there was no reasonable suspicion that the person was or had been engaged in criminal activity. In this case, the Court held: "[T]he fact that [a person] was in a neighborhood frequented by drug users, standing alone, is not a basis for concluding that [he] himself was engaged in criminal conduct." Essentially, the Court invalidated the seizure of Brown in the absence of suspicion of any wrongdoing.

Dunaway v. New York
442 U.S. 200 (1979)

An informant implicated Dunaway in a murder but could not provide sufficient information to justify the issuance of a warrant. However, the police took Dunaway into custody at his neighbor's home and without his consent transported him to the police station in a squad car. Although he was never told that he was under arrest, there was evidence that "he would have been physically restrained if he had attempted to leave." At the station, Dunaway was placed in an interrogation room and subjected to extensive custodial interrogation. During this time, after receiving his Miranda warnings, he made incriminating statements implicating himself in the murder. Dunaway was charged with and then convicted of the murder. The U.S. Supreme Court, in an opinion written by Justice William Brennan for six justices, held that a suspect cannot be detained and transported to a police station for interrogation without probable cause to arrest.

Delaware v. Prouse
440 U.S. 648 (1979)

At 7:20 p.m. on November 30, 1976, a New Castle County, Delaware, patrolman in a police cruiser stopped the automobile occupied by the respondent. The patrolman smelled marijuana smoke as he was walking toward the stopped vehicle, and he seized marijuana which was in plain view on the car floor. The respondent was subsequently indicted for illegal possession of a controlled substance. At a hearing on the respondent's motion to suppress the marijuana seized as a result of the stop, the patrolman testified that prior to stopping the vehicle, he had observed neither traffic nor equipment violations nor any suspicious activity and that he had made the stop only in order to check the driver's license and registration. The patrolman was not acting pursuant to any standards, guidelines, or procedures pertaining to document spot checks promulgated by either his department or the state attorney general. Characterizing the stop as "routine," the patrolman explained, "I saw the car in the area and wasn't answering any complaints, so I decided to pull them off." The trial court granted the motion to suppress, finding the stop and detention to have been wholly capricious and therefore in violation of the Fourth Amendment. The Delaware Supreme Court affirmed, noting first that "the issue of the legal validity of systematic, roadblock-type stops of a number of vehicles for license and vehicle registration check is not now before the Court." The court further held that "a random stop of a motorist in the absence of specific articulable facts which justify the stop by indicating a reasonable suspicion that a violation of the law has occurred is constitutionally impermissible and violative of the Fourth and Fourteenth Amendments to the United States Constitution." The U.S. Supreme Court, in an 8-1 decision, its opinion written by Justice White, held that police officers may not stop the driver of a vehicle in order to check his or her driver's license and car registration absent at least reasonable suspicion that the driver is unlicensed, that the vehicle is unregistered, or that it is otherwise subject to seizure for violation of the law.

References

Bartollas, C. (1988). *American criminal justice: An introduction.* New York: MacMillan.

Black, H. C. (1979). *Black's law dictionary* (5th ed.). St. Paul, MN: West.

City agrees to change stop-and-frisk rules. (2003, September 19). *The New York Sun,* p. 2.

del Carmen, R. V. (1991a). *Civil liabilities in American policing: A text for law enforcement personnel.* Englewood Cliffs, NJ: Prentice Hall.

del Carmen, R. V. (1991b). *Criminal procedure: Law and practice.* Pacific Grove, CA: Brooks Cole.

del Carmen, R. V. (2004). *Criminal procedure: Law and practice* (6th ed.). Belmont, CA: Wadsworth/Thomson Learning.

Dressler, J. (2002). *Understanding criminal procedure* (3rd ed.). Newark, NJ: LexisNexis.

Gaines, L., & Miller, R. (2004). *Criminal justice in action: The core* (2nd ed.). Belmont, CA: Wadsworth/Thomson Learning.

Inciardi, J. A. (1987). *Criminal justice* (2nd ed.). Orlando, FL: Harcourt Brace Jovanovich.

Maclin, T. (1998). Race and the Fourth Amendment. *Vanderbilt Law Review, 51* (March), 347.

Moskovitz, M. (2000). *Cases and problems in criminal procedures: The practice* (3rd ed.). New York: Lexis.

Peoples, E. E. (2003). *Basic criminal procedures* (2nd ed.). Upper Saddle River, NJ: Prentice Hall.

Scheb, J. M., & Scheb, J. M. (1999). *Criminal law and procedure* (3rd ed.). Belmont, CA: West/ Wadsworth.

Stuckcy, G. B., Robcrson, C., & Wallacc, H. (2004). *Procedures in the justice system* (7th ed.). Upper Saddle River, NJ: Pearson-Prentice Hall.

Weston, P. B., & Wells, M. (1976). *Criminal evidence for police* (2nd ed.). Englewood Cliffs, NJ.: Prentice Hall.

Cases Cited

Adam v. Williams, 407 U.S. 143 (1972)

Alejandre v. State, 903 P. 2d 794 (Nev. 1995)

Alabama v. White, 496 U.S. 325 (1990)

Brown v. Texas, 443 U.S. 47 (1979)

City of St. Paul v. Uber, 450 N.W. 2d 623 (1990)

Delaware v. Prouse, 440 U.S. 648 (1979)

Dunaway v. New York, 442 U.S. 200 (1979)

Florida v. J. L., 529 U.S. 266 (1999)

Florida v. Royer, 460 U.S. 491 (1983)

Hayes v. Florida, 470 U.S. 811 (1985)

Illinois v. Gates, 462 U.S. 213 (1983)

Illinois v. Wardlow, 528 U.S. 119 (2000)

Mapp v. Ohio, 367 U.S. 643 (1961)

Maryland v. Wilson, 519 U.S. 408 (1997)

Michigan v. Chesternut, 486 U.S. 567 (1988)

Michigan v. Long, 463 U.S. 1032 (1983)

Minnesota v. Dickerson, 508 U.S. 366 (1993)

New Jersey v. T. L. O., 469 U.S. 325 (1985)

Pennsylvania v. Bruder, 488 U.S. 9 (1988)

People v. Coulombe, 86 Cal. App. 4th 52 (2000)

People v. George, 914 P. 2d 367 (2002)

Rochin v. California, 342 U.S. 165 (1952)

State v. Hjelmstad, 535 N.W. 2d 663 (1995)

State v. Merklein, 388 So 2d 218 (Fla.2d DCA 1980)

State v. Werner, 129 Wn.2d 485 (1996)

Terry v. Ohio, 392 U.S. 1 (1968)

United States v. Aruizu, 534 U.S. 266 (2001)

United States v. Cortez, 449 U.S. 411 (1981)

United States v. Hensley, 469 U.S. 221 (1985)

United States v. Montgomery, 561 F.2d 875 (1977)

United States v. Place, 462 U.S. 696 (1983)

United States v. Sharpe, 470 U.S. 675 (1985)

United States v. Smith, 799 F.2d 704 (11th Cir. 1986)

United States v. Sokolow, 490 U.S. 1 (1989)

Weeks v. United States, 232 U.S. 383 (1914)

Whren v. United States, 517 U.S. 806 (1996)

CHAPTER 6

Searches and Seizures

Focal Points

- The Legal Basis for Searches and Seizures
- A *Search* and a *Seizure* Defined
- Types of Searches and Seizures
- Searches and Seizures with Warrants
    - The Probable Cause Requirement
    - The Supporting Affidavit
    - Specificity of a Search Warrant
    - Signature of a Magistrate
- Anticipatory Search Warrants
- Executing the Search Warrant
    - Announcing the Warrant
- Searches and Seizures without Warrants
- Exceptions to the Search Warrant
    - Searches Incidental to a Lawful Arrest
    - Searches with Consent
    - Exigent Circumstances
    - Stop and Frisk
    - Automobiles
    - Items in Plain View
    - Searches of Airports, Borders, and Abandoned Property
- Some Pertinent Cases

Introduction

Searches of people and places are activities in which police officers routinely engage (Senna & Siegel, 1998). In fact, in their capacity to prevent law violations, they must detect and investigate crime. When their searches are successful, officers may seize people and items derived from the search to link their suspect to the crime. After a seizure, officers may turn over articles of evidence to criminal prosecutors to help the state build its case against a suspect. While police are detecting and investigating crime, their behaviors are guided by rules and procedures found in state constitutions, in the U.S. Constitution, as well as in case law and departmental policies (Champion, 1998; Senna & Siegel, 1998). Unlike the police officers in movies such as *Dirty Harry*, *Beverly Hills Cop*, and *Die Hard*, police officers in real life cannot haphazardly and recklessly collect evidence to bring suspects to justice. Instead, they must work within the parameters of the law. Light (1999) contends that police officers must carefully safeguard and not violate the suspect's right to due process. Both the Fifth and Fourteenth Amendments provide U.S. citizens with due process protection. The Fifth Amendment provides protection in the federal system, while the Fourteenth Amendment ensures protection on the state level. The due process clause of the Fourteenth Amendment has been interpreted by the courts to mean that the rights found in the Bill of Rights are incorporated into the Fourteenth Amendment and therefore apply to state as well as federal courts. Essentially, due process ensures that U.S. citizens will be treated fairly and justly and not be subjected to arbitrary and unreasonable practices from governmental officials (Rush, 2000).

Chapter 6 is divided into several sections. Part One explains the legal basis for searches and seizures. Part Two defines a *search* and a *seizure*. Part Three first presents the elements of a lawful search warrant. Second, it explains the types of searches and seizures conducted by police officers: those with a search warrant and those without a search warrant. Third, the section addresses several exceptions to the search-warrant requirements that the courts have created to allow the admission of evidence collected by legitimate police investigation. Part Four provides some pertinent cases.

PART ONE:
THE LEGAL BASIS FOR SEARCHES AND SEIZURES

Unlike a stop and frisk, the legal basis for searches and seizures is explicitly stated in the Fourth Amendment to the U.S. Constitution:

> The right of the people to be secure in their persons, houses, papers and effects, against unreasonable searches and seizures, shall not be violated, and no Warrants shall issue, but upon probable cause, sup-

ported by oath or affirmation, and particularly describing the place to be searched, and the persons or things to be seized.

The Amendment does not protect U.S. citizens from all searches and seizures; rather, it protects them from unreasonable governmental intrusions. It does not apply to searches and seizures conducted by private individuals. In fact, in *State v. Jacobsen*, the U.S. Supreme Court held "that the Fourth Amendment is wholly inapplicable to a search or seizure, even in unreasonable ones, effected by a private individual not acting as an agent of the Government or with the participation of knowledge of a governmental official." The Court's position was restated in *Skinner v. Railway Labor Executive's Association*.

The legality of searches and seizures is determined by their reasonableness. The Fourth Amendment requires that searches and seizures be conducted when officers have established probable cause to believe that a person has either engaged in a crime or will engage in a crime or that articles of evidence can be found in a specific location. Probable cause exists when a set of facts and circumstances within an officer's knowledge would lead a reasonable or prudent man to believe that an offense has been or is being committed (Black, 1979). del Carmen (1999) contends that the degree of certainty which an officer needs to establish probable cause is more than 50 percent. Once an officer has established probable cause, his or her actions have satisfied the reasonableness requirement of the U.S. Constitution. At this point, he or she is acting within the parameters of the law. However, if a search or seizure of a person or item is conducted without probable cause, the officer is operating outside the scope of the law. As a result, any search or seizure of people or items will probably be ruled as unreasonable within the meaning of the Constitution and will be viewed as a violation of the person's right to privacy. Thus, the defendant's attorney will make a motion to suppress the evidence under the exclusionary rule. To sum up, a search-and-seizure is viewed as unreasonable when an officer exceeds the scope of police authority, generally because he or she lacks the facts and circumstances that would lead a reasonable and prudent person to believe that an illegal act has been committed (Gaines & Miller, 2004).

The Fourth Amendment also stipulates that in order to conduct a search of persons, papers, and effects, police officers must procure a warrant from a neutral and detached magistrate. However, the officer must establish and show probable cause to convince a magistrate that a crime was committed by a particular suspect and/or that specific items (evidence) can be retrieved at a specified location. The officer usually conducts this procedure by using an affidavit. After the magistrate reads the affidavit alleging either that a crime has been committed by a particular suspect or that articles of evidence can be found at a particular location, he or she must be satisfied that probable cause exists. If the magistrate does not find probable cause wanting, he or she will issue a warrant. If the affidavit is based on reasonable suspicion or a hunch, and therefore lacks probable cause, the magistrate will not issue a warrant.

The warrant is an order issued by a magistrate commanding an officer to seize the person or property named in the warrant. Legal scholars contend that the obvious advantage to the warrant is that courts are more inclined to admit evidence secured in this manner (Bartollas, 1988). Searches and seizures conducted with a warrant find greater acceptance at trial and offer greater protection for officers against civil and/or criminal liability (Adler, Mueller, & Laufer, 1994). A warrant can order the seizure of property taken in a crime or tools used in the commission of a crime; it can also order the seizure of persons named in the warrant. There are two types of searches: those with a warrant and those without a warrant. Nevertheless, a warrant is not often used by patrol officers in major cities because of exigent circumstances that preclude them from initially getting a warrant from a magistrate.

The Fourth Amendment requires that the warrant describe the place to be searched and the person or items to be seized as a result of the search (Gaines & Miller, 2003). A warrant must be limited in scope because, by its very nature, it is supposed to be as particularized as possible. In addition, it is supposed to be as matter-of-fact as possible. Indeed, a warrant does not provide police officers with an occasion to go on a "fishing expedition." In *Chimel v. California*, the U.S. Supreme Court narrowed the permissible scope of searches incident to lawful arrests. Under *Chimel*, police may search the body of an arrestee and the area within that person's immediate control. The area of immediate control is defined as the area within the "grasp" or "wing span" of the arrested person (del Carmen, 1999).

PART TWO: A *SEARCH* AND A *SEIZURE* DEFINED

While commonly used together in the context of warrants, a *search* and a *seizure* actually represent different actions. *To search* means to look for and *to seize* means to take possession of (del Carmen, 2003). Within the context of the Constitution, *to search* means to examine or probe into areas where a person enjoys a reasonable expectation of privacy in order to discover contraband that may link a person to a law violation and that may therefore be used in a criminal prosecution of that person. These areas include an individual's house or other premises, his or her person, or his or her vehicle or aircraft. However, in *Katz v. United States*, the U.S. Supreme Court moved beyond the traditional areas where people are ordinarily believed to have a reasonable expectation of privacy and considered whether people in other kinds of areas also enjoy some degree of constitutional protection. In this case, Charles Katz was a bookie who ran his betting operation from a public telephone booth. FBI agents were aware of his illegal behavior and the phone booth that he frequented, so they attached a listening device to the outside of the booth. At Katz's trial, the government introduced into evidence recordings of phone conversations in which Katz and others discussed placing bets. In *Katz*, the Court had to decide whether the government's recording of conversations constituted an unreasonable search-and-seizure in violation of the Fourth Amendment. The Court created a two-pronged test to determine conditions under which one has a reasonable expectation of privacy. First, the person has to exhibit an actual or subjective expectation of privacy within a specific area. Second, society has to recognize the expectation as reasonable. The Court held that Katz had met the two conditions. Therefore, the FBI agents had violated Katz's Fourth Amendment rights because the amendment protects not simply areas but people within areas. After the *Katz* decision, search-and-seizure questions could not focus exclusively on the basis of the area that was searched; rather, they had to focus also on whether a person has a reasonable expectation of privacy in a specific area.

Part Three: Types of Searches and Seizures

Searches and Seizures with Warrants

A *warrant* is a legal order from a neutral and detached magistrate that commands an officer to arrest the person and/or to seize the property of the person whose name appears on the warrant (del Carmen, 1991). The Constitution requires that police officers demonstrate, by sworn testimony, that probable cause exists to believe that a crime has occurred or that articles of evidence, as the result of a crime, can be found in a specific location. As a general rule, experts argue that a search-and-seizure is valid under the Fourth Amendment when it is made with a warrant. Some searches, however, do not require a warrant or enjoy any constitutional protection. For example, the Fourth Amendment does not apply to border searches or searches conducted outside the United States. The amendment does not apply to searches of open fields or abandoned property. The amendment does not apply to areas where people do not have a reasonable expectation of privacy. Scheb and Scheb

(1999) contend that the warrant requirement to conduct a search or seizure is designed to ensure that the impartial magistrate is interposed between the citizen and the state. There are four essential elements of a valid search warrant: (1) probable cause; (2) the supporting affidavit; (3) the specificity of the search; and (4) the signature of a magistrate.

The Probable Cause Requirement

A search warrant requires that both an officer and a judge determine the existence of probable cause. For example, the officer must be certain that probable cause exists to request the search warrant, and the magistrate, after reading the sworn affidavit, must also be certain that probable cause exists before he or she grants a warrant. Probable cause consists of a greater degree of certainty than suspicion. It exists when prudent and cautious police officers have trustworthy information that leads them to believe that a crime has been committed or that evidence of a crime might be obtained at a particular location. In *Illinois v. Gates*, the U.S. Supreme Court stated that other courts should view the determination of probable cause as a "commonsense, practical question" that must be decided in light of the totality of the circumstances in a given case. The *Gates* decision has been echoed by lower federal courts. For example, in *United States v. Fama*, a court stated that even though an innocent explanation might be consistent with the facts alleged in an affidavit seeking a search warrant, this does not negate probable cause. It also appears that most state courts have followed the ruling in *Gates*. For example, in *State v. George*, the Ohio Supreme Court ruled that an affidavit by a police agent stating that he had observed a tall marijuana plant growing in an enclosed space provided probable cause for a magistrate to conclude there was marijuana or related paraphernalia in the residence nearby. Other states have not accepted *Gates* and have decided to provide their citizens with more protection than that allowed by the federal decision (see *Commonwealth v. Upton* and *State v. Jacumin*).

The Supporting Affidavit

Another essential element of a warrant is the supporting affidavit. An *affidavit* is a sworn, written statement made by a police officer in the presence of an authorized official, usually a magistrate (Anderson, Mangels, Langsam, & Dyson, 2002). Scheb and Scheb (1999) define an *affidavit* as a signed document attesting under oath to certain facts of which the person submitting the affidavit has knowledge. Affidavits may be recorded and transmitted in multiple formats, including electronic recordings and the telephone. For example, in *State v. Yoder*, the Idaho Supreme Court ruled that electronically recorded testimony was no less reliable than a sworn, written statement. The court also ruled that the word *affidavit*, under the Idaho constitution, was sufficiently broad enough to include tape recordings of oral testimony. Moreover, in California, the law allows police officers to complete affidavits over the telephone to expedite the issuance of a warrant (West's Ann. Cal. Pen. Code 1526(b)).

After reading the affidavit, the magistrate must find a showing of probable cause to believe that a crime has been committed or that items related to a crime can be found at a specified location. If the magistrate is satisfied that probable cause exists, he or she will issue a warrant that validates a search. The magistrate must ensure that the affidavit supporting a search warrant precisely describes the place or person to be searched and the things to be seized as a product of the search. Thus, the affidavit must contain specific facts that establish probable cause to justify a search (see Moskovitz, 2000). The affidavit cannot establish probable cause for the issuance of a warrant if the officer has relied upon mere suspicion; rather, it must present facts and circumstances justifying the officer's belief. Some legal experts argue that the information provided in the affidavit must be fresh and not dated to ensure that the items to be seized are still located on the premises expected to be searched (Scheb & Scheb, 1999). This issue has been a source of litigation in the past. For example, in *State v. Pulgini*, the court held a search warrant invalid because there had been an unexplained delay of twenty-three days between the last alleged facts and the issuance of the warrant. However, in *United States v. Rosenbarger*, the court ruled that a twenty-one-day lapse between the observation of the receipt of the stolen property and the issuance of the warrant did not invalidate the warrant because the magistrate could determine there was a reasonable probability that the stolen goods were still in the defendant's home. Nevertheless, no set rule has been created concerning this issue.

Specificity of a Search Warrant

The Fourth Amendment states, in part: "[N]o Warrants shall issue, but upon probable cause … and particularly describing the place to be searched, and the persons or things to be seized." The warrant must describe with a reasonable degree of certainty the place where the search will be conducted. For example, in *Garrison v. State*, the court ruled that a search warrant specifying that the search was to take place on a certain third-floor apartment was insufficient to permit the search of an adjacent apartment when police officers mistakenly entered the wrong apartment. Specifically, the address alone of the apartment building was not sufficient. However, in *Lyon v. Robinson*, the court ruled that the mistake of inadvertently listing the address of a residence to be searched as "325 Atkinson Street" rather than "325 Short Street" did not render the warrant invalid since the mistake was not misleading or confusing: the streets intersected in front of the residence and the warrant provided an accurate physical description of the premises to be searched. In another case, the court ruled that a warrant describing property to be seized as "various long play phonographic albums, and miscellaneous vases and glassware" was insufficient. However, in *State v. Nall*, the court approved seizure of items described as "a set of antique ceramic book ends in the shape of horses and advertising rolling rock beer." Del Carmen (1991) contends that items for seizure must be described with sufficient particularity so that police officers will recognize which items are retrievable. For example, a warrant cannot simply list "stolen goods." Such language would be viewed as too general and would allow an officer to "fish around" until he or she discovers something to be used as evidence. Despite the particular nature of search warrants, courts seem less strict and officers are given leeway when they search for drugs and contraband. Some believe that courts seem less strict because drugs can be hidden in many obscure places.

Signature of a Magistrate

As stated earlier, search warrants must be issued only by a neutral and detached magistrate. In *Johnson v. United States*, the U.S. Supreme Court claimed: "[I]nferences must be drawn by a neutral and detached magistrate instead of being judged by the officer engaged in the often competitive enterprise of ferreting out crime." Therefore, only a magistrate has the right to grant a search warrant. Some states and the federal government may allow oral warrants rather than written ones. Typically, such warrants are initially drawn and then authorized through recordings. A police officer petitions for a warrant either in person or by telephone, stating, under oath, the facts and circumstances that helped him or her to establish probable cause. The judge then orally authorizes the warrant. Some legal scholars contend that this practice remains within the parameters of the Fourth Amendment since the Amendment does not specify that the affidavit must be written (del Carmen, 1999).

Anticipatory Search Warrants

Largely fueled by the "war on drugs" and thus the need to stop the flow of drugs, *anticipatory search warrants* have emerged (which, by the way, are not limited to raids for drugs) (Scheb & Scheb, 1999). Anticipatory search warrants are a radical departure from traditional search warrants. Before a traditional warrant can be granted, a judge must read a supporting affidavit and find a showing of probable cause. However, under anticipatory search warrants, probable cause does not have to exist until the warrant has been executed and the search has been conducted. For example, in *Bernie v. State*, Supra, a freight delivery service notified police that a package had come open during transit and revealed a suspicious substance that later proved to be cocaine. An anticipatory warrant was issued to search the residence to which the package was addressed. Police were on the scene when the freight company delivered the package. The warrant was served, the cocaine was seized, and the defendant was taken into custody. At trial, the defense moved to suppress the evidence, but the court allowed its introduction and the defendant was convicted. On appeal, the Florida Supreme Court ruled that neither the federal nor the state constitution prohibited search warrants to be served at a future date in anticipation of delivery of contraband. Despite *Bernie*, the U.S. Supreme Court has not yet ruled on whether a search based on an anticipatory warrant is valid under the Fourth Amendment. Some federal and state courts appear to follow the *Bernie* decision, since they have upheld the basic concept that contraband does not have to be currently located at the place described in a search warrant if probable cause exists to believe that, at some point, the contraband will be there. For example, in *United States v. Hale*, the Ninth Circuit Court of Appeals held that an anticipatory search warrant is permissible "where the contraband to be seized is on a sure course to its destination." Similarly, in *United States v. Dornhofer*, the Fourth Circuit Court of Appeals upheld an anticipatory search warrant authorizing an inspector to search an apartment for child pornography after the magistrate who issued the warrant had claimed it was valid on the condition that the contraband would be placed in the mail. The court reasoned that after the mailing had been accomplished, the contraband was on a certain course to its destination.

Executing the Search Warrant

A search warrant is directed to a law-enforcement officer commanding him or her to carry out the stated intent of the warrant. Its execution is governed by applicable federal and state laws and rules of criminal procedure (Scheb & Scheb, 1999). For example, Rule 41 (c) (1) of the Federal Rules of Criminal Procedure provides the following:

> [The warrant] shall command the officer to search, within a specified period of time not to exceed 10 days, the person or place named or

the property or person specified. The warrant shall be served in the daytime, unless the issuing authority ... authorizes its execution at times other than daytime.

Rule 41 defines *daytime* as the time occurring between 6:00 a.m. and 10:00 p.m. (Scheb & Scheb, 1999). del Carmen (1991) mentions that sometimes, depending on the nature of the search warrant, some states require that warrants be served at night. States may also vary in the time frame given to police officers to execute a warrant. For example, some states specify ten days (California), and other states allow less time (Texas specifies three days). When the search is executed, the officer executing the warrant must provide a copy of the warrant and a receipt for any property seized to the party from whom it is taken. If the person is not at home, the officer must leave a copy and a receipt on the premises, indicating that police entered the premises and seized certain items. The officer must also file a report and submit it to his or her police department and place the seized item (or items) into inventory (del Carmen, 1991).

Announcing the Warrant

The law requires that when an officer is executing a warrant, he or she must announce his or her purpose and authority before entering the premises of another person. The general purpose of the announcement is to allow for voluntary compliance with the warrant. In addition, the announcement alerts the homeowner or renter that it is the police or authorities who are about to enter the premises. del Carmen (1991) contends that, depending on the state and how a jury may decide a case, if police break into a person's premises to execute a warrant, the warrant and search may be invalidated. However, sometimes, when officers execute a warrant, the experience could endanger the officers, and suspects could attempt to destroy evidence. In fact, the U.S. Supreme Court has recognized that officers could face danger or lose evidence when executing warrants. Therefore, the Court has allowed exceptions to the "knock and announce" requirement. Since the Constitution does not specify if an announcement should be made before the execution of a warrant, state law and court decisions typically govern officers' behavior. For example, in *Wilson v. Arkansas*, the Court stated that there are cases in which, because of exigent circumstances, an announcement is not required or necessary. Such circumstances typically include the following: 1) when announcing could present a strong threat of violence or danger to the officer; 2) when contraband or other property might be destroyed; 3) when the officers reasonably believe that the persons within the premises are in imminent peril of bodily harm; 4) when officers reasonably believe that those in the dwelling are engaged in the process of destroying evidence or escaping because they are aware of the police presence; or 5) when police officers believe the person to be arrested is in the process of committing the crime. In *Wilson*, though the Court did not create exceptions to the "knock and announce" requirement, it left the determination of such exceptions to the lower courts:

> For now, we leave to the lower courts the task of determining the circumstances under which an unannounced entry is reasonable under the Fourth Amendment. We simply hold that although a search or seizure of a dwelling might be constitutionally defective if police officers enter without prior announcement, law enforcement interests may also establish the reasonableness of an announcement entry.

Searches and Seizures without Warrants

Though searches and seizures without warrants were meant to be the exception, in reality this practice is the rule. The Constitution states that searches and seizures are to be made with the authority of a warrant. However, like most arrests, they are in fact made without a warrant (Gaines & Miller, 2004). The courts have recognized that it is not practical to expect police officers to procure a warrant before making an arrest or a search when they are faced with "exigent circumstances." As a result, courts have upheld warrantless searches. However, police would do well to procure a warrant or jeopardize successful prosecution. The U.S. Supreme Court has said that probable cause is needed to justify a search-and-seizure without a warrant. When an officer makes an arrest, a warrantless search is justified. Consequently, warrantless searches incident to a lawful arrest outnumber searches made with a warrant (see del Carmen, 1991). When an arrest is made, the arresting officer has the burden of proving to a magistrate that probable cause existed. Essentially, courts have said to police officers, "Make the arrest, conduct a search, and show cause later." For example, in *County of Riverside v. McRaughlin*, the U.S. Supreme Court ruled that a judicial determination of probable cause must occur within forty-eight hours after the arrest, even if this two-day period occurs during a weekend or a series of two holidays. There are generally seven exceptions to searches and seizures made without a warrant. They include (1) searches incidental to a lawful arrest; (2) searches with consent; (3) exigent circumstances; (4) stop and frisk; (5) automobiles; (6) items in plain view; and 7) searches of airports, borders, and abandoned property.

Exceptions to the Search Warrant

Searches Incidental to a Lawful Arrest

After a lawful arrest has been made, officers can legally search a suspect and seize any evidence found on that person and use it to criminally convict the offender. Making a "search incidental to a lawful arrest" is commonly practiced when officers operate with or without a warrant. In order for this practice to pass muster constitutionally, two conditions must be met. First, the arrest itself must be lawful: either the arresting officer must have a valid warrant (based on probable cause) or, to effect an arrest without a warrant, the arresting officer must have probable cause to believe that the suspect engaged in or was about to engage in a crime. Second, the search must be limited in scope or reasonable enough to ensure the safety of the arresting officer and to prevent the destruction of evidence or contraband. Prior to *Chimel*, courts allowed police great latitude in searching the premises of suspects. For example, in *United States v. Robinowitz*, the U.S. Supreme Court upheld a warrantless search of an entire home incidental to a lawful arrest. However, the Court retreated from this position in *Chimel v. California*. In, this case, the Court ruled that once a lawful arrest has been made, officers may search any area within the suspect's "immediate control," or any area where the suspect may be able to access a weapon or destroy evidence. Therefore, a search incidental to an arrest does not allow officers to go on a "fishing expedition" by searching a suspect's entire dwelling place. Officers would do well first to make an arrest and then to obtain a search warrant. In some cases, an arrest is made after a search reveals incriminating evidence. In these cases, the search will be upheld as one incidental to an arrest if officers can prove that probable cause existed for an arrest before a search was conducted (*Baily v. United States*). However, in *United States v. Jones*, the U.S. Supreme Court refused to uphold a search after it was shown that the arrest had been a mere pretext to conduct a warrantless search.

Searches with Consent

Another exception to the search warrant occurs when consent is given to the officer to conduct a search. When a party consents, there are no Fourth Amendment protections (Stuckey, Robinson, & Wallace, 2004). Warrantless searches are viewed as valid when consent is voluntarily and intelligently given to a government agent—that is, when the person freely agrees to a search and at the same time understands the consequences of his or her actions. If incriminating evidence is found and later challenged in court, the burden of proof is placed on the officer to show that consent was voluntarily and intelligently given and was not the product of force or coercion. In *Schneckloth v. Bustamonte*, the U.S. Supreme Court held that although the subject's knowledge of a right to refuse is a factor to be taken into account, it is not a requirement for establishing a voluntary search. Del Carmen (1991) contends that voluntariness and intelligence are determined when one looks at the "totality of the circumstances." For example, before consent was given, how did officers ask permission to search? Did they command or make a request? When consent is voluntarily and intelligently given, officers should put this permission in writing, in the presence of other officers. If necessary, this written permission can be presented as evidence in court to prevent the defense from moving to suppress articles of evidence taken by a consent search.

Exigent Circumstances

This exception comprises emergency circumstances that preclude officers from acquiring a search warrant. The exception is generally a catchall category of emergencies that makes getting a warrant impractical. Such circumstances include, but are not limited to, the following: hot pursuits; danger of physical harm to the officer; destruction of evidence; and intoxicated drivers. Since police frequently respond to crimes in progress, they do not have time to stop and visit a judge for a warrant. As a consequence, courts have given police leeway in effecting searches without warrants as long as the officer has probable cause to justify his or her actions. For example, in *Warden v. Hayden*, the U.S. Supreme Court held that officers may enter a dwelling without a warrant in response to screams for help. The Court stated that the Fourth Amendment does not require officers to delay their investigation if doing so will gravely endanger their lives or the lives of others. In *Schmerber v. California*, the U.S. Supreme Court ruled that police may, without a search warrant and by force if necessary, take a blood-alcohol test from a person arrested for driving while intoxicated as long as the setting and procedure are reasonable (i.e., when the blood is drawn by a doctor at a hospital). The Court viewed the forcible blood test as a "minor intrusion" and noted it was performed by medical personnel. Moreover, the Court reasoned that exigent circumstances existed since the alcohol in the suspect's bloodstream might diminish during the time required to procure a warrant. In addition, the Court held that police are not required to obtain a warrant while in the process of apprehending a suspect, even if the suspect enters a house. The general rule is that as long as police have reason to believe that the suspect is in the house, a warrantless search is reasonable within the meaning of the Fourth Amendment. Subsequently, in *Welsh v. Wisconsin*, the U.S. Supreme Court ruled that the destruction of evidence does not constitute exigent circumstances if the underlying offense is relatively minor. As a result of *Welsh,* lower courts have routinely disagreed over what constitutes a "relatively minor" offense. In *State v. Curl,* the Idaho Supreme Court ruled that police erred when, acting on probable cause but without a warrant, they entered a home and seized marijuana they believed was to be destroyed. The court viewed the possession of marijuana as a minor offense.

Stop and Frisk

A *stop and frisk* is a routine law-enforcement practice that allows police officers to briefly stop and question suspects and sometimes pat down their outer garments. *Terry v. Ohio* is the leading case concerning this practice. In *Terry,* the U.S. Supreme Court upheld the authority of police officers to briefly detain a suspect; to ask for his or her name and address and an explanation of his or her actions; and to frisk or pat down the suspect if the officer had safety concerns. Because the practice is such a limited intrusion, the Court allows the stop and the warrantless search for weapons on less than probable cause. Since the stop is narrow in scope, it requires only that an officer have reasonable suspicion (Scheb & Scheb, 1999). While a Terry stop allows an officer to pat down a suspect for safety reasons, sometimes this limited kind of search leads to the discovery of a weapon. For example, in *Michigan v. Long,* the U.S. Supreme Court ruled that the seizure of contraband other than a weapon while engaging in a legal Terry stop is justified under the "plain view" doctrine. Subsequently, in *Minnesota v. Dickerson,* the Court stated that police officers may seize nonthreatening contraband detected by their touch during a protective pat down as long as the pat down stays within the parameters of a Terry search and if the contraband's contour is immediately apparent. However, the Court agreed that the actions of the officer in "squeezing, sliding and otherwise manipulating the contents of the defendant's pocket" to identify a lump of crack cocaine that weighed one-fifth of a gram went beyond what was permissible. This extension of *Terry* is referred to as the "plain feel" exception to the warrant requirement of the Fourth Amendment.

Automobiles

Another exception to the warrant requirement is searches conducted in automobiles. Police do not violate the Fourth Amendment if they stop a motorist when they have adequate grounds to believe that the driver is ill or has fallen asleep (see *State v. Pinkham*). Moreover, warrantless searches of automobiles have been a long-standing practice: since automobiles are mobile, they do not enjoy the same degree of protection as areas where one has a reasonable expectation of privacy. Indeed, they enjoy less expectation of privacy. The U.S. Supreme Court has ruled that if a police officer has probable cause to believe that a vehicle contains contraband or evidence of a crime, he or she can stop the vehicle and effect a search (*Carroll v. United States*). Moreover, if the officer is lawfully present at the vehicle and observes or smells contraband, such activity does not constitute a search within the meaning of the Fourth Amendment. However, police officers do not need probable cause to stop a vehicle. When officers make routine traffic stops, they need only a reasonable belief that a motorist has committed a driving infraction. Nevertheless, any stop, though limited, represents a seizure within the meaning of the Constitution. While the stop is limited and the detention is brief, police officers need at least a reasonable suspicion to justify an investigatory stop of a motor vehicle. In fact, the U.S. Supreme Court has ruled that police cannot simply stop people or drivers on a hunch or in good faith but that their actions must be guided by an articulable suspicion of wrongdoing—either an offense already committed or an offense in prospect (see *United States v. Montgomery*). However, when police make valid stops, they may engage in searches when they see illegal items in plain view. These searches may include those of the driver, the vehicle, and even the passengers in the vehicle. For example, in *Wyoming v. Houghton*, the Court ruled that when automobiles are stopped, any container that belongs to one or more passengers (as long as the container is capable of hiding contraband) can be searched. The Court has also stated that when police engage in warrantless searches of automobiles under exigent circumstances, they may continue the search after the vehicle has been taken to the police station (see *Chambers v. Maroney*). Despite the Court's ruling in *Chambers*, several state supreme courts have not complied with it, contending that once a car is impounded, exigent circumstances that may justify a roadside automobile search disappear (see *State v. Kock*; *State v. Larocco*; and *State v. Miller*).

The U.S. Supreme Court has also upheld the legality of automobile stops based on pretexts. In *Whren v. United States*, the Court ruled that a police officer could stop an automobile for a traffic violation even if the officer's intent was to search the car for drugs. If the officer happens to discover contraband, he or she can use the evidence to effect an arrest and to gain a criminal conviction. In *Maryland v. Wilson*, the Court ruled that an officer could order passengers, as well as the driver, out of the car during traffic stops without establishing either probable cause or reasonable suspicion.

Concerning automobile searches, the courts have had to address whether some items (e.g., closed containers) in the automobile enjoy any protection.

In *United States v. Ross*, the U.S. Supreme Court ruled that warrantless searches of closed containers found in an automobile are valid. In *United States v. Johns*, the Court held that a warrantless search of a plastic container seized during an automobile search was valid even though the police waited several days before opening the container. The Court ruled that the search of the container was not unreasonable because it was merely delayed.

Items in Plain View

Another exception to the search warrant is items found within the police officer's plain view. del Carmen (1991) contends that plain view is not a search within the meaning of the Fourth Amendment because the officer merely seizes what he or she sees. The items are not those for which the officer had to search. Since there is no reasonable expectation of privacy, the Constitution provides no protection to items found in plain view (see *Harris v. United States*), and the courts do not expect police officers to ignore contraband such as drugs, the tools of a crime, or weapons. Illegal items can be seized within the meaning of the Constitution when police officers either observe them in a routine traffic stop or upon the execution of a warrant at a suspect's dwelling place. In *Coolidge v. New Hampshire*, the U.S. Supreme Court ruled that police are permitted to seize evidence without a warrant under the following circumstances: (1) when the officer has a legal justification to be in a constitutionally protected area when the seizure occurs; (2) when the evidence seized is in the plain view of the officer who comes across it; and (3) when it is apparent that the object is evidence of a crime. Essentially, *Coolidge* established the "plain view doctrine." Under this doctrine, when an officer makes a legal stop or an arrest and immediately recognizes evidence, he or she can seize it. The nature of the items seized in plain view is based on an "inadvertent discovery." The officer must accidentally discover items in plain sight. He or she cannot engage in a search. However, in *Horton v. California*, the U.S. Supreme Court stated that the inadvertence requirement was not an essential part of the plurality opinion in *Coolidge*. Despite *Horton*, some state courts continue to insist that the inadvertence requirement is a limitation on the plain view exception (see *State v. Halczyszak*).

In *United States v. Pacelli*, the U.S. Supreme Court stated that the plain view doctrine applies in two instances: (1) when the item is seized before the search is commenced and (2) when illegal evidence is immediately recognized by an officer conducting an otherwise valid search or entry. In *Pacelli*, the Court upheld the seizure of illegal chemicals found during a search based on a warrant to search for heroin. The warrant gave police officers the right to enter and search the premises; items of contraband found in plain view during the search for heroin were deemed properly seized. However, in *Arizona v. Hicks*, the U.S. Supreme Court retreated from *Pacelli*. A police officer had lawfully entered an apartment to search for weapons and noticed stereo equipment that seemed out of place given the condition of the apartment. His suspicion aroused, the officer manipulated the equipment to locate the serial numbers. A check of the numbers revealed that the equipment was stolen. The Court ruled that the equipment had been illegally seized, reasoning that the serial numbers were not in the officer's plain view.

Searches of Airports, Borders, and Abandoned Property

Because of the need to stop the flow of contraband, especially drugs, and to thwart terrorism, law-enforcement officers do not need a warrant to search international borders (*United States v. Martinez-Fuerte*), seaports, and travelers and their baggage at airports. Since the tragic terrorist attacks of September 11, 2001, airport searches have become more frequent and intrusive. For example, airlines across the country now engage in both random and preselection searches, whereby any passenger can be stopped and asked to remove articles of clothing and to open carry-on bags. Many passengers of Arabic descent or those with names that sound Arabic are preselected for searches. Some have complained that they have been targeted or singled out. They view these stops and searches as instances of racial profiling or "traveling while Arabic." Despite what appears to be disparate treatment, the courts have upheld airport searches (either by inspection or by X-ray) on the basis of balancing the need for the search with its limited scope. Because the United States has experienced many degrees of alertness with respect to the threat of terrorism, passengers are aware of the possibility of airport searches. Some experts argue that because of the threat of terrorism, most Americans have accepted an intrusion into some of their civil liberties (Gaines & Miller, 2004; Stuckey et al., 2004). Proponents of airport searches argue that travelers can avoid the possibility of a search by opting not to fly but to use another means of travel.

del Carmen (1991) argues that searches of immigration borders are regulated not by the Fourth Amendment but by immigration laws and agency policies. As a result, law-enforcement personnel on border patrol can search people and motor vehicles crossing the border when they have reasonable suspicion. They need neither a warrant nor probable cause to engage in a search. In *Ramsey v. United States*, the U.S. Supreme Court held that searches at the border are reasonable per se because of the right of the sovereign nation to protect itself by stopping and searching persons and property entering its soil. Therefore, officers may search persons and property entering the country without obtaining a warrant or establishing probable cause. For example, law-enforcement officers from the Bureau of Citizenship and Naturalization Services, (formerly, Immigration and Naturalization Services), as well as officers from the Drug Enforcement Agency, routinely make warrantless stops of U.S. citizens and aliens if they are suspected of either smuggling drugs or illegal aliens into the United States. Such stops are a form of balancing the national interest of preventing illegal persons and goods from entering the United States with the limited intrusion that occurs when a person decides to cross the border.

While the Fourth Amendment offers protection in areas where people have a reasonable expectation of privacy, some scholars wonder if it offers protection to items or property discarded by a previous owner. For example, when citizens discard items by placing them at the curbside to be picked up by trash collectors, are those items in the trash protected by the Constitution? If a police officer decides to retrieve items that he or she believes can be used to connect a suspect to a crime, will the items be admissible in court or will the court move to suppress them because the police officer failed to procure a search warrant? In *Abel v. United States*, the U.S. Supreme Court created the "abandoned property exception." In this case, a hotel manager gave consent to an FBI agent to search a room that had been previously occupied by the petitioner. During the search, police found incriminating evidence in a wastepaper basket. During trial, Abel argued that the evidence should have been suppressed since officers did not have a warrant to search the hotel room. The Court ruled that once Abel vacated the room, the hotel had exclusive rights to its possessions and could freely give consent to a search. Therefore, *Abel* established that any property that has been discarded or left behind in a hotel room may be searched and seized by police officers without a warrant. Moreover, in *California v. Greenwood*, the Court held that evidence of the defendant's drug use collected from his garbage that had been placed on the sidewalk for pickup by the trash collector was properly admitted since the defendant had demonstrated intent to abandon the property. In *Greenwood*, the Court ruled that when people place garbage on the sidewalk to be collected by a trash collector, the items in the trash enjoy no reasonable expectation of privacy. Essentially, the Court has ruled that the Fourth Amendment does not prohibit a warrantless search-and-seizure of garbage left for collection outside the curtilage of a home.

Part Four: Some Pertinent Cases

Stoner v. California
376 U.S. 483 (1964)

Stoner became a suspect in an armed robbery investigation when police discovered a checkbook on the ground near the robbery scene. The checkbook contained Stoner's name and checks made out to a hotel in another city. They went to the hotel and discovered that Stoner was living there. Though Stoner was not in his room, the hotel clerk admitted officers into Stoner's room without an arrest or search warrant. The police found evidence linking Stoner to the robbery. The petitioner was arrested two days later in another state. The evidence taken from the hotel was admitted into trial and he was subsequently convicted of robbery. The case was appealed to the U.S. Supreme Court. The Court held that the search of defendant's hotel room without his consent and with neither search nor arrest warrants violated his constitutional rights, even though the search was conducted with the consent of the hotel clerk. *Stoner* has been interpreted to mean that a hotel clerk cannot give consent to search a room that is still occupied by a guest staying at the hotel. Therefore, hotel guests are no less entitled to protection than home owners.

Bumper v. North Carolina
391 U.S. 543 (1968)

Bumper, an African-American male, was a suspect in a rape case. In North Carolina, rape was an offense punishable by death or life imprisonment. Furthermore, the law allowed the prosecution to challenge for cause any prospective juror who openly admitted to being opposed to capital punishment. During their investigation of Bumper, four police officers went to his home and advised his grandmother that they had a search warrant and wanted to come in and look around. The police did not have a warrant. Nevertheless, the grandmother gave her consent, and police entered the home and found a .22 caliber rifle that linked Bumper to the rape. The defense argued that the rifle should be suppressed from trial since the officers never had a search warrant. The evidence was admitted and Bumper was convicted of rape. He avoided the death penalty: the jury recommended life imprisonment. The state supreme court affirmed the conviction. Bumper appealed and the U.S. Supreme Court granted certiorari. In *Bumper*, the Court held that the search was unjustified because consent was given only after officers had asserted they possessed a warrant to search the house. Therefore, consent was not intelligently and voluntarily given. The owner of the home had not been made aware that her grandson was the prime suspect in a rape case. Therefore, the search was invalid and the weapon retrieved from the search should have been suppressed during trial.

Almeida-Sanchez v. United States
413 U.S. 266 (1973)

Almeida-Sanchez, a Mexican citizen with a valid work permit, was driving twenty-five miles from the Mexican border. Border patrol officers stopped his car and conducted a search. Officers admit that at the time of the search, they lacked probable cause or consent. They found marijuana and charged Almeida-Sanchez with possession of a controlled substance. He was subsequently charged and convicted in federal court. On appeal, the defense challenged the constitutionality of a warrantless boarder search conducted without probable cause or consent. The government justified the search and conviction on the basis of the Immigration and Nationality Act which allows for warrantless searches of automobiles and other conveyances "within a reasonable distance from any external boundary of the United States." The U.S. Supreme Court held that a search of an automobile more than twenty miles from the Mexican border at a roving border-patrol checkpoint, without a search warrant, consent, or probable cause to believe there was evidence in the automobile, violated the Fourth Amendment. The search could not be justified on the basis of any special rules applicable to automobile searches since probable cause was lacking, and it could not be justified by analogy with administrative inspections since the officers had no warrant or reason to believe that petitioner had crossed the border or committed an offense; finally, no consent had been given by the petitioner. Moreover, the Court held that the search was not a border search or the equivalent.

Schneckloth v. Bustamonte
412 U.S. 218 (1973)

Police officer James Rand observed an automobile with a broken taillight and stopped it. The driver had no driver's license and was asked to step out of the car, together with several other occupants. One passenger, Alcala, had a driver's license and told Rand and other officers present that the automobile belonged to his brother. The officers asked if they could search the vehicle and Alcala consented. While conducting their search, the officers discovered a stolen check and arrested one of the passengers, Bustamonte. The evidence was used to convict Bustamonte of unlawfully possessing a check. He was convicted and sentenced. The case was appealed to the Ninth Circuit Court of Appeals. The court reversed the conviction of the district court, holding that the prosecution had failed to prove that Bustamante, pursuant to the Fourth and Fifth Amendments, gave consent to the search with the understanding that it could be freely withheld. The case was appealed to the U.S. Supreme Court. The Court held that advisement of Fourth Amendment rights is unnecessary as a prerequisite to a consent search in a noncustodial situation. The standard for consent is voluntariness as determined from all the circumstances.

United States v. Matlock
415 U.S. 164 (1974)

Matlock was wanted in connection with a bank robbery. On the basis of probable cause, police officers went to Matlock's residence, where they arrested him in his front yard. A Mrs. Graff also lived in the home. She admitted officers into the home at their request. Though they did not have a search warrant, they asked Mrs. Graff if they could look in various rooms, and she agreed. They also looked in the bedroom that Mrs. Graff admitted sharing with Matlock. Subsequently, the officers discovered money in Matlock's bedroom closet. The officers believed the money was taken in the robbery. On the basis of the evidence, Matlock was indicted for bank robbery. At trial, the respondent moved to suppress the money as evidence. In this case, the district court held that when consent of a third party is relied on to effect a search, the state must show that when consent was given, the officer reasonably believed the person who gave it had the authority to permit a search and the person who consented did have actual authority to permit a search. The district court held the government had failed to show that Mrs. Graff had such authority. The Seventh Circuit Court of Appeals affirmed the lower court's ruling, and the U.S. Supreme Court granted certiorari. The Court reversed and remanded the case, holding that the lower court had erred. The government had sustained its burden of proof concerning Mrs. Graff's authority to consent to the search. The Court also held that evidence seized during the warrantless search of a bedroom because the common-law wife or the defendant had consented to the search was admissible.

United States v. Brignoni-Ponce
422 U.S. 873 (1975)

The border patrol near the Mexican border stopped a vehicle containing persons apparently of Mexican descent. Officers asked about their citizenship and immigration status and other matters and searched the vehicle—a search which yielded contraband. The result was a conviction. The U.S. Supreme Court held that at roving border-patrol checkpoints, a vehicle may be briefly stopped for questioning and may be investigated if the officer's observations establish reasonable suspicion that the vehicle contains aliens illegally in the country. The officer may question the driver and passengers about their citizenship and immigration status and may ask them to explain suspicious circumstances, but any further detention or search must be based on consent or probable cause.

United States v. Ortiz
422 U.S. 891 (1975)

Ortiz was stopped at a border-patrol checkpoint about sixty-six miles north of the Mexican border. Officers requested to search Ortiz's vehicle, but Ortiz refused. The officers searched anyway and discovered illegal aliens. Ortiz was convicted of transporting them. The case was appealed, and the U.S. Supreme Court granted review. The Court held that the search of a vehicle at a fixed checkpoint required consent, probable cause, or a warrant. Searches must not be made on a random basis. The Court further ruled that a checkpoint so far removed from the Mexican border was unreasonable.

United States v. Martinez-Fuerte
428 U.S. 543 (1976)

The border patrol established checkpoints for illegal Mexican aliens at various places along a major interstate highway. Martinez-Fuerte was apprehended at one of the recovery checkpoints. Martinez-Fuerte was convicted of transporting illegal aliens. He appealed to the U.S. Supreme Court. The Court held that the Fourth Amendment was not violated by stops of vehicles at permanent border checkpoints for brief questioning of their occupants regarding immigration status, even though there was no reason to believe that the particular vehicle contained illegal aliens. Fixed checkpoints do not need to be authorized in advanced by a judicial warrant.

United States v. Ramsey
431 U.S. 606 (1977)

Charles W. Ramsey and James W. Kelly started a heroin-by-mail business in the area of Washington, D.C. They procured heroin which was mailed in letters from Bangkok, Thailand, and sent to several locations in the District of Columbia. Two of their suppliers, located in West Germany, were engaged in international narcotics trafficking during 1973 and 1974. They were also being investigated. Intercepted transatlantic conversations between Bailey and Charles W. Ramsey established the existence of an international network. Title 19 U.S.C. 482 and specific postal regulations authorize customs officials to inspect incoming international mail when they have a "reasonable cause to suspect" that the mail contains illegally imported merchandise, although the regulations prohibit the reading of correspondence absent a search warrant. Acting pursuant to the statute and the regulations, as well as on the basis of the facts above, a customs inspector, having noticed that certain incoming, letter-sized airmail envelopes were from Thailand, a known source of narcotics, and that the envelopes were bulkier and much heavier than those used for usual airmail letters, opened the envelopes for inspection at the General Post Office in New York City, considered a "border" for border-search purposes. Ultimately, the envelopes were found to contain heroin. Ramsey and others were subsequently indicted and charged with narcotics offenses. During trial, Ramsey sought suppression of the evidence, but the lower court denied the motion. On appeal, the court of appeals reversed the decision, and the U.S. Supreme Court granted certiorari. The Court held that customs officers could open and search mail entering the U.S. without probable cause.

United States v. Cortez
449 U.S. 411 (1981)

Border patrol officers were investigating the trafficking of illegal aliens over the Mexican-United States border. They discovered a path entering into the United States and some distinctive shoe prints and tire tracks indicating a particular kind of truck. They stopped the truck and questioned Cortez, the truck driver, and his passengers, who happened to be wearing shoes matching the prints made at the illegal border crossing. The case was reviewed by the U.S. Supreme Court. The Court held that border patrol officers investigating a specific person for smuggling aliens into the U.S. could stop a vehicle based on reasonable suspicion for the purpose of questioning the occupants about their citizenship, immigration status, and the reasons for their presence in the area.

United States v. Villamonte-Marquez
462 U.S. 579 (1983)

United States customs officials were patrolling a water channel connecting Lake Charles, Louisiana, with the Gulf of Mexico, when they observed an anchored forty-foot sailboat. Customs officers noticed that a passing vessel caused the boat to rock violently. When officers asked the respondents aboard the sailboat if everyone was all right, their suspicions grew when the respondents shrugged their shoulders in a unresponsive manner. A customs officer and a Louisiana state police officer boarded the sailboat and asked to see the documentation for it. While viewing a document, they smelled marijuana and saw, through an open hatch, a large quantity of marijuana wrapped in burlap. The respondents were then arrested and given Miranda warnings. A subsequent search of the vessel revealed more narcotics. At trial, the respondents were convicted of federal drug violations. On appeal, the circuit court reversed, holding that officers violated the respondents' Fourth Amendment rights when they boarded the sailboat without having reasonable suspicion that a crime had been committed. The case was reviewed by the U.S. Supreme Court, which had granted certiorari. The Court held that the Fourth Amendment is not violated when customs agents board vessels to conduct document checks without having a suspicion that a statute is being violated.

Texas v. Brown
460 U.S. 730 (1983)

A police officer of Fort Worth, Texas, stopped Brown at a routine driver's license checkpoint. Brown was asked to show the officer his driver's license, and while he was fumbling for it, a party balloon dropped out of his pocket. It appeared to be tied at one end. The officer, as well as other officers present, knew or had strong reason to believe that such balloons were often receptacles for drugs such as cocaine. Brown continued to search for his license, and he reached into his glove compartment. When he did so, the officer shined his flashlight into the compartment and saw in plain view other party balloons, as well as envelopes containing a white substance. One balloon was retrieved by an officer and examined more closely. The balloon contained cocaine, and Brown was subsequently arrested for possession of cocaine. At trial, Brown moved to suppress the evidence, but the court denied the motion. He was subsequently convicted for possession. The Texas Court of Criminal Appeals reversed the conviction, holding that the seizure of the evidence had violated the Fourth Amendment. The appeals court rejected the state's claim of the plain view exception. Instead, the court relied on *Coolidge v. New Hampshire*, reasoning that in order for the plain view doctrine to apply, the officer must legitimately have been in a position to view the object and it must have been immediately apparent to the police that incriminating evidence existed. The case was appealed to the U.S. Supreme Court. The Court held that seizure of evidence in plain view did not violate the warrant requirement of the Fourth Amendment.

Immigration and Naturalization Services v. Delgado
466 U.S. 210 (1984)

Immigration and Naturalization Services (INS) agents conducted two factory surveys of the workforce in search of illegal aliens. A third factory survey was conducted with the employer's consent at another garment factory. These surveys typically last from one to two hours. While these surveys are conducted, some INS officers are positioned near factory exits, and others move systematically through the factory, where they approach each employee and question him or her on matters of citizenship and ask for identification. When satisfied with an employee's answers, officers move on to the next employee. While surveys are being conducted, employees have the option of moving freely in the factory or to continue working. In this case, the respondents alleged that the factory surveys violated their Fourth Amendment rights and sought declaratory relief. The district court granted summary judgment for the INS, but the court of appeals reversed, holding that the surveys constituted a seizure of the entire workforce and that the INS could not question an individual employee unless its agents had reasonable suspicion that all the employees were illegal aliens. The case was appealed to the U.S. Supreme Court. The Court held that "factory surveys" or interrogations by law-enforcement officers do not by themselves constitute a seizure within the meaning of the Fourth Amendment since the entire workforce of each factory was not seized for the duration of a survey.

Oliver v. United States
466 U.S. 170 (1984)

Acting on information that the petitioner was growing marijuana on his farm, Kentucky state police went to Oliver's farm to investigate. After arriving at the suspect's farm, officers approached a "No Trespassing" sign at the beginning of a path. Without a search or an arrest warrant, they followed the path about a mile until they came to some marijuana plants growing in the middle of a field. Oliver was arrested and indicted for manufacturing a controlled substance in violation of a federal statute. At trial, the defense moved to suppress the evidence. The district court agreed and suppressed the discovery of the marijuana field. The case was appealed to the U.S. Supreme Court. The Court held that open fields are not afforded the same protection under the Fourth Amendment as that extended to land immediately surrounding and associated with the home. The asserted expectation of privacy in open fields is not an expectation that society recognizes as reasonable.

Dow Chemical Company v. United States
476 U.S. 227 (1986)

The petitioner operates a 2,000-acre chemical plant that consists of numerous covered buildings with equipment between various buildings exposed to visual observations from the air. The petitioner has elaborate security around the perimeter of the complex, barring ground-level public view of the facility. After the petitioner refused the request of the Environmental Protection Agency (EPA) for an on-site inspection of the facility, the EPA did not seek an administrative search warrant; instead, it used a commercial aerial photographer to take photographs of the facility from various altitudes which were within lawful navigable airspace. As a result, the petitioner filed a lawsuit in federal district court alleging that the EPA had violated the Fourth Amendment and had gone beyond its administrative authority. The district court granted summary judgment to the petitioner, but the court of appeals reversed, holding that the EPA did not exceed its investigatory authority and that the aerial photography taken without a warrant did not violate the defendant's Fourth Amendment rights. The case was appealed to the U.S. Supreme Court. The Court held that the EPA's aerial photography of Dow's 2,000-acre complex from navigable airspace without a warrant was not a search under the Fourth Amendment. The Court also reasoned that the use of aerial observations and photography is within EPA's statutory authority. The EPA needs no explicit statutory provision to employ methods of observation commonly available to the public at large.

California v. Ciraolo
476 U.S. 207 (1986)

Santa Clara Police received an anonymous tip that Ciraolo was growing marijuana in his backyard. Acting on the information, officers went to Ciraolo's home to look around. Since a view of the yard was obstructed by a high fence, the officers flew over Ciraolo's home in an airplane and photographed the backyard from an altitude of 1,000 feet. After viewing the photographs and detecting marijuana plants, officers obtained a search warrant for Ciraolo's premises, where they seized seventy-three marijuana plants. Ciraolo was arrested. At trial, he moved to suppress the evidence on the grounds that aerial photography constituted an illegal search within the meaning of the Fourth amendment. The evidence was admitted and he was subsequently convicted of cultivating marijuana. The case was appealed to the California Court of Appeals. The court reversed the conviction, holding that the aerial observation was illegal. The case was appealed and the U.S. Supreme Court granted certiorari. The Court held that the Fourth Amendment was not violated by a warrantless aerial observation from an altitude of 1,000 feet of a fenced backyard within the curtilage of a home. Furthermore, the search was nonintrusive and occurred within public navigable air space.

Arizona v. Hicks
480 U.S. 321 (1987)

One evening, occupants in an apartment reported that someone from an apartment above had fired a bullet through their ceiling, injuring one of the occupants. Police investigated the upstairs apartment, rented by Hicks. While investigating without a warrant, they discovered weapons and a stocking-cap mask. They also noted that the apartment was run-down. But new stereo equipment stood in plain view. They moved the equipment and wrote down its serial numbers. Later, when the stereo items were compared with those listed in another crime report, the items were found to have been stolen. A search warrant was obtained to search Hicks's apartment. He was arrested, charged with, and convicted of robbery. On appeal, the U.S. Supreme Court held that although the mere recording of serial numbers does not constitute a "seizure," moving a stereo found in plain view in order to obtain its serial number came within the Fourth Amendment as a "search" independent of actions that justified exigent entry into the dwelling. The Court also held that a violation of the Fourth amendment occurred because officers acted on reasonable suspicion rather than having probable cause to believe the items were stolen.

United States v. Dunn
480 U.S. 294 (1987)

In 1980, Drug Enforcement Administration agents investigated Dunn, who was suspected of manufacturing drugs in large quantities in a private laboratory located on his property. Agents placed a beeper in a container used by Dunn to transport drugs. Agents also relied on aerial photographs of the ranch that showed the truck backed up to a barn behind the ranch house. The ranch was completely encircled by a perimeter fence and contained several interior barbed-wire fences, including one around the house approximately fifty yards from the barn. There was also a locked wooden fence enclosing the barn. Without a warrant, officers crossed the perimeter fence, several of the barbed-wire fences, and the wooden fence in front of the barn. They were led to the barn by the smell of chemicals, and they could hear a motor running inside it. They did not enter the barn but stopped at the locked gate and, shining their flashlights, observed what they thought was a drug laboratory. They then left the ranch but returned twice the next day to make further observations. They secured a search warrant and entered the barn, where they seized a quantity of illegal drugs. Dunn was convicted of drug manufacturing. Dunn moved to suppress the evidence, claiming a violation of the Fourth Amendment. The district court denied the motion pursuant to the warrant, and the respondent was convicted of conspiracy to manufacture controlled substances. The case was appealed. The court of appeals reversed the conviction, holding that the barn was protected under the Fourth Amendment since it was within the residence's curtilage. The U.S. Supreme Court granted certiorari and held that peering into the front of a barn without a search warrant did not violate the Fourth Amendment because the barn was not within the curtilage of a dwelling and observations made from open fields do not violate any privacy expectations.

California v. Greenwood
486 U.S. 35 (1988)

While police were acting on information that Billy Greenwood was engaged in trafficking in narcotics, they inspected the trash cans he had discarded and left at the curbside for pickup. Police engaged in this practice for several days and discovered sufficient incriminating evidence giving them probable cause to obtain a search warrant of the premises. A search of Greenwood's house yielded large quantities of cocaine and hashish and resulted in Greenwood's arrest. At trial, Greenwood moved to suppress the evidence against him, contending that the seizure of items taken from his trash cans constituted a violation of his rights. He was subsequently convicted on felony narcotics charges. He appealed the conviction. Because probable cause was established after police had searched Greenwood's trash cans, the state supreme court, pursuant to *People v. Krivde*, dismissed the charges, holding that warrantless trash searches violated the Fourth Amendment and the California state constitution. The case was appealed and the U.S. Supreme Court granted certiorari. The Court held that the Fourth Amendment does not prohibit warrantless searches and seizures of garbage left for collection outside the curtilage of a home since those who relinquish ownership of discarded items no longer have a reasonable expectation of privacy concerning those items. The Court also held that Greenwood's contention that the California constitutional amendment violates the due process clause of the Fourteenth Amendment was without merit.

Illinois v. Rodriguez
497 U.S. 177 (1990)

Gail Fischer called police and reported that she had been beaten by her boyfriend, Rodriguez. The police went with Fischer to Rodriquez's apartment. She allowed them entry since she lived there and had a key. She maintained that the apartment was "ours." Indeed, her clothes, furniture, and other personal effects were in the apartment as proof of her statement. When police entered, they saw containers in plain view. Upon checking the containers, they found drugs in them and then made an arrest. The police then seized the drugs. At trial, Rodriguez moved to suppress the evidence, arguing that the search had violated his Fourth Amendment rights. The trial court agreed and granted the motion, holding that at the time Fischer allowed police entry, she lacked the common authority to do so since she had moved out of the apartment. The court also rejected the state's claim that even if Fischer lacked common authority, there was no Fourth Amendment violation if police reasonably believed at the time of entry that she possessed the authority to give consent. The state appealed the case to the appellate court. The court affirmed the decision. The case was appealed to the U.S. Supreme Court and it granted review. The Court held that a consent search was valid when consent was obtained from a third party who the police at the time of the entry reasonably believed possessed common authority over the premises but who in fact did not have such authority.

Horton v. California
496 U.S. 128 (1990)

Horton was suspected by California police for committing an armed robbery. He was visited by the police, who arrived with a valid search warrant specifically authorizing them to look only for stolen property, not the weapons used in the robbery. During the search, police did not find any stolen property. However, they discovered some weapons that were in plain view. The officers seized the weapons, believing them to be the weapons used in the robbery. At trial, Horton moved to suppress the evidence, but the court refused. He was subsequently convicted of robbery. He appealed, and the California Court of Appeals affirmed the conviction. The case was appealed to the U.S. Supreme Court. The Court held that police do not violate the Fourth Amendment by arriving at a place where evidence is inadvertently discovered, because it is immediately apparent that the evidence has an incriminating character. Police can seize the evidence under the plain view doctrine.

Florida v. Bostick
501 U.S. 429 (1991)

Terrance Bostick was a passenger on a bus from Miami to Atlanta. Sheriff department officers for Broward County, Florida, regularly boarded the bus without any suspicion to ask passengers for permission to search their luggage with the intent to catch drug smugglers. They approached Bostick, asked him a few questions, asked to see his ticket, and asked if they could search his bag. He was advised that he could refuse, but he gave consent. They discovered cocaine in the bag and he was subsequently arrested on drug-trafficking charges. He filed a motion to suppress the evidence, arguing that it had been unlawfully obtained, but the trial court refused. He was convicted of possession of cocaine. The case was certified to the Florida State Supreme Court. The court held that the bus searches were unconstitutional per se because police did not afford passengers the opportunity to "leave the bus" in order to avoid questioning. Florida appealed the case to the U.S. Supreme Court. The Court held that a police officer may approach a person on a bus without cause and request consent to search luggage. The Court further held that when deciding if a search request is overly coercive, one must look at whether a party felt free to decline or terminate the search encounter. It also held that in the absence of intimidation or harassment, Bostick could have refused the search request. Whether consent is given depends on the totality of the circumstances.

Florida v. Jimeno
500 U.S. 248 (1991)

Enio Jimeno was overheard by a police officer arranging a drug transaction over the telephone. The officer followed Jimeno and stopped his car when Jimeno committed a traffic violation. The officer advised Jimeno that he had reason to believe that Jimeno had narcotics in his possession and asked for permission to search the car. Jimeno consented to the search and the officer found a brown paper bag of cocaine in a closed container within the car. Jimeno was arrested. At trial, Jimeno argued that the evidence should be suppressed since his consent of the car search did not extend to the closed container. The trial court agreed, holding that the drugs were the product of an unconstitutional search within the meaning of the Fourth Amendment. The Florida District Court of Appeals and the Florida Supreme Court both affirmed. The case was appealed and the United States Supreme Court granted certiorari. The Court held that the search did not violate the Fourth Amendment prohibition against unreasonable searches and seizures. The search was objectively reasonable for the police to conclude that the general consent to search the respondent's car included the consent to search containers within the car which might bear drugs. A reasonable person may be expected to know that narcotics are generally carried in some containers. The Court also held that a consent to search a vehicle includes a consent to search closed containers found in the vehicle unless restrictions were placed on the consent when it was given.

California v. Hodari
499 U.S. 621 (1991)

Hodari, a juvenile, was observed by police late at night with others huddled around a vehicle in a high-crime neighborhood of Oakland, California. Everyone fled in different directions when seeing the approaching police vehicle. One officer, Pertoso, drove around the block to intercept one of the fleeing persons, Hodari. Pertoso intercepted him and a brief scuffle ensued. Hodari broke free, began to run away again, and threw away what appeared to be a small rock. The officer tackled and arrested him. The recovered rock turned out to be crack cocaine. Hodari was arrested. In the juvenile proceeding, Hodari argued for a motion to suppress the evidence. He was convicted and he appealed. The state court of appeals reversed the decision, holding that Hodari had been seized when he saw Pertoso running toward him and that therefore the seizure was unreasonable under the Fourth Amendment. The case was appealed to the U.S. Supreme Court. The Court held that Hodari was untouched by Pertoso before he dropped the drugs. When no physical force has been applied, there is no seizure within the meaning of the Fourth Amendment. Further, the Court held that the seizure of an item discarded by a person who has been pursued by the police does not violate the Fourth Amendment when the police have not touched the person in order to make an arrest at the time the item was discarded.

Ohio v. Robinette
519 U.S. 33 (1996)

After stopping Robinette for speeding, an Ohio deputy sheriff gave him a verbal warning, returned his driver's license, and then asked whether he was carrying contraband such as drugs or weapons in his car. The defendant replied, "No," but consented to a search of the car. The search revealed some marijuana and a pill that later proved to be a controlled substance. He was arrested. At trial, he moved to have the evidence suppressed, but the motion was denied. He was subsequently found guilty. He appealed and the Ohio Court of Appeals reversed, holding that the search resulted from an unlawful detention. The state supreme court affirmed. The case was appealed to the U.S. Supreme Court. The Court held that the Fourth Amendment does not require that a lawfully seized defendant be advised that he is "free to go" before his consenting to a search. The Amendment is based on reasonableness, which is measured in objective terms by examining the totality of the circumstances.

United States v. Montoya de Hernandez
473 U.S. 531 (1985)

Montoya de Hernandez, a female drug smuggler, operated as a "mule." Based upon a reliable informant's tip, DEA agents established surveillance and intercepted Montoya de Hernandez at the Los Angeles Airport when she exited a flight from Bogota, Colombia. She was detained incommunicado for almost sixteen hours before customs officials sought a court order authorizing a pregnancy test (she had claimed to be pregnant), an X-ray, and a rectal examination. During the sixteen hours, she was given the option of retuning to Columbia on the next available flight, but she refused. She was also given the opportunity to use the airport's toilet facilities—but, again, she refused. She also refused to be X-rayed. In keeping with the court order, the pregnancy test was conducted at a hospital and proved to be negative. A rectal examination was given, which revealed an attempt to smuggle eighty-eight cocaine-filled balloons in her alimentary canal. She was arrested and charged with drug trafficking. At trial, she sought to suppress the evidence, claiming a violation of her Fourth Amendment rights. The district court refused and she was subsequently convicted of various federal narcotics offenses. She appealed the ruling and the court of appeals reversed, holding that the respondent's detention violated the Fourth Amendment because the customs officials did not have a "clear indication" of alimentary-canal smuggling at the time of detention. The U.S. Supreme Court granted certiorari and held that the detention of a traveler at the international border that went beyond the scope of the routine customs search and inspection is justified at its inception if customs agents, considering all the facts surrounding the traveler and his or her trip, reasonably suspect that the traveler is smuggling contraband in his or her alimentary canal. Incommunicado detention for almost sixteen hours to allow the suspect to be X-rayed (a procedure she refused) and to have a bowel movement (an opportunity she refused) prior to seeking a search warrant was justified under the circumstances.

REFERENCES

Adler, F., Mueller, G. C., & Laufer, W. S. (1994). *Criminal justice.* New York: McGraw-Hill.

Anderson, J. F., Mangels, N., Langsam, A., & Dyson, L. (2002). *Criminal justice and criminology: Concepts and terms.* Lanham, MD: University Press of America.

Barkan, S. E., & Bryjak, G. J. (2004). *Fundamentals of criminal justice.* Boston: Pearson/Allyn and Bacon.

Bartollas, C. (1988). *American criminal justice: An introduction.* New York: Macmillan.

Black, H. C. (1979). *Black's law dictionary: With pronunciations.* St. Paul: MN: West.

Champion, D. (1998). *Criminal justice in the United States* (2nd ed.). Chicago: Nelson-Hall.

del Carmen, R. V. (1991). *Civil liabilities in American Policing: A text for law enforcement personnel.* Englewood Cliffs, NJ: Brady/Prentice Hall.

del Carmen, R. V. (1999). *Criminal procedures: Law and practice* (4th ed.) Belmont, CA: Wadsworth.

del Carmen, R. V. (2001). *Criminal procedure: Law and practice.* Stamford, CT: Wadsworth/ Thomson Learning.

del Carmen, R. V. (2003). *Criminal procedures: Law and practice* (6th ed.) Belmont, CA: Wadsworth.

Gaines, L., & Miller, R. L. (2004). *Criminal justice in action: The core.* Belmont, CA: Thomson/Wadsworth.

Israel, J. H., Kamisar, Y., & LaFave, W. R. (1991). *Criminal procedure and the Constitution: Leading Supreme Court cases and introductory text.* St. Paul, MN: West.

Klein, I. J. (1997). *Law of evidence for criminal justice professionals* (4th ed.). Belmont, CA: West/Wadsworth.

Light, S. C. (1999). Understanding criminal justice. Belmont, CA: West/Wadsworth.

More, H. W. (1981). *Critical issues in law enforcement.* Cincinnati: Anderson.

Moskovitz, M. (2000). *Cases and problems in criminal procedures: The police* (3rd ed.). New York: Lexis.

Rush, G. E. (2000). *The dictionary of criminal justice* (5th ed.). New York: Duskin/McGraw-Hill.

Scheb, J. M., & Scheb, J. M. (1999). *Criminal law & procedure.* Belmont, CA: West/ Wadsworth.

Senna, J. J., & Siegel, L. J. (1998). *Essentials of criminal justice* (2nd ed.). Belmont, CA: West/Wadsworth.

Stuckey, G. B., Robinson, C., & Wallace, H. (2004). *Procedures in the justice system.* Upper Saddle River, NJ: Pearson-Prentice Hall.

West's Ann. Cal. Pen. Code 1526(b).

Cases Cited

Abel v. United States, 362 U.S. 217 (1960)

Almeida-Sanchez v. United States, 413 U.S. 266 (1973)

Arizona v. Hicks, 480 U.S. 321 (1987)

Baily v. United States, 389 F. 2d 305 (D.C. Cir. 1967)

Bernie v. State, 524 So. 2d 988 (Fla. 1988)

Bumper v. North Carolina, 391 U.S. 543 (1968)

Burdeau v. McDowell, 256 U.S. 465 (1921)

California v. Ciraolo, 476 U.S. 207 (1986)

California v. Greenwood, 486 U.S. 35 (1988)

California v. Hodari, 499 U.S. 621 (1991)

Carroll v. United States, 267 U.S. 132 (1925)

Chambers v. Maroney, 399 U.S. 42 (1970)

Chimel v. California, 395 U.S. 752 (1969)

Commonwealth v. Upton, 476 N.E. 2d 548 (Mass. 1985)

Coolidge v. New Hampshire, 403 U.S. 443 (1971)

County of Riverside v. Mc Raughlin, 500 U.S. 44 (1991)

Dow Chemical Company v. United States, 476 U.S. 227 (1986)

Florida v. Bostick, 501 U.S. 429 (1991)

Florida v. Jimeno, 500 U.S. 248 (1991)

Garrison v. State, 494 A. 2d 193 (Md. 1985)

Harris v. United States, 390 U.S. 234 (1968)

Horton v. California, 496 U.S. 128 (1990)

Illinois v. Gates, 462 U.S. 213 (1983)

Illinois v. Rodriquez, 497 U.S. 177 (1990)

Immigration and Naturalization Services v. Delgado, 466 U.S. 210 (1984)

Johnson v. United States, 333 U.S. 10 (1948)

Katz v. United States, 389 U.S. 347 (1967)

Lyon v. Robinson, 783 F. 2d 737 (8th Cir. 1985)

Maryland v. Wilson, 117 U.S. 882 (1997)

Michigan v. Long, 463 U.S. 1032 (1983)

Minnesota v. Dickerson, 508 U.S. 366 (1993)

New York v. Belton, 453 U.S. 454 (1981)

Ohio v. Robinette, 519 U.S. 33 (1996)

Oliver v. United States, 466 U.S. 170 (1984)

Ramsey v. United States 431 U.S. 606 (1977)

Schmerber v. California, 384 U.S. 757 (1966)

Schneckloth v. Bustamonte, 412 U.S. 218 (1973)

Skinner v. Railway Labor Executive's Association, 489 U.S. 602

State v. Curl, 869 P.2d 244 (Idaho, 1993)

State v. George, 323 S.C. 496, 476 S. E.2d 903 (1996)

State v. Halczyszak, 496 N.E. 2d 925 (Ohio 1986)

State v. Jacobson, 466 U.S. 109 (1984)

State v. Jacumin, 778 S.W. 2d 430 (Tenn. 1989)

State v. Kock, 725 P. 2d 1285 (Ore. 1986)

State v. Larocco, 592 P. 2d 460 (Utah 1990)

State v. Miller, 630 A. 2d 1315 (Conn. 1993)

State v. Nall, 379 Sc.2d 731(La. 1980)

State v. Pinkham, 565 A. 2d 318 (Me. 1989)

State v. Pulgini, 366 A. 2d 1198 (Del. Super. 1976)

State v. Yoder, 534 P.2d 771 (1975)

Stoner v. California, 376 U.S. 483 (1964)

Terry v. Ohio, 392 U.S. 1 (1968)

Texas v. Brown, 460 U.S. 730 (1983)

United States v. Brignoni-Ponce, 422 U.S. 873 (1975)

United States v. Cortez, 449 U.S. 411 (1981)

United States v. Dornhofer, 859 F. 2d 1195 (4th Cir. 1988)

United States v. Dunn, 480 U.S. 294 (1987)

United States v. Fama, 758 F.2d 834 (2d Cir. 1985)

United States v. Hale, 784 F. 2d 1465 (9th Cir. 1986)

United States v. Johns, 469 U.S. 478 (1985)

United States v. Jones, 452 F. 2d 884 (8th Cir. 1971)

United States v. Martinez-Fuerte, 428 U.S. 543 (1976)

United States v. Matlock, 415 U.S. 164 (1974)

United States v. Montgomery, 561 F 2d 875 (1977)

United States v. Montoya de Hernandez, 473 U.S. 531 (1985)

United States v. Ortiz, 422 U.S. 891 (1975)

United States v. Pacelli, 470 F. 2d 67 (2d Cir. 1972)

United States v. Ramsey, 431 U.S. 606 (1977)

United States v. Robinowitz, 339 U.S. 56 (1950)

United States v. Rosenbarger, 536 F. 2d 715 (6th Cir. 1976)

United States v. Ross, 456 U.S. 798 (1982)

United States v. Villamonte-Marquez, 462 U.S. 579 (1983)

Warden v. Hayden, 387 U.S. 294 (1967)

Welsh v. Wisconsin, 466 U.S. 740 (1984)

Whren v. United States, 517 U.S. 806 (1996)

Wilson v. Arkansas, 514 U.S. 927 (1995)

Wyoming v. Houghton, 526 U.S. 295 (1999)

CHAPTER 7

Arrests

Focal Points

- Principles Governing an Arrest
  - Specificity of Probable Cause
  - Establishing Probable Cause
  - Officer's Firsthand Observations
  - Information Provided by an Informant
  - Information plus Corroboration
- The Elements of an Arrest
  - The Intent to Arrest a Suspect
  - The Authority to Arrest
  - Seizure and Detention
  - The Understanding of the Arrestee
- Arrests with and without a Warrant
  - Arrests with a Warrant
  - Service of an Arrest Warrant
  - Search Warrants and Third-Party Premises
  - Legal Authorizations Analogous to an Arrest Warrant
  - Specificity of an Arrest Warrant
  - Arrests without a Warrant
  - Concerning Felonies
  - Concerning Misdemeanors
  - Concerning Traffic Violations
  - Concerning Minor offenses Not Punishable with a Jail Term
- Legal Consequences of False Arrests and False Imprisonment
  - Civil Liability under State Tort Law
  - Civil Liability under Federal Law
  - A Private Citizen's Right to Make an Arrest
  - Inadmissibility of Evidence Obtained

INTRODUCTION

A critical practice of police work is an officer arresting a suspect. Such an action occurs more commonly than one might imagine. Experts estimate that as many as 15 million arrests are made each year (Neubauer, 1999; Senna & Siegel, 2000). Arrests typically occur when an officer has either firsthand information or other evidence connecting a suspect to a crime. For example, if an officer observes a person breaking the law, probable cause to effect an arrest is automatically established. An arrest can also occur after witnesses come forward and provide police with sufficient information or evidence that leads the police to believe that a particular suspect was involved in criminal behavior (Senna & Siegel, 2000). After either action occurs, a police officer can legally make an arrest of the suspect (Inciardi, 1987, 1999).

Arrest in the United States is complex and, in some respects, problematical. First, the laws governing an arrest vary from jurisdiction to jurisdiction. In addition, in American criminal justice, "arrest" is constitutionally based: it has been judicially recognized that an arrest constitutes a seizure of the person, thereby implicating the Fourth Amendment protection of the right of the people to be secure in their persons against unreasonable searches and seizures. An arrest is also a key initiatory phase in the criminal-justice process. Hence, one cannot explore the meaning of an arrest for the purposes of examining American criminal procedure without putting the concept in both its constitutional and criminal-justice contexts. This observation has two key implications: first, a constitutional or legal arrest may impact favorably the prospect of a conviction in every criminal case tried in an American criminal court; second (which is the converse of the first), an unconstitutional or illegal arrest may impact adversely the prospect of a conviction in a criminal case. Put slightly differently, the legality of an arrest is often crucial in determining the admissibility of evidence in American criminal trials. Indeed, it is well established in American criminal jurisprudence that both evidence obtained as a result of an illegal arrest and other evidence emanating from such an arrest are, generally, subject to suppression under the exclusionary rule.

The effect of an arrest is the legal deprivation of an individual's liberty. Hence, mere words do not constitute an arrest. There must be some overt police conduct, in the form of physical restraint, both manifesting the intention to arrest and actually making the arrest. In addition, the law-enforcement measure must leave no doubt that the person is not free to leave on his or her own volition. And it must leave no option that the person is free to leave. It is immaterial whether the measure is characterized as an "arrest" or a "detention" under state law. Thus, according to the law, when a person has been taken into custody against his or her will for criminal prosecution or interrogation, an arrest has been effected within the meaning of the Fourth Amendment constitutional protection against unreasonable searches and seizures.

An arrest occurs when a police officer takes a suspect into custody or deprives him or her of freedom in a significant manner. Stated another way, an arrest is made when someone is taken into custody and restrained from movement until he or she is brought before a court to answer charges about involvement in a crime (see Dressler, 2002; del Carmen, 1991; del Carmen & Walker, 2004; Senna & Siegel, 2000; Rush, 2003). Anderson and Newman (1993) argue that an arrest is the point of intake for the criminal-justice process. It is also the point at which the power of the government actually touches the arrested person and compels him or her to conform to its practice. Some experts even argue that an arrest has occurred when a suspect understands that he or she is not free to leave the scene of a police stop.

Because an arrest is an intrusion placed on a person by police authority, it is governed by the Fourth Amendment protection against unreasonable searches and seizures. (Indeed, Worrall [2004] considers an arrest the most intrusive form of seizure.) Therefore, it is vitally important that officers make legal arrests and not violate a suspect's constitutional rights. Such violation is prohibited by law and could serve as the basis of a lawsuit filed against a police officer and his or her department or agency (Kappeler, 2006). Thus, law-enforcement officers must be aware of the legality governing an arrest within the meaning of the U.S. Constitution. They must be aware that the Fourth Amendment protects citizens' reasonable expectations of privacy. Specifically, the Amendment states:

> The right of the people to be secure in their persons, houses, papers, and effects, against unreasonable searches and seizures, shall not be violated, and no Warrants shall issue, but upon probable cause, supported by oath or affirmation, and particularly describing the place to be searched, and the persons or things to be seized.

The Fourth Amendment means that an arrest can be made if police are armed with a warrant or if police on their own initiative establish probable cause that a suspect has committed a serious crime (Senna & Siegel, 2000). However, the Fourth Amendment protects only against searches and seizures that are deemed unreasonable (Rush, 2000, 2003). Worrall (2004) and Inciardi (1987) argue that, in regard to the Fourth Amendment, reasonableness is determined by whether law-enforcement officers' behavior and actions have been governed by probable cause. Simply put, if an officer has probable cause when making a felony arrest, his or her actions will be upheld as legal and constitutional within the meaning of the Fourth Amendment. However, if the officer fails to establish probable cause, the arrest will be held as illegal and can be challenged in court, since such failure is considered arbitrary and capricious (Inciardi, 1987; Kappeler, 2006).

Chapter 7 provides a general discussion of the Fourth Amendment as it pertains to arrests. It is divided into several parts. Part One presents a detailed discussion of the principles governing an arrest. Part Two lists and explains the elements of an arrest. Part Three distinguishes between types of arrests conducted by police: those made with a warrant and those made without a warrant. Part Four discusses the legal consequences of false arrests and false imprisonment. Part Five describes invalid actions of officers during arrests and legitimate actions of officers after arrests. Part Six presents an overview of principles governing the law of arrest. Part Seven provides some pertinent Fourth Amendment cases related to arrest procedures.

Part One: Principles Governing an Arrest

Throughout the United States, each state has its own set of laws that provides law-enforcement officers with specific instructions governing when and how to effect a valid arrest (Peoples, 2003). Experts claim that police can effect an arrest under one of the following circumstances. First, an officer is legally authorized to make an arrest when he or she establishes probable cause to believe that a suspect has committed a felony or a misdemeanor (Bohm & Haley, 1999). However, state law specifies that if the officer intends to make an arrest in a misdemeanor case, he or she must have observed the law violation. (Such observation is not required in felony cases). Second, a law-enforcement officer is free to make an arrest if he or she has reason to believe that a suspect has committed a felony—even though the officer did not actually observe the suspect's behavior. Third, the officer is acting within the scope of the law if he or she effects an arrest while acting on the authority of an arrest warrant (Peoples, 2003).

State law not only specifies the criteria for making a valid arrest; it also provides officers with rules governing the time period when arrest warrants should be executed. For example, because of the threat posed by dangerous felons, most states require that felony arrests be effected at any time during the day or night. States recognize the pressing need to apprehend felons quickly before they commit more crimes. Moreover, in keeping with the traditions of common law, most states require that law-enforcement officers, when executing a warrant, knock and announce their purpose (Fagin, 2003). This practice allows voluntary compliance and minimizes the use of police force. Concerning arrests for misdemeanors, the process of serving a warrant is relaxed. Because of the nonserious nature of misdemeanors, some states advise that warrants for such crimes be served between the hours of 10 p.m. and 6 a.m., unless the suspect is observed by police in the open public. If the suspect is seen on the street, police officers can quickly make an arrest. There is no need to arrest the suspect at his or her home (Fagin, 2003).

The Specificity of Probable Cause

While already discussed at length in Chapter 3, probable cause requires further discussion here since it is the legal concept which legitimizes arrests. Law-enforcement officers must be aware of probable cause for several reasons. Chief among them is that it is a constitutional requirement specifically stated in the Fourth Amendment, which governs searches and seizures (Neubauer,

1999; Moskovitz, 2000). In part, the Fourth Amendment states that "no Warrants shall issue, but upon probable cause." In fact, if a search or seizure lacks probable cause, the court will likely rule either course of action as invalid and charges will be dropped against the suspect (Dressler, 2002). Hence, an arrest or investigation could hinge on whether the arresting officer had probable cause before he or she took the suspect into custody or searched the arrested person or his or her belongings and retrieved illegal items. Therefore, the legality of a search, seizure of evidence, or an arrest is premised on probable cause (Dressler, 2002). But what is *probable cause*? Rush (2003) defines the concept as a set of facts and circumstances that would lead a reasonable and prudent person to believe that a specific person had committed a particular crime. In *Brown v. State*, the Georgia Court of Appeals stated that the "test of probable cause is whether it would justify a man of reasonable caution in believing that an offense has been or is being committed, and thus requires merely a probability less than a certainty but more than a mere suspicion or possibility." Stated plainly, probable cause requires probabilities, not certainties. When law-enforcement officers believe that a specific person has committed a particular crime, probable cause is established. At this time, officers can effect an arrest since the courts equate the establishment of probable cause with satisfying the reasonableness requirement of the Fourth Amendment (see Gaines & Miller, 2004). del Carmen (1991) contends that the concept is important to police work because it must be present before officers can execute many of their duties. In *Michigan v. Summers*, the U.S. Supreme Court ruled: "A warrant to search for contraband founded on probable cause implicitly carries with it the limited authority to detain the occupants of the premises while a proper search is conducted. Because it was lawful to require respondent to reenter and to remain in the house until evidence establishing probable cause to arrest him was found, his arrest and the search incident thereto were constitutionally permissible."

Establishing Probable Cause

Probable cause is often misunderstood by lay persons. The confusion has much to do with the concept of *reasonable suspicion* (Worrall, 2004; Peoples, 2003). Unlike probable cause, reasonable suspicion requires a lower degree of proof than probable cause (Bohm & Haley, 1999; Moskovitz, 2000). Reasonable suspicion is a commonsense, nontechnical concept that concerns the factual and practical consideration of everyday life upon which reasonable and prudent men act (del Carmen, 1991). It is also a standard of proof needed for officers to conduct minor, minimally intrusive procedures such as a stop and frisk (i.e., a brief pat down of the outer garments of a suspect) (Bohm & Haley, 1999). However, searches and seizures require a higher standard of proof. Nevertheless, the U.S. Supreme Court has given law-enforcement officers latitude in establishing probable cause. In *United States v. Ortiz*, the Court ruled that in order to establish probable cause, police officers are entitled to draw reasonable inferences both from the facts surrounding an investigation and from their prior experiences. In *Ortiz*, the Court stated that, given the experience of police officers, they are better qualified than the average lay person to evaluate and make deductions concerning facts and circumstances. Hence, what a lay person may not recognize as probable cause may constitute this degree of certainty to a trained and experienced police officer. del Carmen (1991) contends that police officers must consider the "totality of circumstances" when establishing probable cause. Essentially, police must quickly evaluate the facts that have led them to believe that a particular person has engaged in a specific crime or that a crime is about to be committed. The totality of circumstances usually includes a combination of factors, such as the suspect's reputation, race, clothes, suspicious behavior, neighborhood (especially if the area is known for drugs and other crime), the time of day, tips from informants, calls from concerned citizens, etc. (Champion, 1997; Light, 1999). An officer should be aware of such factors and should report his or her determination of probable cause, since it will be needed to procure a search or an arrest warrant or if any of the officer's actions are later challenged in court. Regarding the determination of probable cause, experts warn that it is better for police officers to have too much information rather than too little in order to justify any actions they take (del Carmen, 2004). Daniel (1991) argues that to allow a lesser degree of certainty in police work would leave law-abiding citizens at the mercy of an officer's whim or caprice.

As stated earlier, the U.S. Supreme Court has given law-enforcement officers leeway in determining probable cause. Some common criteria that officers use to justify searches and arrests are: (1) the officer's firsthand observations or knowledge regarding the facts and circumstances of a crime; (2) information given to officers by a reliable source or informant; and (3) corroboration of the information given by a reliable source or informant.

Officer's Firsthand Observations

Because most police work occurs after crimes are committed, rare is the occasion when officers discover offenders in the commission of crime (Gaines & Miller, 2004). However, when officers make firsthand observations of offenders engaging in crime, they can quickly effect an arrest since probable cause is automatically established. del Carmen (2004) contends that officers can use their five senses to establish probable cause. For example, if an officer sees a suspect fleeing a bank, hears gunshots coming from a certain area, smells marijuana or other drugs after making a routine traffic stop, touches a weapon or contraband after making a search incidental to a lawful arrest, or even tastes alcohol or another illegal substance, he or she can determine probable cause. In *Berry v. State*, a Georgia appeals court held that an officer who had a degree in chemistry, who had received special training in drug identification, who knew the odor of hydrochloric acid, and who knew that hydrochloric acid is used to process cocaine and heroin, had probable cause to arrest a person fitting the drug-courier profile when he detected the odor of hydrochloric acid. Any of these firsthand experiences can lead to the determination of probable cause, which, in turn, can lead to a valid arrest of a suspect. Essentially, to make a valid warrantless arrest, the police officer must have made a personal observation. In addition, the manner of the observation must have been lawful. Hence, the information that leads to the determination of probable cause must be lawfully obtained (Daniel, 1991).

Information Provided by an Informant

Law-enforcement agencies and courts welcome the assistance of the community. They have always embraced information from citizens that could help solve crime. When police officers assess the trustworthiness of the information in their determination of probable cause, the U.S. Supreme Court has stated that an objective standard must be used and not simply a reliance on good faith (Daniel, 1991). The information is better received when the informant lacks a criminal record. However, if the informant has a criminal history, it does not necessarily mean that the informant is not trustworthy. In *Aguilar v. Texas*, the U.S. Supreme Court addressed this issue by examining whether information from an informant with a criminal past can be used to help police establish probable cause. In *Aguilar*, the Court created a two-pronged test—i.e., two independent tests—to determine if police officers can use information from informants with a criminal history to establish probable cause. The first test focused on the reliability of the informant. The second addressed the reliability of the informant's information. In the first test, the Court was concerned with whether the informant had been used in the past and whether he or she had proved reliable. In the second test, the Court was concerned with whether the informant had actually witnessed the commission of the crime. Both tests had to be established in an affidavit and had to prove reliable to a neutral and detached magistrate. Therefore, if both tests were satisfied, the informant's testimony could be used to determine probable cause; if not, it could not be used for that determination. The Court's decision in *Aguilar* was reiterated in *Spinelli v. United States*. Spinelli's conviction was overturned on his challenge that the information in the affidavit had failed to establish probable cause justifying a warrant to be issued for his arrest (see also Inciardi, 1987, 1999). The U.S. Supreme Court agreed, ruling that, as determined in *Aguilar*, neither the reliability of the informant nor the reliability of the informant's information had been established. *Aguilar* was overturned by *Illinois v. Gates*. In *Gates*, the Court abandoned the two-pronged test and decided that a more effective way to determine the reliability of the information from an informant was to use a test regarding the totality of the circumstances. Essentially, under *Gates*, the Court created a new standard, which required that police establish three items in their affidavit. First, police had to show that the informant had been reliable in the past. Second, the informant had actually witnessed the crime. Third, the informant's information had been corroborated by independent police work. Under *Gates*, magistrates evaluated the merits of affidavits by examining the facts and circumstances that had led an officer to establish probable cause. If they agreed with the officer, they issued an arrest or a search warrant.

In *Gates*, the Court did not require police officers to reveal the identity of the informant in the affidavit. This position was challenged and then reaffirmed in *McCray v. Illinois*. In this case, the Court ruled that a warrantless arrest, search, and seizure are valid even if the arresting police officer does not reveal the identity of the informant: the evidence at trial would prove that the police had corroborated the information given by a reliable informant. The Court also held that the issue in *McCray* was whether probable cause exists, not the defendant's guilt or innocence—unless the informant's identity is germane or material to the defendant's guilt or innocence. If such proves to be the case, the informant's identity must be revealed or prosecutors must consider dropping the case and dismissing the charges against the defendant.

Information plus Corroboration

While the U.S. Supreme Court has given police flexibility in establishing probable cause, which includes using information from informants, it has not allowed police to rely solely on such information. Indeed, the Court has ruled that probable cause cannot be established exclusively by information from an informant. The police must also conduct an investigation to corroborate claims made by informants. By using information from informants together with corroboration of such information, police can obtain sufficient evidence to justify making an arrest, as was the case in *Draper v. United States*. In *Draper*, police received information from an informant claiming that the petitioner had gone to Chicago to get three ounces of heroin and would return with the drugs to Denver, Colorado, on September 8. The informant also provided the narcotics agents with a detailed physical description of Draper and the clothes that he would be wearing. With this information, police set up surveillance of all trains coming from Chicago on the mornings of September 8 and 9. After observing a man fitting his description, the police arrested Draper. Police seized heroin and a syringe in the search. During trial, Draper argued that the evidence taken from him should have been suppressed on the grounds that the information given to the police had failed to establish probable cause. The Court disagreed, holding that any information received from an informant that has been corroborated by an officer's independent investigation is sufficient to establish probable cause for an arrest, even though such information was hearsay and would not otherwise have been admissible in a criminal trial. The Court has also long recognized that probable cause can be established by the collective knowledge of police officers when there is communication among them rather than by the exclusive efforts of the police officer who effects the arrest (Daniel, 1991).

Part Two: The Elements of an Arrest

As mentioned earlier, false arrest and false imprisonment can be challenged because they violate civil liberties and constitutional rights (Kappeler, 2006; del Carmen, 1991). When either false arrest or false imprisonment occurs, police officers can be legally liable to the injured party. The suspect can take legal action, citing a violation of his or her rights. Specifically, the suspect files either a Section 1983 claim or a civil tort action, alleging a violation of the Fourth Amendment protection against unreasonable searches and seizures and a denial of due process under the Fourteenth Amendment. Since the actions of police officers are governed by the U.S. Constitution, state constitutions, and state penal codes, it is essential that officers work within the framework of the law or risk facing legal litigation in the form of criminal or civil penalties. Therefore, officers must be aware of the elements associated with a valid or legal arrest. According to Gaines, Kaune, and Miller (2000); Klotter (2002); and del Carmen and Walker (2004), there are four elements of an arrest: (1) the intent to arrest a suspect; (2) the authority to arrest; (3) seizure and detention; and (4) the understanding of the arrestee.

The Intent to Arrest a Suspect

Every day, police officers routinely stop vehicles, ask drivers to step out of their vehicles and present their licenses, give traffic citations to drivers who have violated traffic laws such as speeding, failure to wear a seat belt, failure to signal properly when changing lanes or turning corners, driving with a cracked headlight or taillight, or having an expired tag. When police officers stop drivers of motor vehicles, they are usually operating with reasonable suspicion or probable cause to believe that the operator of the vehicle has violated a driving ordinance. These brief encounters or temporary detentions do not typically constitute an intent by an officer to make an arrest. However, what begins for an officer as reasonable suspicion may easily escalate into probable cause that justifies an arrest and a search incidental to a lawful arrest. How can one determine if an officer has an intent to make an arrest? The U.S. Supreme Court has said that *intent* is a subjective term in that even if a police officer has not articulated to a suspect that he or she is under arrest, this lack of articulation has no bearing on whether the suspect is in custody. In *Berkemer v. McCarty*, the Court ruled that if a police officer never articulates to a suspect that he or she is in custody, the suspect's status is to be determined by what a reasonable person in the suspect's position would conclude from the circumstances. del Carmen (1991) argues that, according to the *McCarty* decision, even if the police do not articulate the intent to effect an arrest, a suspect can consider himself or herself under arrest if, considering the totality of the circumstances, the suspect does not believe that he or she has the freedom to leave the scene of the police stop. This ruling was reiterated in *Michigan v. Chesternut*, when the Court ruled that the police can be considered to have seized an individual "only if, in view of the circumstances surrounding the incident, a reasonable person would have believed that he was not free to leave."

The Authority to Arrest

The authority to arrest is of critical importance. When there is none, what may have the semblance of an arrest may well turn out, both in fact and in law, to be either an illegal detention or even a kidnapping or some other form of unlawful seizure. The situation can become legally precarious especially when the person attempting to effect an arrest is a private individual. When there is authority to arrest, the deprivation of liberty is justified. Conversely, when authority is lacking, the deprivation of liberty is unjustified. In the former case, the arrest is valid; in the latter, it is invalid. A problem related to the authority to arrest is the nature and extent, if any, of the authority of a police officer to effect an arrest while not on duty. The law is somewhat complex in that it varies from state to state. In some states it is permissible for a police officer not on duty to effect an arrest for a crime that he or she witnesses; in other states it is not permissible.

Since the police are considered law-enforcement officers, states empower them to arrest citizens for criminal law violations (Fagin, 2003; Gaines et al., 2000). However, the authority can be actual or assumed. When the authority to arrest is actual, the arrest is considered valid. But if the authority is merely assumed, the arrest is considered invalid. del Carmen (1991) argues that there are several instances when authority is merely assumed—that is, when proper authority is lacking. These include the following: (1) when the officer mistakenly assumes that he or she has the power to arrest when that power does not exist and (2) when the officer goes beyond his or her authority to make an arrest when there is no justification for such behavior. For example, if an officer arrests a suspect for committing a misdemeanor without having observed the illegal act or if an officer arrests someone on an invalid warrant, the arrest is merely assumed and therefore invalid. Klotter (2002) argues that when an officer makes an arrest or restrains a suspect's freedom of movement under assumed or pretended authority, the arrest is illegal and the officer can be sued or even jailed for the violation. Furthermore, the authority to arrest varies from state to state and sometimes from jurisdiction to jurisdiction within certain states. Some states and jurisdictions authorize police officers to make an arrest at any time—that is, when the officer is either on duty or off duty. Other states prohibit off-duty officers from effecting an arrest. The authority to arrest is governed by state laws and departmental policy.

Seizure and Detention

Seizure and *detention* are concepts essential to a police officer making an arrest. There are two types of seizure: constructive and actual. In a seizure, the suspect submits to the authority of the police officer. The suspect can submit voluntarily (a constructive seizure) or he or she can be forced to do so. del Carmen (1991) refers to the latter as an actual seizure, in which the suspect is taken into custody with the use of handcuffs or firearms. As mentioned above, an arrest can also be effected if the suspect voluntarily submits to the officer's authority. del Carmen (1991) refers to this form of seizure as constructive since it is accomplished without any physical touching, grabbing, holding, or applying direct force. Some experts argue that words alone do not constitute an arrest. For example, if an officer tells a suspect that he or she is under arrest, the person is not yet in the physical custody of police. Therefore, the officer's words must be followed by the physical restraint of the suspect. In other words, the suspect must be seized by the officer.

Actual restraint is the act of physically taking the person targeted for the arrest into custody—either by the use of hand signals or firearms or by merely touching the suspect. The former involves the use of force without actually touching the suspect; the latter clearly entails touching the suspect. By contrast, *constructive restraint*, as the term implies, takes place when the person targeted for the arrest voluntarily submits to the will and control of the arresting officer. Even when the seizure is constructive, neither words alone nor the mere possession of authority to arrest constitutes a lawful arrest. The case *California v. Hodari* illustrates this view of the law. In *Hodari*, the U.S. Supreme Court stated the law as follows: "[T]o constitute a seizure of the person … there must be either the application of physical force, however slight, or where that is absent, submission to the officer's 'show of authority' to restrain the subject's liberty." The Court found: "No physical force was applied in this case, since Hodari was untouched by [Officer] Pertoso before he dropped the drugs. Moreover, assuming that Pertoso's pursuit constituted a 'show of authority' enjoining Hodari to halt, Hodari did not comply with that injunction and therefore was not seized until he was tackled. Thus, the cocaine abandoned while he was running was not the fruit of a seizure."

In *Berry v. Bass*, a court warned that a person can no more arrest another by simply telling him to consider himself under arrest and then turning on his heel and leaving the other free to go his own way than a person can commit a homicide by telling another to consider himself dead. The person said to be under arrest has to be in actual custody and under the control of the officer (Klotter, 2002). If the suspect voluntarily submits to the control of the officer, the arrest is just as valid as if the suspect were subdued and handcuffed. The arrest is not contingent on the use of physical force, manual touching, or physical restraint visible to the eye (Klotter, 1996). A voluntary seizure minimizes injury to everyone involved; the use of force increases the likelihood of injury to a suspect as well as a police officer. However, if it is determined that a police officer used excessive force to arrest a suspect, the officer's behavior can serve as the basis of a lawsuit filed against him or her for using excessive force or making an unreasonable seizure, within the meaning of the Fourth and Eighth Amendments, respectively (Scheb & Scheb, 1999).

The Understanding of the Arrestee

The arrested person must understand that he or she is under the control and custody of the police (Peoples, 2003). A police officer can clarify this understanding by saying to the suspect, "You are under arrest," then touching his or her weapon, placing handcuffs on the suspect, and restraining his or her freedom of movement. A restraint of the arrested person's liberty can also be communicated through actions rather than words. For example, if an officer tackles or subdues a fleeing suspect, places handcuffs on him or her, and places the suspect into a patrol vehicle, the officer has demonstrated the intent to make an arrest, even though no words have been spoken. Thus, the arrestee's understanding that he or she is no longer at liberty can be conveyed through police officers' words and actions. However, the law dispenses with this requirement of understanding under three circumstances: 1) when the suspect is either intoxicated or under the influence of drugs; (2) when the suspect is insane; and (3) when the suspect is unconscious. In each of these circumstances, mental incapacity, temporary or permanent, negates any inference of understanding by the suspect.

Part Three: Arrests with and without a Warrant

Arrests with a Warrant

Law-enforcement officers can make an arrest either with or without a warrant. However, before effecting an arrest, the officer must have probable cause to believe that a certain suspect committed a particular crime (del Carmen & Walker, 2004). Ideally, when an officer establishes probable cause, he or she typically completes an affidavit that identifies the suspect by name if known (or by "John Doe") and that presents the facts and circumstances of the crime. Some experts argue that a warrant consists of both an affidavit and an order that an officer arrest an offender and present him or her to a judicial officer (Daniel, 1991). The affidavit is submitted to a judge or magistrate, who is responsible for ensuring that probable cause does exist to arrest a suspect. If the magistrate finds probable cause, he issues an arrest warrant that commands the police officer to seize the person whose name is on the warrant (Gaines et al., 2000; Gaines & Miller, 2004). However, if the magistrate finds no probable cause, he or she does not issue the arrest warrant. Daniel (1991) notes that the verified facts provided to the magistrate need not all be presented in the affidavit but that additional facts may be given in verified oral testimony or in another affidavit (p. 21). Though states vary in their procedures for filing an affidavit, most state statutes require that the affidavit give the county in which the offense was committed, the time and date it was committed, the place of the offense, the party against whom the offense was committed, and a statement describing the offense (Daniel, 1991). Moreover, if the offense was larceny, the affidavit must also describe the property which was alleged to have been stolen, the owner of the property, the value of the property, and the name of the person who was in possession of the property before it was stolen (Daniel, 1991). To understand the law concerning warrants, it is necessary to begin with a precise definition of an *arrest warrant*. In its technical sense, an arrest warrant is a writ or precept issued by a magistrate, a justice of the peace, or other competent authority, which is addressed to a sheriff, a constable, or other officer and which requires him or her to arrest the person named therein and to bring that person before the magistrate or court to answer, or to be examined, concerning some offense which he or she is charged with having committed (Black, 1979). Senna and Siegel (2000) define an arrest warrant as an order issued by the court that directs the officer to arrest a suspect to answer accusations about his or her involvement in a crime. Nevertheless, some experts argue that in 95 percent of all felony arrests, police officers act without a warrant (Senna and Siegel, 2000; Anderson and Newman, 1993; del Carmen, 1991).

Furthermore, in most states in the United States and within the federal jurisdiction, issuing an arrest warrant is the exclusive prerogative of a judge or other judicial officer. Hence, as a matter of law, an arrest warrant can be vitiated if someone other than a judicial officer authorizes its issue, although in some states, clerks may be statutorily empowered to do so. In addition, the law requires that a judicial officer issuing an arrest warrant be neutral and detached: the judicial officer must not be biased in favor of the police or the prosecutor's position in the case. The meaning and the scope of this requirement have been the subjects of some case law.

While an arrest is constitutionally valid when effected with a warrant, it may be made without a warrant under three circumstances: first, when the crime is committed in the presence of a police officer; second, when the arresting officer establishes probable cause that a crime has been committed or is to be committed and that the suspect is the person who has committed the crime or is about to commit it; third, when the law of a given jurisdiction allows the officer to effect an arrest without a warrant. For example, some states allow police to make a warrantless arrest under specific circumstances—for example, when domestic violence has occurred and when officers have observed someone stalking a victim. When a police officer lawfully makes an arrest without a warrant, the arrestee must be promptly taken before a magistrate for a probable cause hearing (see *Riverside v. McLaughlin*).

del Carmen (1991) and Scheb & Scheb (1999) argue that the officer making a warrantless arrest has the burden of proving that the arrest was based on probable cause and that the arrest warrant was not necessary since the arrest was effected under one of the exceptions to having a warrant. If the police fail to establish probable cause, the suspect is released and is no longer subject to the criminal justice system. If police can determine probable cause, the suspect is detained and the justice process continues.

The purpose of an arrest warrant is twofold. First, it serves to protect private citizens from police harassment, unjustified arrest and incarceration, and even false criminal prosecutions, since the authority to arrest is derived from a warrant (Klotter, 2002). Second, it protects law-enforcement officers from civil liability because it carries the presumption that probable cause exists (del Carmen, 1991). In fact, the U.S. Supreme Court held in *United States v. Watson* that law-enforcement officers may find it wise to seek an arrest warrant when it is practicable to do so and that their judgments about probable cause may be more readily accepted when backed by a warrant issued by a magistrate. In short, the Court advised that police would do well to procure a warrant when in doubt about making a search or an arrest.

Service of an Arrest Warrant

Another key issue to be addressed in the context of an arrest warrant is that of proper service. It is a legal imperative. According to its definition, the arrest warrant is usually directed to any law-enforcement officer in the jurisdiction. In some states, however, a private citizen is empowered to effect service. For the purposes of the law, there are two levels of service of an arrest warrant. These are (1) service within a state and (2) service outside a state. Regarding the former, the law states that an arrest warrant issued in a county or judicial district may be served by a law-enforcement officer of any other county or judicial district where the accused is found. However, some states, notably California and Texas, statutorily empower local law-enforcement officers to execute arrest warrants throughout the state.

Regarding service outside a state, the general rule is that an arrest warrant does not have authority outside the territorial boundaries of the state in which it was issued. This lack of authority is predicated on the doctrine that laws, generally, do not have force or binding effect outside their territorial limits. Hence, generally speaking, an arrest warrant issued in one state cannot be effected in another state. There are two exceptions to this rule. First, on the basis of the legal doctrine referred to as "hot pursuit," an arrest warrant issued for a felony in one state can be effected in another state in pursuance of some uniform legislative instrument. Second, an arrest warrant issued in one state can be executed in another state on the basis of what is technically called a "hit." The execution of an arrest warrant on this basis is triggered by a national computer search.

Regarding the time of arrest, the general rule is that an arrest warrant for a felony may be executed either during the day or the night but an arrest warrant for a misdemeanor can be executed only during the daytime. However, in some states an arrest for any crime may be executed at any hour of the day or night. At the time of the arrest warrant's execution, the arresting officer need not have the warrant in his possession. However, the person arrested must be shown the warrant after its execution. Regarding the expiration of the arrest warrant, legally the warrant must be executed without unreasonable delay. However, it remains valid until the time of its execution or withdrawal.

One misconception about the service of an arrest warrant is that law-enforcement officers, upon receiving a warrant, are authorized to enter a dwelling without first announcing themselves. This idea is far from reality (Worrall, 2004). In fact, in *Wilson v. Arkansas*, the U.S. Supreme Court held that police officers must act in a manner consistent with the common law, which requires them to announce their identity and purpose before entering a dwelling to execute a warrant. If they fail to do so, their behavior is tantamount to breaking into someone's premises (Peoples, 2003). This requirement fosters voluntary compliance and reduces the prospect of violence by the resident and the arresting officers. However, in *Wilson*, the Court specified that the "knock and announce" requirement is not written in stone and that officers are not obligated to "announce" under circumstances such as the following: (1) when the suspect is armed and poses a threat to the officer and others inside the premises; (2) when the suspect in the dwelling is about to destroy evidence; (3) when the suspect might attempt an escape; and (4) when a felony is being committed at the time the officer arrives to execute the warrant. Under these circumstances, as well as under others that fit law-enforcement needs, the officer can deviate from the "knock and announce" requirement. del Carmen (1991) contends that exceptions to the announcement requirement are governed by state law, by court decisions, and by police-agency regulations that can vary from state to state. For example, Worrall (2004) maintains that officers can sometimes request a warrant with special authorization to be executed at night and without the need to knock and announce. In sum, police officers should be aware of the laws and procedures governing when and how to properly serve an arrest warrant.

Search Warrants and Third-Party Premises

Arresting persons within the premises of third parties poses quite complex legal problems for law-enforcement officers operating within the constitutional constraints imposed on the American criminal justice system. One problem is whether, barring exigent circumstances, the police have authority to search the premises of third parties while executing an arrest warrant. The case *Steagald v. United States* illustrates this problem. In that case, federal agents learned from an informant that a federal fugitive could probably be found at a certain address. They obtained a warrant for his arrest, but the warrant did not specify the address. On the authority of the arrest warrant, the agents proceeded to the address provided them by the informant. It turned out to be that of the residence of a third party. In *Steagald*, the U.S. Supreme Court held that the arrest warrant could not be used as legal authority to enter the home of a person other than that named in the warrant.

By equivalent reasoning, the U.S. Supreme Court, in *Minnesota v. Olson*, ruled that entering a residence with neither a warrant nor consent to arrest an overnight guest was not justified on the grounds of exigent circumstances and therefore constituted an infringement of the Fourth Amendment protection against unreasonable searches and seizures. In that case, the police suspected a certain Olson of being the driver of a getaway car used in a robbery and murder. They arrested the suspected murderer and recovered the murder weapon. They then surrounded the home of two women with whom they believed Olson had been staying. Without obtaining authorization and with weapons drawn, they entered the home and found Olson hiding in a closet. They arrested him and he implicated himself in the crime. He was convicted. On appeal, Olson sought to exclude his statement on the grounds of lack of exigent circumstances or justification for the warrantless entry. The Court upheld the appeal on the grounds that Olson's status as an overnight guest in the home was sufficient to ensure an expectation of privacy which society would recognize as reasonable. The Court also observed that there were no exigent circumstances justifying the warrantless entry. Consequently, Olson's statement was inadmissible.

Legal Authorizations Analogous to an Arrest Warrant

American criminal procedure recognizes three main types of legal authorizations analogous to an arrest warrant. They are (1) a citation, (2) a bench warrant, and (3) a capias. Technically, a *citation* is a writ from a court ordering a person to appear in court within a specified time. In many states, statutory authority empowers the police to utilize this form of authorization for minor infractions of the law. The advantage of a citation is that the accused does not have to be taken into custody at the time of the violation. If the accused fails to comply with the citation, an arrest warrant will be issued.

A *bench warrant* is a writ emanating from the bench commanding the arrest of a defendant who has failed to appear in court even though he or she knows of the obligation to appear.

Technically, a *capias* is a writ directed to a law-enforcement officer for diverse reasons to apprehend a defendant and take him or her into custody. It is a command of a more generic nature than, for example, a bench warrant in that it can be utilized for noncriminal purposes—for instance, for the protection of a vulnerable witness. A capias can also be used when an accused person jumps bail and when a person is indicted by a grand jury.

Specificity of an Arrest Warrant

There are several essential elements of an arrest warrant that can render it valid or invalid. These elements include the following: 1) the affidavit for the warrant must be supported by probable cause; 2) the affidavit must be supported by oath or affirmation; 3) the affidavit must describe the accused and the nature of the offense; and 4) the warrant must be issued and signed by a neutral and detached magistrate (Klotter, 2002). Therefore, when completing an affidavit to procure a warrant, a police officer must ensure that the warrant is constitutionally correct or it could be challenged in court. A warrant must contain the name of a suspect if known. If the suspect's name is unknown, a description of the suspect must be provided so that the suspect can be identified with a reasonable degree of certainty. In such a case, the name "John Doe" is listed on the warrant followed by a physical description of the suspect—for example, "a 25-year-old white male who is approximately 5' 7'." Experts argue that listing "John Doe" on the warrant without providing a physical description is invalid because the warrant could authorize police to arrest anyone (Daniel, 1991). The warrant must also contain details about the crime that the suspect is alleged to have committed. Essentially, the facts and circumstances written by the police officer must be convincing enough to constitute a show of probable cause. The affidavit must be supported by the sworn testimony of a police officer and presented to and then signed by a neutral and detached magistrate (Klotter, 2002) authorizing the issue of an arrest warrant. If the magistrate is compensated for issuing an arrest warrant and is not compensated if he declines to issue a warrant, it would appear that the magistrate is not objective and is therefore not considered detached (Daniel, 1991).

Arrests without a Warrant

In American criminal justice, there is a strong judicial preference for the use of an arrest warrant as the major initiating accusatory instrument in the criminal justice process. Despite this strong judicial preference, judicial pragmatism and expediency, sometimes dictated by the functional constraints on the criminal investigatory process, have, over time, crystallized into judicial recognition of the legality of warrantless arrests by the police. While courts prefer law-enforcement officers to be armed with a warrant in hand, the U.S. Constitution does not require that a warrant be issued unless a suspect is arrested at his or her home (Israel, Kamisar, & LaFave, 1991). The courts have consistently ruled in this manner to protect the sanctity of the home. Nevertheless, warrantless arrests appear to be the rule rather than the exception. Statistics show that the majority of arrests effected by American law-enforcement agents are warrantless arrests. In fact, an estimated 95 percent of all arrests are made without a warrant. Over the years, however, the common law has tried to balance the rights of individual suspects to be free from unjustified arrests with the need for the community to protect itself. Therefore, the courts have created exceptions to the warrant requirement (Israel, et al. 1991), but such exceptions are meant to be used only if absolutely necessary (Klotter, 2002). For example, in *People v. Jimenez*, a New York court stated:

> Maximum protection of individual rights could be assured by requiring a magistrate's review of the factual justification prior to any arrest, but such a requirement would constitute an intolerable handicap for legitimate law enforcement. Thus, while the court has expressed a preference for the use of arrest warrants when feasible ... it has never invalidated an arrest supported by probable cause solely because the officer failed to secure a warrant.

In fact, del Carmen (1991) argues that though the law varies from state to state, police officers in every state have the power to make arrests without a warrant. State legislatures and courts have been sensitive both to the demands of police work and to the suspect's rights and the interests of the community. Thus, police are given more latitude when responding to felonies. Because felony suspects pose a greater threat to public safety, states have made distinctions regarding how law-enforcement officers can respond to felonies and misdemeanors when they lack a warrant. Under what circumstances, then, is it legally permissible for police officers to effect warrantless arrests? According to the law, there are four major types of arrests which do not require a warrant:

(1) arrests for felonies, (2) arrests for misdemeanors, (3) arrests for traffic violations, and (4) arrests for minor offenses not punishable with a jail term.

Concerning Felonies

Concerning the authority to effect a warrantless arrest for a felony, the law varies according to six circumstances: (1) when a felony is committed in the presence of the officer; (2) when the felony is committed in a public place; (3) when the felony takes place in a private residence; (4) when the felony does not take place in the officer's presence; (5) when exigent circumstances demand that a warrantless arrest be effected for the felony; (6) when the officer perceives danger to his or her safety.

When the felony is committed in the presence of the officer, his or her authority to effect a warrantless arrest is largely statutory at the present time. According to the law, the officer effecting the arrest must have actually perceived the criminal act through any of his five senses.

When the felony is committed in a public place, a police officer is legally not required to obtain an arrest warrant. The case *United States v. Watson* is the authority for this circumstance in both state and federal jurisdictions where the circumstance is regulated by statute.

When the felony takes place in a private residence, it is clearly impermissible, in the eyes of the law, for a police officer to effect a warrantless arrest in such a residence in the absence of consent. The case *Payton v. New York* illustrates the judicial aversion to such arrests. In *Payton*, after two days of intensive investigation, detectives gathered sufficient evidence to show probable cause that Payton had murdered the manager of a gas station. On the basis of such evidence, they proceeded to Payton's apartment to arrest him without a warrant. Under New York law, the police are statutorily empowered to effect a warrantless arrest. After knocking on the metal door and without receiving any response, the detectives called for emergency assistance and then used crowbars to open the door and made an entry into the apartment. They found no one there but immediately spotted in plain view a .30 caliber shell casing. They seized it and subsequently introduced it as evidence at Payton's murder trial. Payton was subsequently convicted. He appealed his conviction on the grounds that the Fourth Amendment required the police to obtain a warrant for effecting a felony arrest in a private residence. The U.S. Supreme Court upheld this view of the law, affirming the necessity for a warrant in cases of this type. The Court declared the New York law unconstitutional, as well as all states' laws of that nature.

When the felony is not committed in the officer's presence, the law still permits a police officer to effect a warrantless arrest when, for instance, a report is immediately made to him by someone who witnessed the commission of the felony.

When exigent circumstances justify a warrantless arrest by a police officer, two major situations illustrate what the law has succinctly characterized as "exigent circumstances." These are (1) the possibility of disappearance of the suspect and (2) what is technically known as the doctrine of "hot pursuit." The exigent circumstance of "hot pursuit" was determined by the U.S. Supreme Court in *Warden v. Hayden*. In *Hayden*, the Court upheld the warrantless entry and search as reasonable on the grounds that delay would have resulted in the suspect's escape. It was immaterial that the chase ended as soon as it began; the chase was still legally a "hot pursuit." Furthermore, it is a requirement of law that, in determining the permissibility of a warrantless arrest in the case of an escaping suspect, due regard must be made to (a) the gravity of the offense committed, (b) the belief that the suspect is armed, and (c) the probability of the suspect's escape.

When the arresting officer perceives danger to his or her safety, a warrantless arrest is clearly permissible. The Court stated quite pointedly in *Hayden*: "The Fourth Amendment does not require officers to delay in the course of an investigation if to do so would gravely endanger their lives or the lives of others."

In keeping with their common-law tradition, all states authorize police officers to make warrantless arrests of suspects when a felony has been committed and the arresting officer has probable cause or reason to believe that the person to be arrested committed the felony (Anderson & Newman, 1993; Peoples, 2003). While rare, it is possible that officers may encounter or observe felonies being committed. When either action occurs, an officer can effect a warrantless arrest since he or she has firsthand knowledge of the crime and the offender (Anderson & Newman, 1993). For example, while on routine patrol, officers observe two persons exchanging a drug for money. Upon making this observation, officers can arrest both the seller and the buyer of the illegal substance.

Another exception to an arrest warrant occurs when police are in "hot pursuit" of felons. Peoples (2003) refers to "hot pursuit" as "fresh pursuit." *Fresh pursuit* occurs when officers are pursuing a felon or a suspect fleeing capture and arrest (Dressler, 2002). Under this exigent circumstance, it is not practical for officers to stop pursuit, procure a warrant, and restart their pursuit (Dressler, 2002; Peoples, 2003). Peoples argues that during a fresh pursuit, an officer's efforts to apprehend a fleeing felon or suspect are viewed as continuous and uninterrupted and may cross into other jurisdictions without impairing or limiting the officer's power to arrest. Consider a fresh pursuit of suspects fleeing capture in Alabama and crossing over the state line into Mississippi. While one would expect Alabama officers in hot pursuit of the suspects to radio ahead for assistance from police in Mississippi, no one would reasonably expect Alabama police to abruptly end their chase when approaching the Mississippi state line.

Concerning Misdemeanors

All states' statutes generally allow a police officer to arrest a suspect for committing a misdemeanor. Most states stipulate that an officer can only arrest a suspect for a misdemeanor when the offense was either committed or attempted in the officer's presence. However, several states—including Arizona, Hawaii, Iowa, Louisiana, New York, and Wisconsin—allow a police officer to make a warrantless misdemeanor arrest when the officer never observed the commission of the misdemeanor (Klotter, 1996). In these states, the officer needs only to establish reasonable grounds to believe that a suspect committed the alleged offense. However, there are exceptions in arresting misdemeanor offenders when the alleged offense has not been witnessed by the arresting police officer. According to Klotter (1996), such exceptions include the following: (1) the offender will flee if not immediately arrested; (2) he or she will destroy or conceal evidence of the offense; (3) he or she may cause injury to self or others; and (4) he or she may damage property if not apprehended. del Carmen (1991) argues that because of the many exceptions in arresting misdemeanor offenders, the idea of first getting a warrant has become meaningless to many police officers.

Concerning Traffic Violations

Regarding traffic violations, a police officer is permitted to effect a warrantless arrest only in situations when there exists express authority to do so. The law or practice varies from jurisdiction to jurisdiction.

Concerning Minor Offenses Not Punishable with a Jail Term

The permissibility of warrantless arrests regarding minor offenses not punishable with a jail term has not yet been determined by the U.S. Supreme Court. The Court missed the opportunity to decide the issue in *Ricci v. Arlington*. In this case, the Court, after having granted certiorari, subsequently dismissed the matter on the grounds that the certiorari "had been improvidently granted." The issue, therefore, remains unsettled.

PART FOUR: LEGAL CONSEQUENCES OF FALSE ARRESTS AND FALSE IMPRISONMENT

According to the Maryland Code of Criminal Procedure (2005), a false arrest occurs when a person is unlawfully taken into custody by a police officer who has either actual or pretended legal authority for the actual or presumed purpose of having the arrestee answer criminal or civil questions. False imprisonment occurs when a person is unlawfully restrained or confined by a law-enforcement officer. In either course of action, an innocent person can invoke a tort action against the arresting officer and his or her agency because an arrest is considered a form of imprisonment (Scheb & Scheb, 1999). In Maryland, in order for the plaintiff (the victim) to prove that the police officer (the defendant) deprived him or her of freedom of movement without consent or probable cause, the plaintiff must show that the officer was operating without legal justification or outside of the scope of his or her authority. As a general rule, an arrest warrant prevents liability because of a false arrest. Oddly enough, if the warrant looks valid on the surface but is later determined as improper, the arresting officer may still avoid liability and the arrest can be considered legal since the mistake may have been attributed to a judicial official. When citizens are the victims of false arrest or false imprisonment by police officers, they can take several actions to seek redress. Civil actions can be taken on the state and federal levels. Civil actions under state law are considered the most common form of redress for punishing police misconduct. For example, when a police officer makes a false arrest or wrongly imprisons a victim, he or she can bring a civil tort action against the officer on the state level.

Civil Liability under State Tort Law

Torts are civil wrongs committed by one party injuring another or damaging the property of another (Anderson, Dyson, Burns, & Taylor, 1998). Concerning police officers, a tort occurs when an officer violates a duty imposed by law. States classify torts into three categories: intentional torts, negligence torts, and strict liability torts. Intentional torts occur when police officers knowingly cause physical or mental harm to another person. False arrest and false imprisonment come under this category. Negligence torts occur when officers engage in conduct that could possibly cause harm to others. This behavior includes an officer's failure to protect and to respond to calls, as well as his or her negligent use of a motor vehicle so that the officer injures innocent bystanders while in pursuit of fleeing motorist suspects. Since strict liability torts occur when manufacturers sell defective products that are unreasonably dangerous to buyers or cause injury, they do not apply to police officers.

Under a state tort claim, the victim typically sues for damages incurred as a result of police misconduct. According to Scheb & Scheb (1999), damages in false arrests and imprisonment claims may include an award for physical injuries, emotional suffering, loss of reputation, loss of earnings, and other recognized harm. Moreover, if it can be shown that officers engaged in gross negligence, malice, or excessive force while effecting a false arrest, the court may also impose punitive damages to send the message that such behavior will not be tolerated in the future by the offending police or law-enforcement agencies. Scheb and Scheb (1999) argue that there are several advantages to using state tort actions that include less of a burden of proof than that required in criminal cases. For example, the plaintiff has to establish only with a preponderance of the evidence that he or she was falsely arrested and imprisoned by the defendant. Also, the plaintiff initiates the action, not the state prosecutor. Furthermore, the victim receives direct compensation for sustained injuries. However, several disadvantages are associated with filing a state tort claim. Fyfe (1998) lists three major ones: (1) filing a claim is a time consuming process; (2) bringing a case to trial is expensive; and (3) the plaintiff may discover that the offending police or law-enforcement agency is protected by immunity. If a victim does not want to pursue legal redress on the state level, he or she may opt to litigate the case in federal court.

Civil Liability under Federal Law

Civil liability under federal law is based on deprivation of rights. Civil remedies for such liability are typically litigated in the form of a Section 1983 claim, which was designed to protect against police misconduct. According to Section 1983, which comes under Title 42 of the U.S. Code,

> any person acting under color of law cannot cause other individuals to suffer a deprivation of rights, privileges, or immunities secured by laws and the U.S. Constitution. Anyone responsible for such actions shall be liable to the injured party.

Since in federal court the discovery procedures are liberal and plaintiffs can recover attorney's fees and receive monetary awards, civil rights actions are the remedy most commonly litigated by plaintiffs. The actions of police officers are considered civil rights violations if they deny constitutionally or federally guaranteed rights to plaintiffs. The basic elements of Section 1983 lawsuits are that the defendant must have been acting under color of law (as a police officer, for example) and that a constitutionally or federally protected right was violated (Kappeler, 2006).

In cases of false arrest and false imprisonment, plaintiffs file a lawsuit alleging infringements on their Fourth and Fourteenth Amendment rights. The Fourth Amendment prohibits unreasonable searches and seizures of persons, houses, papers, and other areas without a valid warrant or probable cause. The Fourteenth Amendment protects against deprivation of life, liberty, or property without due process of law and ensures equal protection. Such lawsuits often affect the offending officer, the supervisor, police organizations, and the community. When civil rights violations (false arrest and false imprisonment) occur, lawsuits can be expensive and the aftermath can have a far-reaching impact on police-community relations (Anderson, Dyson & Burns, 1999). Especially among ethnic minorities, false arrest and false imprisonment betray public confidence in the commitment of police to dispense fair and evenhanded justice (Homes, 2000). To some residents, false arrest and false imprisonment may even indicate selective law enforcement or racial profiling. Moreover, police misconduct has a corrupting effect that taints the policing profession. However, Fyfe (1998) argues that lawsuits can serve as deterrents to police misconduct if the suits require overall changes in departmental and agency policy. Specifically, Fyfe contends that the offending officer alone should not be held liable for his or her behavior but that the officer's department should also be held liable for the misconduct. In reaching this conclusion, Fyfe cited the case *Monell v. Department of Social Services of the City of New York.*

In *Monell,* the U.S. Supreme Court allowed the victims of police misconduct to sue the police department and in their suits to name the municipality as liable for the actions of its employees. Essentially, in *Monell,* the Court ruled that civil rights violations committed by public employees might also impose liability on other government officials if it could be shown that the violations were due to poor training and supervision. Thus, *Monell* created a standard that required police administrators to establish better training and supervisory strategies to ensure that police respond to the public with care. Fyfe also argues that lawsuits which name municipalities have been instrumental and effective in helping to curb police misconduct. While it may have seemed that *Monell* had created a standard that would prevent police misconduct, Fyfe argued that the case also brought up several concerns about municipal liability. First, many police administrators think that liability is merely part of policing and that losing millions of dollars in lawsuits does not have an impact on police operations. Second, police officers are not always made aware of the outcome of lawsuits, so none of the policy implications of lawsuits are acted upon. As a result, while these lawsuits appear to have had a deterrent effect on police misconduct, they would perhaps work better with an administration that demonstrates a commitment to weeding out bad officers. In *Monell*, the Court also held that "a municipality cannot be held liable solely because it employees a tortfeaser." Under the ruling, liability could be imposed only if the municipality caused the injury. A major issue raised by the decision was what constituted a direct causal link between a municipal policy and the alleged misconduct of the police officer. Hence, the Court reexamined the issue of municipal liability in several cases (e.g., *City of Oklahoma v. Tuttle*, *City of Canton v. Harris*, and *Board of the County Commissioners of Bryan County v. Brown*) and finally created a new standard called "deliberate indifference." Under the new standard, in order to prove that a municipality was liable for the actions of its officers, the plaintiff had to establish that the municipality had no concern both for what its officers did on the street and for properly training its officers to undertake their duties in a constitutionally correct manner. Accordingly, liability attaches to a municipality when a plaintiff can show that a particular policy of the municipality was so inadequate that it caused the injury. Specifically, the plaintiff must show that the actions of the municipality were deliberately indifferent to the rights of the person with whom the officer had come into contact. This standard has consistently been reaffirmed by the U.S. Supreme Court.

A Private Citizen's Right to Make an Arrest

Each state allows its citizens the right to make an arrest when crimes are committed. For example, a Georgia law permits a private citizen to make an arrest without having to satisfy the requirements of the U.S. Constitution (O.C.G.A. section 17-4-60 (GCA §27-211). Although, the Constitution protects U.S. citizens from state and federal governmental abuses, it does not protect citizens from intrusions by private citizens. As a general rule, a private citizen may arrest an offender if the offense is committed in his or her presence or within his or her immediate knowledge (Daniel, 1991). Moreover, if the offense is a felony and the offender is escaping or attempting to escape, a private citizen may arrest the offender upon reasonable and probable grounds of suspicion (Daniel, 1991). Therefore, a private citizen, unlike a governmental official, is not burdened by the demands of preparing an affidavit, determining probable cause, or procuring a warrant to arrest someone he or she has witnessed committing a crime. However, with the freedom to make a citizen's arrest comes responsibility. A private citizen making an arrest must "without any unnecessary delay, take the person arrested before a magistrate ... or deliver such person and all effects removed from him or her to a peace officer of the state" (Daniel, 1991, p. 22). Private citizens should be aware that if they mistakenly arrest a person or injure a person in the process of effecting an arrest, they could face legal action against them in the form of a civil tort claim.

Inadmissibility of Evidence Obtained

The second major consequence of an illegal arrest in the American criminal justice system is that, under the exclusionary rule, evidence emanating from any search associated with such an arrest is rendered inadmissible in any criminal proceedings against the accused. However, the exclusion of such evidence does not mean that the accused is exempt from being tried for the crime because of the illegality of his or her arrest. In other words, the jurisdiction of a court to try a person for a crime is not diminished or abrogated by the manner in which he or she was brought into the custody. The case *Frisbie v. Collins* is the authority for this view of the law.

PART FIVE: INVALID ACTIONS OF POLICE DURING ARRESTS AND LEGITIMATE ACTIONS OF POLICE AFTER ARRESTS

Invalid Actions of Police during Arrests

This section of Part Five examines three actions of the police while effecting an arrest that can be legally characterized as invalid or lacking in legitimacy.

The Practice of "Media Ride-Along"

The first action concerns one aspect of the relationship between the police and the media in the sphere of crime investigation and is compendiously referred to as the practice of "media ride-along." In the case *Wilson et al. v. Layne*, the U.S. Supreme Court repudiated this law-enforcement practice. Federal marshals and local sheriff's deputies had invited a newspaper reporter and a photographer to accompany them while executing a warrant to arrest the son of the petitioner in their home. A protective sweep revealed that the son was not in the house. The reporters, who did not participate in executing the warrant, photographed the incident, but their newspaper never published the photographs. The petitioners sued the law-enforcement officers on the grounds that their Fourth Amendment rights had been infringed by the officers' action. The Court ruled in favor of the petitioners, but it did not award them any monetary damages. The Court took the view that, because of the "good faith" defense, the rights that had been infringed at the time of the media ride-along were not yet "clearly established."

Strip or Cavity Search

The second action relevant to this context concerns whether it is permissible for the police to conduct a strip or cavity search of the suspect, and if so, under what circumstances. According to the law, even though the police can legitimately conduct a full-body search of the suspect incidental to arrest, body-cavity searches are not permitted in felony arrests. According to a federal circuit court of appeals in *Kennedy v. Los Angeles Police Department*, any police-department policy authorizing such searches is unconstitutional. In *Kennedy*, the impugned policy mandated the Los Angeles police to conduct a body-cavity search in all felony arrests but restricted such a search in misdemeanor cases to narcotics arrests and to suspects suspected of concealing weapons. The department argued that the policy was necessary for "safety, security, and the proper administration of the jail system." The Ninth Circuit Court of Appeals ruled that such searches in felony and misdemeanor cases are unconstitutional and are permissible only if the police can justify them on the specific ground of "reasonable suspicion that the individual arrested may be likely to conceal a weapon, drugs, or other contraband prior to conducting a body cavity search." It is not difficult to fathom the rationale behind the proscription of such searches in the eyes of the law. It is the preservation of human dignity.

Warrantless Protective Search

The third action relevant to this context concerns whether the police can lawfully conduct what has been succinctly described as a "protective sweep" of other areas beyond those within the immediate control of the suspect following the execution of a warrantless arrest. Legally, protective sweeps incidental to a warrantless arrest are generally prohibited. However, as authoritatively declared by the U.S. Supreme Court in the case *Maryland v. Buie*, protective searches are valid when they are justified. In that case, police officers obtained and executed arrest warrants for Buie and an accomplice in connection with an armed robbery. When they arrived at Buie's house, they went through the first and second floors. One of the officers watched the basement so that no one would surprise the other officers. This officer shouted into the basement and ordered anyone there to come out. A voice asked who was there. The officer ordered the person three more times to come out. Finally, as the person—it was Buie—emerged from the basement, he was arrested. Another officer then went into the basement to see if anyone else was there. While there, he noticed in plain view a red running suit similar to the one that one of the suspects was wearing during the robbery. The running suit was seized and eventually introduced into evidence at Buie's trial despite his objection to its admissibility. Thereupon, he was convicted of robbery with the use of a deadly weapon. He appealed his conviction, challenging the legality of the protective search that had resulted in the discovery of the evidence.

The Court made short shrift of this challenge, holding that "the Fourth Amendment permits a properly limited protective sweep in conjunction with an in-home arrest when the searching officer possesses a reasonable belief based on specific and articulable facts that the area to be swept harbors an individual posing a danger to those on the arrest scene." In effect, according to the law, protective sweeps incidental to arrest are generally impermissible, but they are permissible if they can be justified on the basis of the "specific and articulable facts that the area to be swept harbors an individual posing a danger to those on the arrest scene." In sum, the Court articulated three key limitations on such police action. They are as follows: (1) specific and articulable facts are needed to justify an inference by a reasonably prudent officer that the area targeted for the search harbors a dangerous person; (2) such a search should not necessarily be a full search of the premises; and (3) the search must last no longer than necessary to dispel the perceived danger or to complete the arrest.

Legitimate Actions of Police after Arrests

This section of Part Five explores some of the legitimate law-enforcement options open to a police officer after he or she executes an arrest—one of the key phases of the American criminal justice process. After a police officer has effected an arrest, he or she can take six main legitimate actions—all of which have been approved by the courts. They are as follows: (1) searching the suspect, (2) searching the area within the immediate control of the suspect, (3) searching the passenger compartment of a motor vehicle, (4) handcuffing the suspect, (5) monitoring the movement of the suspect and (6) searching the suspect at the place of detention.

Searching the Suspect

Using this option, technically referred to as "a search incidental to a lawful arrest," the police are empowered to search a suspect irrespective of the nature of his or her offense. The case *United States v. Robinson* is the authority for this power. In *Robinson*, the U.S. Supreme Court stated: "[A] custodial arrest of a suspect based on probable cause is a reasonable intrusion under the Fourth Amendment; that intrusion being lawful, a search incident to the arrest requires no additional justification."

Searching the Area within the Immediate Control of the Suspect

The police are also authorized, incidental to a lawful arrest, to search the area within the immediate control of the suspect. Technically, and legally, that area is the one within which the suspect may reach for a weapon or destroy evidence. This principle was established by the case *Chimel v. California*. In *Chimel*, the U.S. Supreme Court defined the permissible area within the suspect's immediate control for the purposes of a search incidental to a lawful arrest as follows: "When an arrest is made, it is reasonable for the arresting officer to search the person arrested in order to remove any weapons that the latter might seek to use in order to resist or effect his escape…. In addition, it is entirely reasonable for the arresting officer to search for and seize any evidence on the arrestee's person in order to prevent concealment or destruction. And the area into which an arrestee might reach in order to grab a weapon or evidentiary items must, of course, be governed by a like rule."

The concept of the area within the suspect's immediate control has not been entirely free from difficulties of legal interpretation, despite the general acceptability of the concept's legal connotation mentioned above. Another legal connotation of the concept is that it encompasses the area limited to the suspect's wingspan. Hence, some courts have adopted a liberal interpretation concerning the area where the suspect might reach for a weapon. Two examples of such an interpretation are as follows: (1) the area underneath a suspect's bed where the suspect was sitting when arrested was held to be one within the suspect's immediate control and (2) an area of six feet between a kitchen shelf and the place of the suspect's arrest was held to be one within the suspect's immediate control, even though an officer stood between the suspect and the shelf (del Carmen, 1991).

However, an officer is permitted to conduct a warrantless search of areas in residences that are within a suspect's immediate control in two legally recognized situations: (1) when an emergency—such as the possible destruction of evidence—requires an immediate response and taking the time to procure a search warrant would frustrate police action and (2) when the search is geared toward a specific, predetermined object of criminality—for example, contraband located in a specific area.

Searching the Passenger Compartment of a Motor Vehicle

As a law-enforcement action incidental to an arrest, what is the nature and scope of the authority of a police officer to conduct a search of the passenger compartment of a motor vehicle? On the basis of case-law authorities, a police officer, having made a lawful custodial arrest of an occupant of a motor vehicle, is permitted to search the vehicle's entire passenger compartment, including the front and back seats. It is also within the officer's prerogative to open any containers found in the compartment. Significantly, the courts have given a broad, or liberal, interpretation to this power. For example, the case *New York v. Belton* is the authority for the position that this power involves, or extends to, searching "closed or open glove compartments, consoles, or other receptacles located anywhere within the passenger compartment, as well as luggage, boxes, bags, clothing, and the like." But there are major limitations on the exercise of this authority. A search of discovered containers must be based on a reasonable belief that their contents pose some danger to the officer's safety or constitute evidence of the crime for which the suspect was arrested. Also, a police officer is not permitted to search the trunk of a motor vehicle or a locked glove compartment.

Handcuffing the Suspect

In the context of American criminal law enforcement, the use of handcuffs incidental to an arrest has always been a matter of policy governed by departmental regulations. Handcuffing a suspect is essentially discretionary. Generally, using handcuffs is required or recommended in felony cases but not in misdemeanor cases, unless the arresting officer has perceived danger to his or her personal safety.

Monitoring the Movement of the Suspect

Generally, incidental to a lawful arrest, a police officer is permitted to accompany a suspect to his residence if the officer has allowed the suspect to go there before being transported to the police station. In the case *Washington v. Chrisman* the U.S. Supreme Court endorsed the legitimacy of such law-enforcement action, observing: "It is not unreasonable under the Fourth Amendment for a police officer, as a matter of routine, to monitor the movements of an arrested person, as his judgment dictates, following an arrest. The officer's need to ensure his own safety—as well as the integrity of the arrest—is compelling." The Court further held that the officer is permitted to remain with the suspect after the arrest.

Searching the Suspect at the Place of Detention

Searching the suspect at the place of detention is not a problematical matter. After the suspect has been taken to the place of detention, usually a jail or police-detention facility, a police officer is clearly permitted to subject the suspect to a complete search of his or her person, provided no such action was taken at the time of the arrest. Probable cause is not required to support such conduct. Furthermore, this police action is justified by the need for an inventory while the suspect is being booked in jail. As a Fourth Amendment requirement, such a search has three legitimate objectives: (1) to protect the suspect's property while he or she is in jail, (2) to protect the police from groundless claims that they have not adequately safeguarded the detention facility by preventing the introduction of weapons or contraband, and (3) to ascertain or clarify the identity of the person arrested (del Carmen, 1991; Israel, Lafave, & Kamisar, 1991).

The Disposition of Suspects after Arrest

Although discussed extensively in Chapter 2, four key aspects of the criminal justice process require a quick consideration in this section of Part Five. They are (1) what is technically known as the "booking" of the arrested person, (2) the initial appearance of the arrested person (now the accused or the defendant) before a magistrate, (3) the purposes of the initial appearance, and (4) the setting of bail. Booking, the initial appearance, and the setting of bail are the main aspects of the disposition of suspects after arrest.

Booking

As the name of the term implies, *booking* simply means making an entry in the police record or arrest book of the name of the suspect (now the defendant or the accused), the time of arrest, and the nature of his or her offense. If the offense is serious, the usual policy is to photograph the defendant and have him or her fingerprinted. The defendant is also kept in jail or a temporary detention facility until bail, as set by a magistrate, is posted. However, if the charge against the accused is a minor one, he or she may be released on what is technically called "station house bail," in which the accused posts cash and promises to appear in court for trial on a specified date. The process of booking also involves conducting an inventory of the defendant's personal property according to police-department procedures.

Initial Appearance before a Magistrate

As part of the procedural due process rights of every person accused of crime under the American criminal justice system, it is imperative that as soon as a person has been arrested for a crime, he or she should be afforded the opportunity of an initial appearance before a magistrate without unnecessary delay. The notion of "unnecessary delay" has from time to time been fraught with difficulties of legal interpretation because the phrase does not have a fixed meaning. The standard judicial approach to interpreting the phrase is based on the criterion of reasonableness. Guided by this criterion, courts determine, on a case-by-case basis, whether there has been unnecessary delay in bringing an accused person before a magistrate for his or her initial appearance. The case *Riverside v. McLaughlin* sheds some light on this issue. In *Riverside*, the suspect brought a lawsuit challenging the process of determining probable cause for warrantless arrests in Riverside County, California. The county's policy was to combine probable-cause determinations with arraignment proceedings. The policy was similar to the provisions of the California Penal Code, which required that arraignments be conducted without unnecessary delay and within two days (forty-eight hours) of arrest, excluding weekends and holidays. The district court granted an injunction requiring the county to provide a probable-cause hearing within thirty-six hours for all persons arrested without warrants.

The question which was not answered on appeal was whether the Fourth Amendment mandates a judicial determination of probable cause within thirty-six hours after the administrative steps incidental to the arrest have been completed, as the lower court had ordered. The U.S. Supreme Court answered the question in the negative, reasoning that if a probable-cause determination is combined with arraignment, it is presumptively reasonable for the time between the arrest and the hearing to extend up to forty-eight hours. The Court further observed that if more time than the forty-eight hours elapses, the onus is on the government to establish that the delay was reasonable. However, if the time between the arrest and the hearing is less than forty-eight hours, the burden shifts to the accused to establish the unreasonableness of the delay. A further illustration of the problematic aspect of the notion of "unnecessary delay" is the observation by the Court in *Powell v. Nevada* that "were

McLaughlin to be applied retroactively, untold numbers of prisoners would be set free because they were not brought before a magistrate within forty-eight hours."

The Purposes of an Initial Appearance before a Magistrate

The purpose of an initial appearance before a magistrate is essentially three-fold: (1) to warn the accused of his rights—a process which includes administering the Miranda warnings; (2) to determine either that probable cause exists to process the accused further through the criminal justice system or that the magistrate should set the accused free; (3) if probable cause exists, to have the accused processed in order to grant him or her bail if the offense is one for which the accused is entitled to bail. Concerning the Miranda warnings, many local jurisdictions require that the magistrates administer the warnings to the accused persons when they initially appear before them.

The Setting of Bail

If probable cause exists for a suspect to be processed through the criminal justice system, especially to be tried for the offense with which he or she is charged, the next crucial step is that the accused is either sent back to jail or afforded the opportunity of being granted bail. The Constitution does not entitle an accused person to receive bail since some crimes are nonbailable and communities have the right to protect themselves from predatory actions. Put differently, criminal suspects are not legally guaranteed they will receive bail after committing a crime. However, if the arrestee is granted bail, a bail bond may be posted for an amount determined by the magistrate, or the arrestee may be released on his or her own recognizance. If the offense is a grave one, the arrestee may be denied bail.

What, then, is bail—technically called "bail bond"? According to Black (1979), bail is

> a written undertaking, executed by the defendant or one or more sureties, that the defendant designated in such instrument will, while at liberty as a result of an order fixing bail, appear in the designated criminal action or proceeding when his attendance is required and otherwise render himself amenable to the orders and processes of the court, and that in the event he fails to do so, the signers of the bond will pay to the court the amount of money specified in the order fixing bail.

Briefly, there are two types of bail bond: (1) cash bail bond and (2) unsecured bail bond. The former is a "sum of money in the amount designated in an order fixing bail, posted by a defendant or by another person on his behalf with a court or other authorized public officer upon condition that such money will be forfeited if the defendant does not comply with the directions of a court requiring his attendance at the criminal action or proceeding involved and does not otherwise render himself amenable to the orders and processes of the court" (Black, 1979). The latter is "a bail bond for which the defendant is fully liable upon failure to appear in court when ordered to do so or upon breach of a material condition of release, but which is not secured by any deposit of or lien upon property" (Black, 1979).

As the name of the term implies, "release on one's own recognizance" means that an accused is granted "a pre-trial release based on the person's own promise that he will show up for trial" (Black, 1979); such a release does not require any bond. If the accused does not fulfill his or her promise, the usual option of the court is to issue a warrant for his or her arrest.

Part Six: Overview of Principles Governing the Law of Arrest

This part of the chapter provides a summary of the principles of the law concerning arrest in American criminal justice. First, an unlawful arrest or detention, without probable cause, has no significant impact on the subsequent prosecution of the offense in question. The remedy available to an aggrieved person for an illegal arrest is a civil lawsuit for damages. However, evidence sought to be introduced as incidental to a lawful arrest and other types of evidence emanating from an unlawful arrest will be inadmissible under the exclusionary rule. Second, an arrest has been correctly characterized as a restriction of an individual's liberty by the government. Any action by a police officer which indicates to the suspect that the latter is not free to leave if he or she wishes constitutes an arrest. A lawful arrest must be premised on probable cause. Third, the concept of probable cause in the context of an arrest is an objectively defined standard. The concept is established when there are reasonable grounds to believe that the suspect has committed an offense. A misapprehension of the facts allegedly underlying the determination of probable cause does not vitiate the arrest if the misapprehension was reasonable. Fourth, an arrest warrant is not required to effect an arrest in public when the arresting officer has probable cause to believe that a felony has been or is being committed by the suspect or when the officer witnesses the commission of a misdemeanor. However, the officer must have a warrant to make an arrest inside a private residence, unless there are exigent circumstances. Finally, the police are required to comply with the "knock and announce" requirement before making an entry to effect an arrest. However, the law dispenses with this requirement if the police have reasonable suspicion that compliance with it might result in the escape of the suspect, danger to some person, or the destruction of evidence.

PART SEVEN: SOME PERTINENT CASES

Frisbie v. Collins
342 U.S. 519 (1952)

Without the benefit of an attorney, Collins (the petitioner), acting on behalf of himself, filed a habeas corpus claim in federal court seeking release from a Michigan state prison where he had been sentenced for life after having allegedly committed a murder. According to Collins, while living in Chicago, he was accosted by Michigan police officers who forcibly handcuffed and blackjacked him and then abducted him back to Michigan. In this case, the petitioner alleged that both the trial and the conviction violated both his due process protection under the Fourteenth Amendment and the Federal Kidnapping Act. Hence, his conviction and detention were unconstitutional. In *Frisbie*, the U.S. Supreme Court stated: "[T]his Court has never departed from the rule announced in *Ker v. Illinois* that the power of a court to try a person for crime is not impaired by the fact that he had been brought within the court's jurisdiction by reason of a 'forcible abduction.' No persuasive reasons are now presented to justify overruling this line of cases. They rest on the sound basis that due process of law is satisfied when one present in court is convicted of crime after having been fairly apprized of the charges against him and after a fair trial in accordance with constitutional procedural safeguards. There is nothing in the U.S. Constitution that requires a court to permit a guilty person rightfully convicted to escape justice because he was brought to trial against his will."

United States v. Santana
427 U.S. 38 (1976)

On August 16, 1974, Michael Gilletti, an undercover officer with the Philadelphia narcotics squad, arranged a heroin "buy" with Patricia McCafferty. McCafferty told him the heroin would cost $115 and said, "We will go down to Mom Santana's for the dope." McCafferty took the money from Gilletti and went inside Santana's house, stopping briefly to speak to the respondent, Alejandro, who was sitting on the front steps. McCafferty came out shortly afterward and got into the car. Gilletti asked for the heroin, and she thereupon extracted from her bra several glossy envelopes containing a brownish-white powder and gave them to him. The officer then placed McCafferty under arrest. When Gilletti asked where the money was, McCafferty replied that Santana had it. While McCafferty was being taken to the police station, other officers drove to Santana's house where they saw Santana standing in the doorway with a brown paper bag in her hand. After they identified themselves as police officers, Santana attempted to escape into her house. The officers chased and caught her. During the ensuing scuffle, two bundles of heroin fell to the floor, which the police recovered. In *Santana*, the issue was whether a warrantless arrest that had begun in a public place and that had ended in a private place was legal. The U.S. Supreme Court ruled that a warrantless arrest that begins in a public place is valid even if the arrest ends in a private place. Moreover, the Court held that the Fourth Amendment did not provide Santana any protection since she was in a public place where people do not have an expectation of privacy. Police officers had probable cause to make an arrest even though Santana was retreating into her home. Essentially, the officers were acting in "hot pursuit" of Santana and the time and circumstances did not permit the officers to get a warrant.

United States v. Watson
423 U.S. 411 (1976)

On the word of an informant, federal postal inspectors arrested Watson in a restaurant for possession of stolen credit cards. Before the arrest, the informant had agreed to meet with Watson and give a signal to the inspectors if Watson had additional credit cards. When the signal was given, officers effected the arrest, removed Watson from the restaurant to a nearby street where he was given his Miranda warnings. Though the arrest was based on probable cause, it was made without a warrant. The arrest was based on the authority of a federal statute which permits law-enforcement officers to make arrests on the basis of probable cause if the officers believe that a suspect has committed a felony or that a felony is in progress. Watson was then searched and the officers found no credit cards. They asked if they could search his automobile, and he agreed. The search yielded an envelope with stolen credit cards. The issue in *Watson* was whether law-enforcement officers could arrest a suspect in a public place without a warrant but with probable cause when there was sufficient time for the officers to procure a warrant. In *Watson*, the U.S. Supreme Court upheld the constitutionality of the federal statute by holding that warrantless arrests for felonies are permitted at common law and that this rule exists in both the state and federal systems. Moreover, the Court cited the 1792 Congressional passage of a law which provides federal marshals with "the same powers in executing the laws of the United States, as sheriffs and their deputies in the several states have by law." Further, the Court held that since sheriffs at that time held the authority to arrest felons without a warrant, the Congressional law demonstrated that the framers of the Constitution saw no inconsistency between the Fourth Amendment and legislation authorizing warrantless felony arrests. According to *Watson*, a felony arrest can be made of a suspect in public if police lack a warrant. Moreover, public arrests can be made of suspects without a warrant even when no exigent circumstances exist that would prevent officers from acquiring a warrant.

Dunaway v. New York
442 U.S. 200 (1979)

After a detective in Rochester, New York, questioned a jail inmate about Dunaway's involvement in a robbery and a homicide, the inmate did not provide the officer with enough information to establish probable cause to procure a warrant. Nevertheless, the detective ordered law-enforcement officers to "pick up" Dunaway and "bring him" to the station for questioning about his involvement in the crimes. Dunaway was taken into police custody but was not informed that he was under arrest. Officers later admitted that if he had tried to resist his "arrest," he would have been physically restrained. At the police station, Dunaway was given his Miranda warnings. He waived his right to have his lawyer present during the interrogation and made incriminating statements. At his trial, the defense moved to suppress his statements. The court denied the motion and Dunaway was subsequently convicted. On appeal, the New York appellate court affirmed the conviction. However, the U.S. Supreme Court granted certiorari. In *Dunaway*, the issue was whether police could make an arrest and interrogate a suspect without first having established probable cause. The Court vacated the judgment, citing *Brown v. Illinois*. In *Brown*, the Court had held: "There is no per se rule that Miranda warnings in and of themselves suffice to cure a Fourth Amendment violation in obtaining inculpatory statements during custodial interrogations following a formal arrest on less than probable cause, and that in order to use such statements, the prosecution must show the statements meet the Fifth Amendment standard of voluntariness in order to break the casual connection between the statements and the illegal arrest. It must be shown that the petitioner's act of free will was sufficient to purge the taint of the unlawful invasion protected by the Fourth

Amendment." Essentially, the Court reversed the ruling of the appellate court because the police officers had lacked probable cause to arrest Dunaway. However, if the officers had had reasonable suspicion, they could have questioned Dunaway in any controlled environment. This procedure would have protected his Fifth and Sixth Amendment rights.

Payton v. New York
445 U.S. 573 (1980)

On January 14, 1970, New York detectives (after two days of intensive investigation) gathered enough evidence to establish probable cause to believe that Payton had murdered a gas station manager two days earlier. At approximately 7:30 a.m. on January 15, six police officers entered Payton's apartment in the Bronx with the intent to arrest him and take him into custody. Despite having probable cause, the officers did not get a warrant to effect Payton's arrest. After arriving at the apartment and hearing music and observing that a light emanated from the apartment, officers knocked on Payton's metal door. There was no answer. Officers called for emergency assistance, and thirty minutes later, they broke open the door with crowbars and entered Payton's apartment. They found that no one was there. However, they found a .30 caliber shell casing in plain view. Payton later turned himself in to police. He was indicted for murder and the evidence was used against him during trial. The defense filed a motion to suppress the evidence, but the trial court allowed the evidence, pursuant to a New York code of criminal procedure. The trial judge held that exigent circumstances justified the officer's omission to announce their purpose before entering the apartment, as required by the New York code. Moreover, the judge held that the officers did not have enough time to procure a search warrant. The New York Court of Appeals affirmed Payton's conviction. The case was appealed to the U.S. Supreme Court and it granted certiorari. In *Payton*, the issue was whether the Fourth Amendment guarantee against unreasonable searches and seizures requires police officers to obtain a warrant for a routine felony arrest when there is time to obtain a warrant. In this case, the Court held that when there are no exigent circumstances forcing police officers to take immediate action, officers must not enter a private home to make a routine warrantless felony arrest. Hence, the evidence should not have been admissible because police had time to obtain a warrant and there were no exigent circumstances justifying their warrantless search. The Court stated: "[I]t is a basic principle of Fourth Amendment law that searches and seizures inside a home without a warrant are presumptively unreasonable. Yet, it is also well settled that objects such as weapons or contraband found in a public place may be seized by police without a warrant. The seizure of property in plain view involves no invasion of privacy and is presumptively reasonable, assuming that there is probable cause to associate the property with criminal activity. The distinction between seizure on private premises was stated in *G. M. Leasing Corp v. United States*."

Michigan v. Summers
452 U.S. 692 (1981)

While executing a search warrant of Summers's house, police officers encountered Summers as he was about to exit it. The house had been under police surveillance because the police believed that it was a central contact point for drug use. As the officers entered the house with a valid search warrant, they also detained Summers. After searching the house for drugs, they found large quantities of narcotics. After the officers confirmed that Summers was the owner of the house, he was quickly arrested and searched. The search led to a discovery of heroin. He was subsequently convicted of possession of heroin. Summers appealed his conviction, contending that the heroin discovered on him should have been suppressed from evidence at trial since it was the product of an illegal search. The defense argued that though police entered the house armed with a warrant, they lacked probable cause to detain Summers initially. The trial judge agreed and granted the motion to suppress the evidence. Both the Michigan Court of Appeals and the Michigan Supreme Court affirmed the decision. The case was appealed and the U.S. Supreme Court granted certiorari. In *Summers*, the Court held that "the initial detention of the respondent, which constituted a seizure and was assumed to be unsupported by probable cause, did not violate his constitutional right to be secure against an unreasonable seizure of his person." The Court added that, according to the Fourth Amendment, a warrant to search a home for contraband carries with it the authority to detain the occupants of the premises while a proper search is conducted. Hence, it was lawful to ask the respondent to reenter the house and to remain there until evidence establishing probable cause to arrest him was discovered. Therefore, since Summers's arrest and the search were constitutionally permissible, the Court reversed the decision of the Michigan Supreme Court.

Michigan v. Chesternut
486 U.S. 567 (1988)

After observing a police car approaching, Chesternut began to run. The police gave chase to "see where he was going," and after catching up with him, officers observed him discard a number of packets. Since the officers were aware that the packets might contain drugs, they collected them and discovered that they contained cocaine. Chesternut was arrested and searched. The search revealed that he had other drugs and a hypodermic needle. He was charged with possession of a controlled substance, in violation of a Michigan law. At the preliminary hearing, a magistrate dismissed the charges, contending that Chesternut had been unlawfully seized during the police pursuit preceding his disposal of the packets. Later, a trial court upheld the dismissal and the Michigan Court of Appeals affirmed. In *Chesternut*, the latter court reasoned that under the Fourth Amendment, any "investigatory pursuit" amounts to a seizure as established in *Terry v. Ohio*, since the defendant's freedom was restricted when the officers began their pursuit. The court also reasoned that Chesternut's flight from the police was insufficient to give rise to the suspicion necessary to justify this kind of seizure. The U.S. Supreme Court granted review in this case. In *Chesternut*, the issue was whether the police officers' investigatory pursuit of Chesternut to "see where he was going" constituted a seizure within the meaning of the Fourth Amendment. The Court held that the officers' pursuit of Chesternut did not constitute a "seizure" that violated the Fourth Amendment protection. Hence, the lower court had erred by improperly dismissing the case. The Court held that there is no bright-line rule applicable to all investigatory pursuits. Rather, the appropriate test is whether a reasonable man viewing the police officers' behavior within the context of the circumstances would have concluded that, on the basis of the officers' action, he was not free to leave the situation. The Court further held that under this test, Chesternut had not been "seized" before he discarded the drug packets. Moreover, a "chase" by the police is insufficient to establish a Fourth Amendment violation since the officers' brief acceleration of their vehicle to catch a fleeing suspect and then driving alongside him would not communicate to a reasonable person that the officers were trying to capture him or intrude on his freedom of movement. The trial records did not reveal that the officers had used their sirens or flashers or that they had ordered the respondent to halt or that they had used their vehicle aggressively. Thus, the conduct of the officers did not have the required objective basis for suspecting Chesternut of criminal activity in order to pursue him.

Brower v. County of Inyo
489 U.S. 593 (1989)

Brower, the decedent, was killed when the car he had stolen crashed into a police roadblock at a high rate of speed as he was fleeing capture. The petitioners, the surviving family members, filed a Section 1983 claim in federal district court, contending that the respondents, in attempting to apprehend Brower under color of law, had violated Brower's Fourth Amendment rights by effecting an unreasonable seizure with excessive force. According to the complaint, the respondents had placed an eighteen-wheeler across the highway in the path of Brower's flight, around a curve, with a police cruiser's headlights aimed in such a manner as to blind Brower while he tried to elude capture. The complaint also charged that the fatal collision was a "proximate result" of police conduct. The district court dismissed the lawsuit for failure to state a claim, concluding that the roadblock was not unreasonable under the circumstances. The case was appealed and a federal court of appeals affirmed the ruling on the grounds that the police had not made a "seizure" of Brower. The case was later appealed to the U.S. Supreme Court. In *Brower*, the Court reversed and remanded the case back to the federal appeals court. In its holding, the Court stated: "[C]onsistent with the language, history and judicial construction of the Fourth Amendment, a seizure occurs when governmental termination of a person's movement is effected through means intentionally applied." In *Brower*, the Court disagreed with the findings of the lower courts and found that the roadblock did in fact constitute an unreasonable seizure within the meaning of the Fourth Amendment. In fact, the Court stated: "[P]etitioners can claim the right to recover for Brower's death because the unreasonableness alleged consists precisely of setting up the roadblock in such a manner as to be likely to kill him."

California v. Hodari
499 U.S. 621 (1991)

On April 23, 1988, Hodari and four or five other youths fled as they were approached by police in an unmarked car on a street in Oakland, California. As the youths fled, officer Pertoso, wearing a jacket with "police" embossed on its front, got out of his car and gave chase to the young men. Hodari, unlike the other youths, was not aware of officer Pertoso's exact location as he was chased. He ran west through an alley while the others fled south. Soon Pertoso and Hodari came face to face and Hodari tossed away a small rock. Officer Pertoso tackled him and retrieved the rock, which he immediately determined was crack cocaine. The officer arrested Hodari and used the crack cocaine as evidence. During Hodari's juvenile proceeding, the defense moved to suppress the evidence, but the trial court refused. Hodari was subsequently found guilty of possession of cocaine. He appealed the decision of the lower court. On appeal, the state court of appeals reversed the decision of the lower court, holding that Hodari had been "seized" within the meaning of the Fourth Amendment when he saw officer Pertoso running toward him but that the seizure was "unreasonable" because, as the state agreed, at the time officer Pertoso gave chase of the young men, he did not have the "reasonable suspicion" required to justify a stop. Therefore, the cocaine evidence should have been suppressed since it was the fruit of an illegal seizure. The case was appealed to the U.S. Supreme Court. In *Hodari*, the issue before the Court was whether at the time Hodari dropped the drugs he was "seized" within the meaning of the Fourth Amendment. The Court held that in order for a seizure to have occurred, physical force, however slight, must have been applied, or if such force had not been applied, a suspect's liberty should have been restrained by his or her submission to an officer's authority. In this case, no physical force was used since Hodari was untouched by officer Pertoso before he dropped the drugs. Further, if one is to assume that officer Pertoso's pursuit constituted a "show of authority" signaling Hodari to halt, Hodari instead opted to take flight. Therefore, he was not seized until he was tackled. Hence, he discarded the cocaine while he was running and not seized. Therefore, the cocaine was not fruit of the seizure. The Court thus reversed and remanded the decision of the California Court of Appeals.

Riverside County v. McLaughlin
500 U.S. 44 (1991)

McLaughlin was arrested without a warrant and detained for several days over a weekend in the Riverside County Jail in California. Pursuant to a Riverside County arrest and detention policy, the suspect must be arraigned without unnecessary or undue delay—specifically within forty-eight hours after persons are arrested, excluding weekends and holidays. This practice satisfies the Fourth Amendment. In this case, the issue was whether Riverside County's policy violated the U.S. Supreme Court's holding in *Gerstein v. Pugh*, which required prompt determinations of probable cause. The Court held that Riverside County's policy did not comply with the *Gerstein* ruling. However, the Court determined that a forty-eight-hour period is presumptively reasonable, provided that an arraignment immediately follows the determination of probable cause. If an arraignment does not immediately follow, the government bears the burden of showing why a period beyond forty-eight hours is a reasonable time for the detention of an accused person. If the period of detention lasts less than forty-eight hours, the burden shifts to the accused to show unreasonable delay. The Court also ruled that intervening weekends or complicated pretrial proceedings were not legitimate reasons for a delay.

Illinois v. McArthur
531 U.S. 326 (2001)

In 1997, Tera McArthur asked two police officers to accompany her to her trailer where she lived with her husband Charles McArthur. She wanted to peacefully remove her belongings since she had plans to leave Charles. While at the trailer, Tera informed the police officers that her husband had marijuana hidden under the couch. One of the officers asked Charles McArthur if he could search under the couch, but permission was denied. Charles told the officer that if he intended to search, he needed to get a warrant. Officers told Charles that he could not reenter his trailer unless he was accompanied by a police officer. Afterward, one of the officers stood outside the door to observe Charles when he went into the trailer. Two hours later, a search warrant was obtained. After a search, officers found drug paraphernalia and marijuana, and Charles McArthur was arrested. During trial, McArthur moved to have the evidence suppressed on the grounds that it was the "fruit" of an unlawful seizure—namely, the officers' refusal to allow him to reenter his trailer unaccompanied by an officer, an action which he admitted would have permitted him to destroy the marijuana. In this case, the trial court granted the motion to have the evidence suppressed; the Appeals Court of Illinois affirmed the trial court's decision; and the Illinois Supreme Court denied the state's petition for leave to appeal. The U.S. Supreme Court heard the case. In *McArthur*, the issue was whether officers with probable cause violated the Fourth Amendment by not allowing a man unaccompanied entrance into his home for two hours while they obtained a warrant, since they believed he would destroy drug evidence. The Court held that, given the nature of the intrusion and law-enforcement interests, the brief two-hour seizure of the premises was permissible under the Fourth Amendment. Moreover, the Court stated: "We have found no case in which this Court has held unlawful a temporary seizure that was supported by probable cause and was designed to prevent the loss of evidence while the police diligently obtained a warrant in a reasonable period of time."

Atwater v. City of Lago Vista
532 U.S. 318 (2001)

In 1997, Gail Atwater was driving her truck, which contained her two children. They were coming from soccer practice in Lago Vista. She was driving at a speed of fifteen miles per hour through a residential neighborhood. Gail and her two children were sitting in the front seat but were not wearing their seat beats. Officer Bart Turek observed Atwater as she drove past him, so he stopped her. During the stop, Turek screamed at Atwater that he had stopped her and given her a warning several months before because he had suspected that her son was not wearing a seat belt. Officer Turek was mistaken. Ultimately, Atwater was arrested and taken into custody for violating the city's seat-belt law. She was placed in jail and she posted bond. Officer Turek had arrested Atwater pursuant to a Texas Transportation Code, which makes failure to wear a seat belt a misdemeanor, with a maximum punishment of $50. Under Texas law, officer Turek had the discretion either to issue a citation for the offense or to effect an arrest. Witnesses at the scene reported that officer Turek had gone on a tirade while taking Atwater into custody: he handcuffed her behind her back and refused her request that she be allowed to take her six-year-old daughter and four-year-old son to a neighbor's house near the police stop. At the police station, Atwater was required to empty her pockets, remove her shoes and glasses, and have her picture taken. She was placed in a jail cell for an hour before she was taken to a magistrate, who released her after she posted bond. Atwater filed suit, alleging that Turek's actions violated her Fourth Amendment right to be free from unreasonable seizures. She also alleged that the incident caused her and her children extreme emotional distress that required medication and counseling. Atwater's suit was a Section 1983 claim against the Lago Vista Police Department. In granting the city summary judgment, the district court ruled that the claim was meritless. In affirming, the en banc court of appeals held that the arrest was not unreasonable under the Fourth Amendment since no one disputed that Turek had established probable cause to make the arrest and there was no evidence showing that the arrest had been conducted in a manner harmful to Atwater's privacy. The case was reviewed by the U.S. Supreme Court. In *Atwater*, the issue was whether the Fourth Amendment, either by incorporating common-law restrictions on misdemeanor arrests or otherwise, limits a police officer's authority to arrest an individual without a warrant for minor criminal offenses. The Court held that the Fourth Amendment does not prohibit a warrantless arrest for a minor criminal offense such as, in this case, a misdemeanor seat-belt violation punishable only by a fine. The Court ruled: "If an officer has probable cause to believe that an individual has committed even a very minor criminal offense, in his presence, he may, without violating the Fourth Amendment, arrest the offender."

REFERENCES

Anderson, P. R., & Newman, D. J. (1993). *Introduction to criminal justice* (5th ed.). New York: McGraw-Hill.

Anderson, J. F., Dyson, L., & Burns, J. (1999). Preventing excessive force litigation. *The Justice Professional, 12* (1), 83–94.

Anderson, J. F., Dyson, L., Burns, J., & Taylor, K. (1998). Preemployment screening and training could reduce excessive force litigation. *Journal of Police and Criminal Psychology, 13* (1), 12–24.

Black, H. C. (1979). *Black's law dictionary: With pronunciations.* St. Paul: MN: West.

Bohm, R., & Haley, K. N. (1999). *Introduction to criminal justice* (2nd ed.). New York: Glencoe/McGraw-Hill.

Champion, D. J. (1997). *The Roxbury dictionary of criminal justice: Key terms and major court cases.* Los Angeles: Roxbury.

Daniel, W. W. (1991). *Georgia criminal trial practice.* Norcross, GA: Harrison.

del Carmen, R. V. (1991). *Civil liabilities in American policing: A text for law enforcement personnel.* Englewood Cliffs, NJ: Brady.

del Carmen, R. V. (2004). *Criminal procedure: Law and practice* (6th ed.). Belmont, CA: Wadsworth.

del Carmen, R. V., & Walker, J. T. (2004). *Briefs of leading cases in law enforcement* (5th ed.). Cincinnati: Anderson.

Dressler, L. (2002). *Understanding criminal procedure* (3rd ed.). New York: LexisNexis.

Fagin, J. A. (2003). *Criminal justice.* New York: Allan & Bacon.

Fyfe, J. (1998). Good judgment: Defending police against civil suits. *Police Quarterly, 1* (1), 91–117.

Gaines, L. K., & Miller, R. L. (2004). *Criminal justice in action.* Belmont, CA: Wadsworth/Thomson Learning.

Gaines, L. K., Kaune, M., & Miller, R. L. (2000). *Criminal justice in action: The core* (2nd ed.). Belmont, CA: Wadsworth/Thomson Learning.

Homes, M. (2000). Minority threat and police brutality: Determinants of civil rights criminal complaints in municipalities. *Criminology, 38,* 343–68.

Inciardi, J. A. (1987). *Criminal justice* (2nd ed.). New York: Harcourt Brace Jovanovich.

Inciardi, J. A. (1999). *Criminal justice* (6th ed.). New York: Harcourt Brace Jovanovich.

Israel, J. H., Kamisar, Y., & LaFave. W. R. (1991). *Criminal procedure and the Constitution: Leading Supreme Court cases and introductory text.* St. Paul, MN: West.

Kappeler, V. (2006). *Police civil liability: Supreme Court cases and materials* (2nd ed.). Cincinnati: Waveland.

Klotter, J. C. (1996). *Legal guide for police: Constitutional issues* (4th ed.). Cincinnati: Anderson.

Klotter, J. C. (2002). *Legal guide for police: Constitutional issues* (6th ed.). Cincinnati: Anderson.

Light, S. C. (1999). *Understanding criminal justice.* Belmont, CA: West/Wadsworth.

Moskovitz, M. (2000). *Cases and problems in criminal procedures: The police* (3rd ed.). New York: Lexis.

Neubauer, D. W. (1999). *America's courts and the criminal justice system* (6th ed.). Belmont, CA: West/Wadsworth.

O.C.G.A. section 17-4-60 (GCA §27-211)

Peoples, E. E. (2003). *Basic criminal procedures* (2nd ed.). Upper Saddle River, NJ: Prentice Hall.

Scheb, J. M., & Scheb, J. M. (1999). *Criminal law & procedure* (3rd ed.). Belmont, CA: West/Wadsworth.

Senna, J. J., & Siegel, L. J. (2000). *Essentials of criminal justice* (3rd ed.). Belmont, CA: Wadsworth/Thomson Learning.

Rush, G. E. (2000). *The dictionary of criminal justice with summaries of Supreme Court cases affecting criminal justice* (5th ed.). New York: Dushkin/McGraw-Hill.

Rush, G. E. (2003). *The dictionary of criminal justice with summaries of Supreme Court cases affecting criminal justice* (6th ed.). New York: Dushkin/McGraw-Hill.

West (2005). *West's annotated Code of Maryland.* Thomson/West.

Worrall, J. L. (2004). *Criminal procedure: From first contact to appeal.* New York: Pearson/Allyn & Bacon.

Cases Cited

Aguilar v. Texas, 378 U.S. 108 (1964)

Atwater v. City of Lago Vista, 532 U.S. 318 (2001)

Berkemer v. McCarty, 468 U.S. 420 (1984)

Berry v. Bass, 157 La. 81 (1924)

Berry v. State, Ga. App. 205 (1982)

Board of the County Commissioners of Bryan County v.

Brown, 520 U.S. 397 (1997)

Brower v. County of Inyo, 489 U.S. 593 (1989)

Brown v. Illinois, 422 U.S. 590 (1975)

Brown v. State, 151 Ga. App. 830 (1979)

California v. Hodari, 499 U.S. 621 (1991)

Chimel v. California, 395 U.S. 752 (1969)

City of Canton v. Harris, 489 U.S. 378 (1989)

City of Oklahoma, v. Tuttle, 471 U.S. 808 (1985)

Draper v. United States, 358 U.S. 307 (1959)

Dunaway v. New York, 442 U.S. 200 (1979)

Frisbie v. Collins, 342 U.S. 519 (1952)

G. M. Leasing Corp. v. United States, 429 U.S. 338 (1977)

Gerstein v. Pugh, 420 U.S. 103 (1975)

Illinois v. Gates, 462 U.S. 213 (1983)

Illinois v. McArthur, 531 U.S. 326 (2001)

Kennedy v. Los Angeles Police Department, 667 F. Supp. 697 (Cd. Cal. 1987)

Ker v. Illinois, 119 U.S. 436 (1886)

Maryland v. Buie, 494 U.S. 325 (1990)

McCray v. Illinois, 386 U.S. 300 (1967)

Michigan v. Chesternut, 486 U.S. 567 (1988)

Michigan v. Summers, 452 U.S. 692 (1981)

Minnesota v. Olson, 495 U.S. 91 (1990)

Monell v. Department of Social Services of the City of New York, 436 U.S. 658 (1978)

New York v. Belton, 453 U.S. 454 (1981)

Payton v. New York, 445 U.S. 573 (1980)

People v. Jimenez, 619 N.Y. S2d 519 (1994)

Powell v. Nevada, 511 U.S. 79 (1994)

Ricci v. Arlington, 523 U.S. 613 (1998)

Riverside County v. McLaughlin, 500 U.S. 44 (1991)

Spinelli v. U.S., 393 U.S. 410 (1969)

Steagald v. United States, 451 U.S. 204 (1981)

Terry v. Ohio, 392 U.S. 1 (1968)

United States v. Ortiz, 422 U.S. 891 (1975)

United States v. Robinson, 414 U.S. 218 (1973)

United States v. Santana, 427 U.S. 38 (1976)

United States v. Watson, 423 U.S. 411 (1976)

Warden v. Hayden, 387 U.S. 294 (1967)

Washington v. Chrisman, 455 U.S. 1 (1982)

Wilson v. Arkansas, 514 U.S. 927 (1995)

Wilson et al. v. Layne, 526 U.S. 603 (1999)

CHAPTER 8

FIELD AND CUSTODIAL INTERROGATIONS

FOCAL POINTS

- The Legal Basis of Custodial Interrogations
- The Fifth Amendment
- Self-Incrimination
    Self-Incriminating Statements
- The Sixth Amendment
    The Right to an Attorney
    From the Investigatory to the Accusatory
    Miranda Rights
- Waiver of Miranda Rights
- Leading Cases in Field and Custodial Interrogations
- The Protection against Self-Incrimination
- Conditions When the Miranda Warnings Are Not Required
- The Erosion of *Miranda v. Arizona*
- Some Pertinent Cases

INTRODUCTION

When suspects are arrested and taken into custody, a critical part of a police investigation is interrogating suspects about their possible involvement in or knowledge about a crime (Samaha, 1994). In *Rhode Island v. Innis*, the U.S. Supreme Court defined an interrogation as "express questioning or its functional equivalent," including "any words or actions on the part of the police that the police should know are reasonably likely to elicit an incriminating response from the suspect." In fact, the strength of the state's case against a suspect depends on the evidence collected by police officers. While building a case, officers typically collect both physical and testimonial evidence. Some legal experts even suggest that there is nothing more compelling to a judge (in a bench trial) or a jury than a signed confession made by a suspect (Gaines & Miller, 2004). Therefore, officers often try to persuade suspects to admit or confess their guilt or involvement in the commission of crime.

While officers are receptive to an admission of guilt, they prefer to have a confession since the two are different. *An admission of guilt* is an acknowledgment of a fact or facts tending to prove guilt, which falls short of an acknowledgment of all the essential elements of the crime. A *confession* is a voluntary statement made by a person charged with a crime, communicated to another person, wherein he or she acknowledges guilt of the offense charged and discloses the circumstances of the act (Black, 1979).

Because a confession is more incriminating for a suspect, serious questions have emerged regarding what practices police officers can legally use to persuade suspects into admitting or confessing their involvement in or guilt of a crime. For example, some legal scholars ask: Can police officers use trickery and deceit to gain a criminal confession? Can officers use physical abuse or inherently coercive tactics to elicit a confession? Can officers engage in psychological manipulation? Can police plant an undercover informant in a jail or holding cell to solicit a confession from a suspect? Can officers deny suspects an attorney prior to interrogating them even after suspects have expressed an interest in their right to having a lawyer present during the interrogation?

As a general rule, in order for custodial interrogations (conducted at the crime scene, station house, or another place) to be valid, they must be conducted in a constitutionally correct manner. The U.S. Supreme Court has stated that after police affect an arrest and take the suspect into custody, before he or she can be questioned about his or her involvement in a crime, police officers must warn the suspect of his or her rights under the Fifth Amendment protection against self-incrimination and the Sixth Amendment right to have legal representation present during the custodial interrogation. Put differently, admissions and confessions must be given voluntarily, knowingly, and intelligently (Weston & Wells, 1976)—that is, the suspect must understand the consequences of giving a confession. Robin (1987) argues that the traditional standard used by American courts for determining the admissibility of a confession is whether it was given voluntarily. Moreover, in *Hopt v. Utah*, the U.S. Supreme Court ruled that for a confession to be admissible as evidence in federal cases, it had to be given voluntarily. Though the Court created this standard for federal courts, it did not apply to courts on the state level (see also Inciardi, 1999).

Confessions cannot be the product of involuntary actions induced by promise, fear, hope, violence, torture, or threat (see Black, 1979). Peoples (2003) contends that a confession may not be coerced or given after a threat or a promise of leniency has been made by police and not until the suspect knows and understands his or her Fifth Amendment protection against self-incrimination and the Sixth Amendment right to have an attorney appointed and present during any questioning. If a suspect chooses to waive his or her Fifth and Sixth Amendment rights, police can use any confession or admission given to them to make a case against the suspect. Moreover, because a suspect may have answered some questions, such action does not prevent him or her of the right to refrain from participating in an interrogation until he or she has consulted an attorney (Weston & Wells, 1976). Subsequently, if officers engaged in improper questioning, any incriminating statements made by the suspect may be excluded from trial (Klotter, 2002).

Chapter 8 is divided into several sections. Part One explains the legal basis of custodial interrogations. Part Two presents leading cases on field and custodial interrogations. Part Three discusses the protection against self-incrimination. Part Four explains the erosion of *Miranda v. Arizona*. Part Five provides some pertinent cases concerning field and custodial interrogations that focus on the admissibility of evidence.

PART ONE: THE LEGAL BASIS OF CUSTODIAL INTERROGATIONS

The legal basis for the protection of citizens regarding custodial interrogations can be found in the Fifth and Sixth Amendments to the U.S. Constitution, along with the landmark cases *Escobedo v. Illinois* and *Miranda v. Arizona*.

The Fifth Amendment

The Fifth Amendment states:

> No person shall be held to answer for a capital, or otherwise infamous crime, unless on a presentment of a Grand Jury, except in cases arising in the land or naval forces, or in the Militia, when in actual service in time of War or public danger; nor shall any person be subject for the same offense to be twice put in jeopardy of life or limb; nor shall be compelled to in any criminal case to be a witness against himself, nor be deprived of life, liberty, or property, without due process

of law; nor shall private property be taken for public use without just compensation.

Self-Incrimination

Self-Incriminating Statements

Besides providing criminal suspects with several forms of protection concerning custodial interrogations, the Fifth Amendment also guarantees them protection against self-incrimination (Gaines & Miller, 2004). Therefore, a suspect's decision to remain silent when, during a police investigation, questions are asked of his or her involvement in or knowledge of a crime cannot be assumed to mean that the suspect is guilty or suppressing evidence, since the Constitution provides that a suspect is not legally obligated to assist the state in making its case against him or her.

The Sixth Amendment

The Sixth Amendment right to an attorney is another legal basis of custodial interrogations. The Sixth Amendment states:

> In all criminal prosecutions, the accused shall enjoy the right to a speedy and public trial, by an impartial jury of the State and district wherein the crime shall have been committed, which district shall have been previously ascertained by law, and to be informed of the nature and cause of the accusation; to be confronted with the witnesses against him; to have compulsory process for obtaining witnesses in his favor, and to have the assistance of counsel for his defense.

The Right to an Attorney

While most American citizens believe that the Fifth and Sixth Amendments go hand in hand, in reality, this has not always been the practice. For example, prior to the 1960s, the Fifth Amendment privilege against self-incrimination and the Sixth Amendment right to counsel were not effectively linked (Inciardi, 1987). In *Brown v. Mississippi*, the U.S. Supreme Court ruled that Brown's confession was inadmissible since the police had forcibly extracted it from him by the use of a whip (see also, Moskovitz, 2000). In *Brown*, the Court stated that "the state may not deny to the accused the aid of counsel." However, in *Crooker v. California*, it appeared that the U.S. Supreme Court had retreated from its decision in *Brown*, for in *Crooker*, the Court held that confessions can be both voluntary and admissible even if obtained from a suspect who was denied the opportunity to consult with legal counsel during interrogation by the police. Legal experts argue that in *Brown* and in *Crooker*, the Court was taking a stand against coerced confessions but was also limiting a suspect's right to counsel. However, in *Massiah v. United States*, *Crooker* was overturned and the Fifth and Sixth Amendments were more closely linked. In *Massiah*, the Court ruled that an indicted person could not be properly interrogated or persuaded to make incriminating statements in the absence of his or her counsel. During this same period of time, the U.S. Supreme Court addressed *Malloy v. Hogan*. In *Malloy*, the Court extended the protection against self-incrimination to state defendants. Legal experts argue that the cases *Massiah* and *Malloy* laid the foundation for one of the landmark cases on custodial interrogation—*Escobedo v. Illinois*.

From the Investigatory to the Accusatory

In *Escobedo*, the U.S. Supreme Court ruled that when police investigations shift from the investigatory to the accusatory, the accused must be permitted to have an attorney present during the police investigation (Inciardi, 1987). Especially when the investigation focuses on the accused and its purpose is to elicit a confession, the accused must be permitted to consult with his or her lawyer. *Escobedo* was heralded as a victory for suspects since the Court had ruled in the defendant's favor on five pivotal conditions concerning the interrogation: (1) if the investigation is no longer a general inquiry into an unsolved crime but has begun to focus on a potential suspect; (2) if the suspect has been taken into police custody; (3) if the police carry out an interrogation that elicits incriminating statements; (4) if the suspect has requested and been denied an opportunity to consult with his lawyer; and (5) if the police have not effectively warned the suspect of his absolute constitutional right to remain silent, more questions are raised for police officers who routinely arrest and interrogate suspects.

After *Escobedo*, police were perplexed over the proper procedures to use during interrogations following an arrest. For example, would police now be required to warn suspects of their right to remain silent? If the suspect requested an attorney, but one was not immediately available, could a police officer legally continue questioning the suspect about his or her involvement in a crime? What were police officers to do if the suspect refused the assistance of a lawyer? How were police to determine at what point during the investigation to focus on a suspect? Did the ruling in *Escobedo* suggest that all of these conditions had to be met before a confession could be admissible (Inciardi, 1987)?

Miranda Rights

Despite the confusion and questions that were raised by *Escobedo*, the U.S. Supreme Court settled them in its ruling in the case *Miranda v. Arizona*.

Miranda v. Arizona
384 U.S. 436 (1966)

Ernesto Miranda, a twenty-three-year-old Mexican with less than a ninth-grade education, was arrested at his home in Phoenix on March 13, 1963, and taken to a local police station for questioning. He was suspected of having kidnapped and raped an eighteen-year-old woman. At the Phoenix police station, Miranda was placed in a lineup and identified by the victim. Then he was interrogated. After officers questioned him, they emerged with a written confession signed by Miranda. At trial, the confession was admitted over Miranda's objections, and he was subsequently convicted of kidnapping and rape. He received a sentence of twenty to thirty years on each count. He appealed the decision. The Arizona Supreme Court affirmed his conviction. The case was then appealed to the U.S. Supreme Court. The Court reversed the lower court's ruling not only on the basis of its view of the relationship between custodial interrogation and genuinely voluntary confessions but also on the basis of the constitutional rights of suspects as promulgated by the Fourth, Fifth, Sixth, and Fourteenth Amendments. The Court held that Miranda's custodial interrogation was inherently coercive and that the procedure of advising suspects of their rights, if such a procedure was followed at all, was rarely sufficiently clear. In a 5 to 4 decision, Chief Justice Earl Warren stated the following:

> Our holding will be spelled out with some specificity in the pages which follow but briefly stated it is this: the prosecution may not use statements, whether exculpatory or inculpatory, stemming from custodial interrogation of the defendant unless it demonstrates the use of procedural safeguards effective to secure the privilege against self-incrimination. By custodial interrogation, we mean questioning initiated by law enforcement officers after a person has been taken into custody or otherwise deprived of his freedom of action in any significant way. As for the procedural safeguards to be employed, unless other fully effective means are devised to inform accused persons of their rights of silence and to assure a continuous opportunity to exercise it, the following measures are required. Prior to any questioning, the person must be warned that he has a right to remain silent,

that any statement he does make may be used as evidence against him, and that he has a right to the presence of an attorney, either retained or appointed. The defendant may waive the effectuation of these rights, provided the waiver is made voluntarily, knowingly, and intelligently. If, however, he indicates that he wishes to consult with an attorney before speaking there can be no questioning. Likewise, if the individual is alone and indicates in any manner that he does not wish to be interrogated, the police may not question him. The mere fact that he may have answered some questions or volunteered some statements on his own does not deprive him of the right to refrain from answering any further inquiries until he has consulted with an attorney and thereafter consents to be questioned.

In deciding *Miranda*, the Warren court explained that when a suspect is held in custody by law-enforcement officers,

the atmosphere and environment of incommunicado interrogation as it exists today is inherently incriminating and works to undermine the privilege against self-incrimination. Unless adequate preventive measures are taken to dispel the compulsion inherent in custodial surroundings, no statements obtained from the defendant can truly be the product of his free choice.

Contrary to popular belief, suspects are not legally required to be given the Miranda warnings upon arrest. The misunderstanding that most citizens share is largely due to the entertainment value of television. A strict interpretation of the case reveals that the Miranda warnings are required only under two conditions: (1) when a suspect is taken into custody and deprived of freedom in a significant way and (2) when a suspect is subjected to questioning by police about his or her involvement in a crime. These two conditions are essential for custodial interrogations. Furthermore, the suspect must be aware that he or she is in custody—either as demonstrated by restrictions placed on his or her freedom of movement or as articulated by the arresting officer (Schmalleger, 2001). If the suspect is not in custody, he or she has the freedom to leave. As a general rule, if the suspect is not in custody, the Miranda warnings are not legally required. But if the suspect is in custody and police wish to interrogate him or her, he or she must first be Mirandized. Each Miranda warning, together with (in parentheses) the constitutional right upon which it is based, includes the following: You have a right to remain silent. Do you understand? (Fifth Amendment right). Anything you say may be used against you in court. Do you understand? (Fifth Amendment right). You have the right to the presence of an attorney before and during any questioning. Do you understand? (Sixth Amendment right). If you cannot afford an attorney, before any questioning, one will be appointed for you free of charge, if you wish. Do you understand? (Sixth Amendment right) (Peoples, 2003).

Some legal experts argue that the statements suspects give to police must be a product of free will and that before officers take those statements, they must advise suspects of their constitutional rights. Essentially, the Miranda warnings are a procedural safeguard that provides an opportunity for police officers to police themselves (Peoples, 2003). In fact, the Warren court suggested that the Miranda warnings should be viewed as an acceptable "preventive measure" with a twofold purpose: (1) to safeguard individual rights from overzealous police officers and (2) to ensure that officers obtain confessions and win convictions in a constitutionally correct manner. In several cases, however, the U.S. Supreme Court has held that the specific wording of the Miranda warnings is not required (the warnings can be given in a general manner) and that the Miranda warnings (though grounded in the Fifth and Sixth Amendments) are not, in themselves, a constitutional right (see *Michigan v. Tucker*; *Edwards v. Arizona*; *New York v. Quarles*; *Duckworth v. Eagan*; *Davis v. United States*; and *Moran v. Burbine*). However, recently, in *Dickerson v. United States*, the U.S. Supreme Court held that the Miranda warnings, in and of themselves, are a constitutional requirement that involves possible civil rights violations if officers continue to interrogate suspects after the latter have invoked their right to counsel and their right to remain silent. In *Dickerson*, the officers had told the suspects that nothing they said during the interrogation would be used against them in court (see also *California Attorneys for Criminal Justice, et al. v. Butts, et al.*). Hence, officers can be legally liable for failing to adhere to a strict application of the Miranda warnings (Peoples, 2003). The Court is primarily concerned that police meet the requirement of providing a suspect with sufficient procedural safeguards to confirm a suspect's knowledge of his or her rights and protection against self-incrimination (Peoples, 2003). The Miranda warnings satisfy this requirement.

Waiver of Miranda Rights

While suspects have the right to voluntarily waive their Miranda rights, they must do so with an understanding of the waiver's consequences. Courts have scrutinized the manner in which waivers are ascertained by police (Scheb & Scheb, 1999). Courts have even stated that if police provide the suspect with his or her Miranda warnings and the suspect agrees to talk without a lawyer present, a confession given as a consequence of coercion, whether physical or psychological, is inadmissible (*United States v. Tingle*). Courts are aware of the possibility of violations of constitutional rights. In fact, some courts are primarily concerned that a waiver of Miranda rights should not be the product of deception or of physical or psychological coercion but that a waiver of Miranda rights or of the right to remain silent should be based on the "totality of circumstances." For example, in *United States v. Carra*, the U.S. Supreme Court ruled that "a voluntary waiver of the right to remain silent is not mechanically to be determined, but is to be determined from the totality of circumstances as a matter of fact." Similarly, in *United States v. Blocker*, a federal district court ruled that a written waiver signed by the accused is not in itself conclusive evidence. In *Blocker*, the U.S. Supreme Court stated: "[T]he court must still decide whether, in view of all the circumstances, the defendant's subsequent decision to speak was a product of his free will."

Under *Miranda*, if a suspect refuses to cooperate in a police investigation, police must accept the refusal. However, police are not legally bound to inform a suspect who is undecided about cooperating that arrangements have been made to provide counsel (Scheb & Scheb, 1999). For example, in *Moran v. Burbine*, police officers arrested a man wanted in connection with a burglary and subsequently linked him to a murder. The suspect's sister, unaware that a murder charge was about to be filed against her brother, arranged for a lawyer to represent him on the burglary charge. The attorney contacted the police to arrange a meeting with her client. At this time, police did not inform the lawyer about the possible murder charge and told the attorney that her client would not be interrogated until the next day. Despite their promise, police questioned Burbine that day but failed to mention to him that a lawyer had been arranged for him and had also tried to contact him that day. During the interrogation, Burbine waived his Miranda rights and confessed to the murder. The U.S. Supreme Court, considering the "totality of circumstances," upheld the confession as admissible evidence.

PART TWO: LEADING CASES IN FIELD AND CUSTODIAL INTERROGATIONS

In the 1960s, Chief Justice Earl Warren and the other justices of the U.S. Supreme Court, known for their protections of civil liberties and constitutional rights, decided several cases in the area of police procedures that would have lasting impact not only on the operations of criminal justice in general but also, in particular, on the manner in which criminal interrogations would be conducted. Unlike other U.S. Supreme Courts, the Warren court not only created policies that the law-enforcement agents were legally obligated to follow but also, for the first time, provided the exact procedures that police must follow to ensure that individual rights be preserved and that law-enforcement officers perform their duties in a constitutionally correct manner (Wasby, 1989). For example, in 1964, the Court reversed its earlier ruling in *Crooker* and ruled in *Massiah v. United States* that an indicted person could not be properly interrogated or persuaded to give incriminating statements without the presence of a lawyer. Moreover, the Court's decision in *Malloy v. Hogan* extended the protection against self-incrimination to state defendants. Despite *Massiah* and *Malloy*, the Court's decisions in the landmark cases *Escobedo v. Illinois, Miranda v. Arizona,* and *Brewer v. Williams* defined and interpreted custodial interrogations. However, before these cases came before the Court, two earlier cases—*Twining v. New Jersey* and *Brown v. Mississippi*—may have arguably influenced the Warren court's decisions in the 1960s and the Burger court's decisions in the 1970s.

Twining v. New Jersey
211 U.S. 78 (1908)

Albert C. Twining and David C. Cornell, executives of the Memmouth Safe and Trust Company, were indicted by a grand jury for having knowingly displayed a false paper to a bank examiner "with full intent to deceive the bank examiner as to the actual condition of their firm." At trial, Twining and Cornell refused to take the stand. Judge Webber A. Heisley addressed the jury as follows:

> Because a man has not gone upon the stand you are not necessarily justified in drawing an inference of guilt. But you have a right to consider the fact that he does not go upon the stand where a direct accusation is made against him.

Both Twining and Cornell were found guilty. On appeal to the U.S. Supreme Court, they argued that the exemption from self-incrimination was one of the privileges and immunities that the Fourteenth Amendment prohibited the states from ignoring. The petitioners claimed that the judge's statement amounted to compulsory self-incrimination and therefore denied them due process. The Court, in its ruling against Twining and Cornell, stated that the protection against self-incrimination was "not fundamental in the due process of law, not an essential part of it." While *Twining* is not considered a case concerning forced confession in a strict sense, since no confession occurred, it still implies that an involuntary confession was made (Inciardi,

1999). Nevertheless, the Court also ruled in *Twining* that defendants in state courts do not enjoy the Fifth Amendment's guarantee of protection against compulsory self-incrimination.

Brown v. Mississippi
297 U.S. 278 (1936)

In *Brown*, three African American men were arrested for the murder of a white man. They were beaten, brutalized, and tortured into confessions of having committed a crime for which there was no other evidence. Specifically, they were tied to a tree, whipped, twice hanged by a rope from a tree, and told that the process would continue until they confessed. Although there was no doubt that torture had been used to elicit the confessions, the duty sheriff later stated that the whipping was "not too much for a Negro; not as much as I would have done it, if it were left to me." At trial, they were convicted solely on the basis of their confessions and sentenced to death. The convictions were affirmed by the Mississippi Supreme Court. On appeal to the U.S. Supreme Court, Mississippi defended its use of the confessions obtained through beatings and torture by citing the *Twining* ruling that defendants in state courts do not enjoy the protection against self-incrimination guaranteed by the Fifth Amendment. The Court agreed with the *Twining* decision but rejected the Mississippi defense, holding that the state's right to withdraw the privilege of self-incrimination was not the issue. In *Brown*, Chief Justice Charles Evans Hughes, speaking for the Court, held that physically coerced confessions could not serve as the basis for a conviction in a state prosecution. Moreover, just as these confessions could not be introduced in federal criminal trials under the Fifth Amendment, neither could they be allowed under the Fourteenth Amendment's due process clause.

Escobedo v. Illinois
378 U.S. 478 (1964)

On the night of January 19, 1960, Mauel Valtierra, the brother-in-law of twenty-two-year-old Danny Escobedo, was fatally shot in the back. Several hours later, Escobedo was arrested without a warrant and was interrogated for fifteen hours. During that period, he made no statements to the police and was released after his attorney had obtained a writ of habeas corpus. Eleven days after the shooting of Valtierra, Escobedo was arrested for a second time and again taken to the Chicago police station for questioning. Shortly afterward, his attorney arrived, but the police would not permit him to see his client. Both the attorney and Escobedo repeatedly requested to see each other, but their requests were continuously denied. Escobedo was told that he could not see his attorney until the police had finished their questioning. During this second period of interrogation, Escobedo made incriminating statements that were construed as a voluntary confession to the crime. Escobedo was subsequently convicted of murder and sentenced to a twenty-two-year prison term. On appeal to the Illinois Supreme Court, Escobedo maintained that he had been told "he would be permitted to go home if he gave the statement and would be granted immunity from prosecution." The statement in question referred to the complicity of his four codefendants, who had all been arrested on the murder charge. The Illinois Supreme Court reversed Escobedo's conviction, but the state petitioned for a rehearing of the case and the court granted it. The decision was again reversed, sustaining the trial court's original conviction, and Escobedo still faced the twenty-two-year prison term. Escobedo appealed the case to the U.S. Supreme Court and it granted certiorari. On June 22, 1964, the Court ruled in favor of Escobedo by a decision of 5 to 4. In delivering the opinion of the Court, Justice Arthur Goldberg noted that it was based on five pivotal facts in the interrogation:

(1) The investigation was no longer a general inquiry into an unsolved crime but had begun to focus on a particular suspect.
(2) The suspect had been taken into police custody.
(3) The police carried out a process of interrogation that led to eliciting incriminating statements.
(4) The suspect had requested and been denied an opportunity to consult with his lawyer.
(5) The police had not effectively warned the suspect of his constitutional right to remain silent.

According to the Court, in *Escobedo*, the accused had been denied "the assistance of counsel in violation of the Sixth Amendment of the U. S. Constitution." The Court further maintained that "[t]he Fourteenth Amendment makes this right applicable to the states and that no statement elicited by the police during the interrogation may be used against a suspect in a criminal trial."

Brewer v. Williams
430 U.S. 387 (1977)

On Christmas eve in 1968, in Des Moines, Iowa, ten-year-old Pamela Powers was abducted, raped, and strangled to death. Two days later, Robert

Williams, who had recently escaped from a mental institution and who resided at the Des Moines YMCA, where the child had last been seen before her abduction, surrendered to police in Davenport, Iowa, some 160 miles away. Williams surrendered after having discussed the matter with his lawyer, Henry McKnight, and when it was learned that a detective would be transporting Williams back to Des Moines, McKnight insisted that no interrogation take place during the trip. The detective agreed. Knowing that Williams was a religious man, the detective addressed him as "Reverend" during the trip; he did not interrogate Williams but presented him with a series of statements referred to in the record as the "Christian burial speech." The policeman stated:

> I want to give you something to think about while we're traveling down the road.... Number one, I want you to observe the weather conditions, it's raining, it's sleeting, it's freezing, driving is very treacherous, visibility is poor, it's going to be dark early this evening. They are predicting several inches of snow for tonight, and I feel you yourself are the only person who knows where this little girl's body is, that you yourself have only been there once, and if you get snow on top of it you yourself may be unable to find it. And, since we will be going right past the area on the way into Des Moines, I feel that we could stop and locate the body, that the parents of this little girl should be entitled to a Christian burial for the little girl who was snatched away from them on Christmas Eve and murdered. And I feel we should stop and locate it on the way in rather than waiting until morning and trying to come back out after a snowstorm and possibly not being able to find it at all.

Shortly after the detective's "Christian burial speech," Williams directed the officer to Pamela Power's dead and frozen body. Williams was subsequently convicted of murder, in spite of his counsel's motion to suppress the evidence resulting from the incriminating statements made by Williams. The Iowa Supreme Court affirmed the conviction. The case was appealed to the U.S. Supreme Court, and Iowa's attorney general, along with the National District Attorneys Association and Americans for Effective Law Enforcement, requested that the Court overturn *Miranda*. By a decision of 5 to 4, the Court ruled that Williams had not waived his right to counsel during his ride from Davenport to Des Moines and that the detective's "Christian burial speech" constituted a "custodial interrogation." Chief Justice William Burger castigated his more liberal colleagues in open court, stating in his strongly worded dissenting opinion that "the result by the Court in this case ought to be intolerable in any society which purports to call itself an organized society."

PART THREE: THE PROTECTION AGAINST SELF-INCRIMINATION

In criminal investigations when a suspect or witness has been taken into police custody and chooses to invoke the Fifth Amendment, or say to an officer that he or she "pleads the Fifth," should the authorities assume this choice to mean that the person knows of the crime or may have even committed it? What can be inferred from such a choice? Meltzer (1972) explains that there are many reasons why an innocent person may wish to invoke the right to remain silent or to refuse to answer questions by the police outright:

> You may have known something, done something, or joined something that was innocent at the time, and might not even be a crime now, but that could provide a link in a chain of evidence against you.
> You may be ready to talk about your own beliefs and actions, but feel obliged to invoke the right for fear any answer may waive the right and force you to inform.
> You may fear that in telling the truth you may expose yourself or someone else to the danger of prosecution for perjury.
> You may detest political witch hunts and feel you cannot cooperate with one in any way. (p. 115)

Despite the reasons offered by Meltzer as to why suspects may invoke the "Fifth," some legal scholars view the Fifth Amendment as so significant that it should be considered fundamental to ordered liberty (Bohm & Haley, 1999). In fact, the protection against self-incrimination is incorporated in the Amendment (Moskovitz, 2000), which stipulates that "[n]o person ... shall be compelled in any criminal case to be a witness against himself." Legal experts contend that the most important procedural safeguard in the Fifth Amendment is the protection against compelled self-incrimination (Bohm & Haley, 1999). When a suspect or defendant invokes his or her protection against self-incrimination, the suspect or defendant attempts to exclude either a confession or an admission of his or her guilt, usually during an interrogation. The protection against self-incrimination is consistent with the notion that the criminal justice system's process is based on the idea that the state must make its own case. In other words, the government must bear the burden of proving the suspect's or defendant's guilt. The suspect or defendant cannot be compelled in any way to assist the state in proving his or her guilt. Furthermore, confessions may not be truthful if they are not made voluntarily. Moreover, the defendant cannot be forced to take the witness stand in court (Bohm & Haley, 1999).

Light (1999) argues that the purpose of the protection against self-incrimination is twofold. First, it is intended to protect innocent citizens from being compelled to give testimony that can be used to falsely accuse them. Moreover, the right to remain silent means that suspects or defendants cannot be forced with physical torture into confessing involvement in a crime. Second, the protection against self-incrimination prohibits citizens from being forced to admit affiliation with groups unfavorable to the government. Moreover, when suspects or defendants decide to exercise their Fifth Amendment right to remain silent, no inference about their guilt or innocence be legally drawn from their decision (Neubauer, 1999). Stated another way, the decision to exercise one's right to remain silent cannot be viewed as a confession of guilt (Meltzer, 1972). Prior to the mid-1960s, though the protection against self-incrimination had been deemed a fundamental right to ordered liberty since its inception in 1791, it was never recognized as a protection that should be extended to criminal suspects whom police encountered after a crime. Before the 1960s, in general, and before the *Miranda* decision, in particular, criminal suspects and defendants were the victims of various forms of misbehavior and illegal practices by police officers in the officers' zeal to solve crime and bring alleged criminal suspects to justice. Robin (1987) reports that the U.S. Supreme Court decided on a case-by-case basis whether a confession was voluntarily or involuntarily taken by police. In its decisions, the Court typically considered the "totality of circumstances" and particularly the length of time of the suspect's detention and interrogation. Adler, Mueller, and Laufer (1996) argue that the "totality of circumstances" would reveal if the interrogation process had broken the suspect's will to resist. For example, if a suspect had been subjected to a deprivation of sleep or food or had been given a beating, the Court considered such subjection as part of the totality of circumstances. Hence, the totality of circumstances was the yardstick the Court used to determine whether confessions were freely given or were the product of coercion.

As mentioned earlier, prior to *Miranda*, police officers in the United States engaged in questionable practices to force suspects to confess their involvement in crimes. In doing so, the officers violated the suspects' Fifth Amendment right to protection against self-incrimination (Senna & Siegel, 1998). Grilliot (1983) finds that suspects or witnesses cannot be forced to give testimony in or out of court that could possibly be used to convict them of a crime. Therefore, if the police are to obtain lawful evidence, such as an admissible confession or testimony, they must extend to suspects or witnesses certain procedural safeguards in order not to violate their right to protection against self-incrimination. If the police fail to do so, the testimony or confession will be excluded from trial pursuant to the exclusionary rule, which prohibits the use of evidence obtained in violation of the U.S. Constitution (Fagin, 2003). The courts frown on admitting illegal testimony since it is viewed as fruit of the poisonous tree. Scheb & Scheb (1999) report that the *Miranda* decision essentially established that the exclusionary rule also applies to statements made by suspects during custodial interrogation (p. 427). Moreover, Robin (1987) concludes that the constitutional protections upon which the U.S. Supreme Court subsequently based its confession decisions were the due process clause under the Fourteenth Amendment, the right to counsel under the Sixth Amendment, and the protection against self-incrimination under the Fifth Amendment. Though critics view the Fifth Amendment protection as a shield that can be used by the accused, it can also guide the state's investigation and preserve the integrity of the criminal justice system (Senna & Siegel, 1998; Weston & Wells, 1976).

Conditions When the Miranda Warnings Are Not Required

Champion (1999) contends that police are not legally required to advise suspects of their rights as long as the criminal investigation has not shifted from the investigatory to the accusatory or "critical" phase, as explained in *Escobedo*. When the shift occurs, the suspect's rights quickly attach and the suspect must be afforded the opportunity to invoke constitutional safeguards. Nevertheless, during detention, police officers do not have to give Miranda warnings under the following circumstances: (1) when they ask a motorist questions during a routine traffic stop; (2) when they do not intend to ask the suspect questions; (3) when they ask nonspecific questions on the scene; (4) when they question witnesses during lineups, field showups, or the shooting of photo IDs; (5) when they ask questions during stop and frisk detentions; or (6) when a suspect volunteers to make a statement (Peoples, 2003; Adler et al., 1996).

PART FOUR: THE EROSION OF
MIRANDA V. ARIZONA

After *Miranda* was decided in 1968, the decision drastically changed the day-to-day practice of policing. But some legal scholars argue that the U.S. Supreme Court was beginning to retreat from its decision as early as 1971, in the case *Harris v. New York*. In *Harris*, the defendant was arrested for selling heroin to an undercover New York police officer on several occasions. Harris's Miranda warnings were incomplete because before police interrogated him, they had failed to advise him of his right to an attorney. However, during the interrogation, Harris confessed both verbally and in writing to selling drugs to an undercover police officer on two occasions. During trial, Harris admitted on direct examination that the first sale to the officer was a sale of heroin but that the second sale was one of baking powder. In an attempt to impeach Harris's credibility, the prosecutor, on cross-examination, referred to Harris's signed confession, which stated that he had sold drugs on both occasions. In this case, the trial judge instructed the jury that the statements allegedly made by Harris during custodial interrogation could be considered only as a means of considering his credibility and not as evidence of his guilt (Robin, 1987). Nevertheless, Harris was subsequently convicted. On appeal, the U.S. Supreme Court held that statements made by the accused in violation of the Miranda warnings are admissible at trial under the following conditions: (1) if the statements were trustworthy; (2) if the testimony of the accused contradicts his or her prior statements to police; (3) if the prior statements of the accused are used not to show guilt but to impeach the credibility of the defendant as a witness in his or her own behalf. The Court also held that when the prosecution had contended that Harris had lied during trial, his statements to the police before trial could be introduced as evidence to prove the contention. The *Harris* decision made it easier for officers to circumvent the tenets of the Miranda warnings—if a suspect voluntarily confessed to a crime before having been informed of his or her right to remain silent. The decision also required that a suspect have an attorney present during his or her interrogation only if juries were instructed that the defendant's confession was not to be considered as evidence of guilt but only as a means of determining whether the defendant was telling the truth if he or she should change his or her testimony at a later day.

Another case that weakened *Miranda* was *Michigan v. Tucker*. In this case, Tucker was arrested for rape, but police failed to give him the full Miranda warnings at the police station. Specifically, Tucker was not advised of his right to a free lawyer. He agreed to be interrogated without a lawyer present. During the questioning, Tucker provided the police with the name of a witness that could provide an alibi for his activities on the night of the rape. However, when police contacted the witness, the witness made statements seriously incriminating Tucker. The case went to trial, and Tucker was subsequently convicted. On appeal to the U.S. Supreme Court, Tucker argued that he had been denied his Fifth Amendment rights because he had been given incomplete Miranda warnings. The Court held that the Fifth Amendment does not require that derivative evidence (namely, statements from a witness providing an alibi) be excluded from trial, even if they were obtained through an interrogation made without the full Miranda warnings. The Court ruled that collateral, derivative, or third-party evidence discovered through a violation of the Miranda rights is admissible at trial, especially when police officers are acting in "good faith" by believing that the witness providing the alibi is trustworthy. In *Tucker*, the Court went so far as to redefine the scope of the Fifth Amendment as including only "genuinely compelled" statements, which were lacking in Tucker's confession (Robin, 1987). Essentially, in *Tucker*, the Court allowed the testimony of a witness whose identity was revealed by the suspect even though the Miranda warnings given the suspect had been incomplete (Senna & Siegel, 1990).

In 1975, the U.S. Supreme Court reviewed the case *Michigan v. Mosley*. Mosley had been arrested in Detroit in connection with two robberies. He was given his Miranda warnings. He informed the officer that he wanted to remain silent, and the officer terminated the questioning. Two hours later, Mosley was visited by a homicide detective who also gave him the Miranda warnings and indicated that he wanted to talk about Mosley's possible involvement in a murder. This time, Mosley did not object to being interrogated. He made incriminating statements and was subsequently convicted of murder. In this case, the Michigan Court of Appeals reversed Moseley's conviction on the grounds that the homicide detective's interrogation was a violation of his Miranda rights since Mosley had initially stated he was not interested in providing any statements to police. The court ruled that to accept Mosley's statements after he had announced his intentions would be a compelled acceptance and thus a violation of the Fifth Amendment. The prosecution appealed the appellate court's ruling to the U.S. Supreme Court, which reversed on the grounds that if Mosley had continued to follow the Miranda warnings, he could have "cut off questioning" at any time. Essentially, the police had presented the Miranda warnings as a safeguard, but the defendant had ignored them. In *Mosley*, the Court's rationale was that "permanent immunity" from interrogating a suspect would transform the Miranda warnings into a wholly irrational obstacle for police. In its holding, the Court used the following criteria to establish if police honored the suspect's rights: (1) clear and complete Miranda warnings were given the suspect at each interrogation; (2) an interrogation ceased immediately if the suspect invoked his right to remain silent; (3) a reasonable period of time had elapsed before the questioning resumed; and (4) the police had a bona fide purpose to resume questioning unrelated to the subject matter that the suspect had previously refused to talk about. The *Mosley* decision upheld the renewed questioning of a suspect who had been given the Miranda warnings and who, during an earlier interrogation, had refused to answer any questions (Adler et al., 1996).

In *Oregon v. Mathiason*, an Oregon state police officer investigating a burglary focused on Carl Mathiason, a paroled suspect. Unable to reach Mathiason, the officer left a note at his apartment asking him to call because "I'd like to discuss something with you." Upon receiving the note, Mathiason called the officer the next day and arranged to meet with him at the state patrol office. Upon meeting Mathiason, the officer told him that he was not under arrest but that he was a suspect in a burglary. The officer then falsely told Mathiason that his fingerprints had been discovered in the burglarized house and that if he cooperated truthfully, the prosecutor and the judge would consider his cooperation positively. At that point, Mathiason admitted to having committed the burglary. The officer then Mirandized Mathiason and taped his confession. At trial, he was convicted of first-degree burglary. He appealed the decision to the Oregon Supreme Court. The court reversed the conviction, holding that "the interrogation took place in a 'coercive environment'" even though, in reality, Mathiason had not been formally arrested or detained. The prosecutor appealed the case to the U.S. Supreme Court. The Court reversed, holding that Mathiason's Fifth Amendment and Miranda rights had not been violated because he was never under arrest or in police custody or "otherwise deprived of his freedom in any significant way." Hence, the circumstances under which Mathiason confessed and made incriminating statements to police officers did not constitute a custodial interrogation.

In 1980, the U.S. Supreme Court weakened the application of the Miranda rights when it ruled in *Rhode Island v. Innis*. In this case, Providence police had arrested Thomas Innis in connection with the sawed-off-shotgun murder of a cab driver and the robbery of another cab driver with the same weapon. The officer advised Innis of his Miranda rights and he replied that he wanted to see a lawyer. The officers transporting Innis to the police station were advised by a captain not to question or intimidate him in any way during the trip. However, on the way to the station, two of the officers conversing between themselves discussed the missing shotgun. One officer even stated that there were "a lot of handicapped children running around in this area" and "God forbid one of them might find a weapon with shells and they might hurt themselves." Innis then interrupted the conversation and directed the officers to turn the car around so he could show them where the gun was hidden. During trial, the gun and Innis's testimony were admitted into evidence despite the objection by the defense, and Innis was subsequently found guilty of robbery and murder. He appealed his conviction to the U.S. Supreme Court. In *Innis*, the Court was concerned with whether the conversation between the two officers was tantamount to an interrogation. If so, it would have violated Innis's right to remain silent under Miranda. In deciding *Innis*, the Court created a two-pronged test to establish a definition of *interrogation*. It held that Miranda safeguards must be given when either "express questioning" or its "functional equivalent" occurs. The Court held that the nature of the police conversation did not constitute an interrogation according to the "express questioning" criterion (Robin, 1987). In its explanation of the "functional equivalent" criterion, the Court held that an *interrogation* refers to any words or actions of police which "they should have known" were reasonably likely to elicit an incriminating response from the suspect. The Court held that the "functional equivalent" criterion was wanting in *Innis*; therefore, his conviction was upheld. *Innis* can be interpreted to mean that safeguards against self-incrimination must be observed "whenever a person in custody is subjected to either express questioning or its equivalent."

In *New York v. Quarles*, the U.S. Supreme Court made further exceptions to Miranda. In *Quarles*, two police officers on routine patrol in Queens, New York, were told by a woman that she had just been raped by an armed man who had then entered a nearby supermarket. The officers sought to apprehend the suspect by following him into the supermarket. Upon entrance, one of the officers quickly spotted the suspect, Benjamin Quarles, near the check-out counter, whereupon the suspect began running toward the rear of the store and was pursued by the officer with a drawn gun. After apprehending and arresting Quarles, the officers noticed that he was wearing an empty shoulder holster. One of the officers asked Quarles, "What did you do with the gun?" Quarles nodded in the direction of some cartons and replied, "The gun is over there." The officer retrieved a loaded .38 caliber revolver. At this time, the officer gave Quarles his Miranda warnings. During trial, Quarles sought suppression of the evidence, and the judge excluded the weapon and Quarles's statement, "The gun is over there," because Quarles had not been Mirandized *before* he made his statement and *before* his weapon was retrieved. On appeal, the New York Court of Appeals affirmed the lower court's ruling. The case was appealed and the U.S. Supreme Court granted certiorari. The Court reversed, and in the process, it established a "public safety" exception to the Miranda requirement that does not depend on the motivation of the officers involved. The Court held that, in this case, "the need for answers to questions in a situation posing a threat to the public safety outweighs the need for the Miranda warning protecting the Fifth Amendment's privilege against self-incrimination." The Court also stated that unless the gun was immediately recovered, it constituted a danger to public safety since shoppers, employees, or an accomplice could find it and make use of it. Under such conditions, the Miranda warnings may be relegated until a later time to protect the public (Robin, 1987). The Court further stated that *Quarles* involved a situation in which concern for public safety must take precedence over literal adherence to the language of Miranda. Therefore, before giving Quarles the Miranda warnings, the officer was justified in asking him the question by "immediate necessity."

In *Nix v. Williams*, the U.S. Supreme Court further weakened Miranda by creating the "inevitable discovery exception." *Nix v. Williams* was a rehearing of *Brewer v. Williams*. Robert Williams had been convicted of the murder of a ten-year-old girl. During the investigation, a detective gave Williams the "Christian burial speech." Though the detective had promised Williams's lawyer that he would not ask any questions during a drive across the state, he asked Williams to consider that the parents of the girl were entitled to provide a Christian burial for their child. As a result, Williams told the detective where he had placed her body. In *Brewer*, the Court had ruled that the detective had violated the suspect's rights by inducing Williams to incriminate himself by questioning him in the absence of his attorney. However, the Court left open the possibility that, in a retrial, the state could introduce the evidence of the body's discovery if the state could establish that the body would have been found even without the defendant's testimony. In *Nix*, the rehearing of *Brewer*, the Iowa court ruled that the body of the girl located by Williams was admissible evidence since it would possibly have been found by search parties anyway. While the interrogation of Williams was illegal, the girl's body did not fall under the exclusionary rule because it would have eventually been found in the same condition. Thus, the Iowa court applied the "inevitable discovery exception" and found Williams guilty. On appeal, the U.S. Supreme Court upheld the conviction, holding that the doctrine of "inevitable discovery" was designed to put the police "in the same, not a worse, position than they would have been in if no police error or misconduct had occurred."

Other cases have continued to erode *Miranda*. For example, *United States v. Leon* created the "good faith exception." In *Leon*, a California district court judge issued a search warrant based on information from a confidential source and on lengthy police investigation. The warrant authorized the search of three houses and several automobiles. The search produced large quantities of cocaine and methaqualone. Defendants filed a pretrial motion to suppress the evidence on the grounds that the affidavit was insufficient to establish probable cause. The district court granted part of the motion and the Ninth Circuit Court of Appeals affirmed. The government petitioned the U.S. Supreme Court for certiorari, asking whether a "good faith exception" to the exclusionary rule should be adopted. In *Leon*, the Court held that evidence which had been obtained by law-enforcement officers acting in reasonable reliance on a search warrant issued by a detached and neutral magistrate but which was ultimately found to be unsupported by probable cause could be introduced into evidence at trial.

In *Moran v. Burbine*, a confession by a murder suspect, Burbine, was admitted into evidence at trial even though police officers had failed to inform Burbine that his sister had already obtained a lawyer to represent his legal interests. In this case, police officers had also assured Burbine's newly retained lawyer that they would not interrogate Burbine until the following day, after the lawyer had provided counseling to the suspect. In *Burbine*, the U.S. Supreme Court ruled that the police do not have to tell a suspect that someone has hired a lawyer for him or her and that they do not have to be honest with the lawyer. They must simply make sure that the suspect knows that he or she has the right to remain silent.

In *Arizona v. Fulminante*, the U.S. Supreme Court considered a murder confession by a prisoner to a fellow inmate who was a police informant. The Court ruled that even if a confession is found to be "coerced," the coerced confession will not automatically cause a mistrial if it can be shown, beyond a reasonable doubt, that the error did not determine the outcome of the trial. A confession often has a tremendous impact on a jury, but it is now possible for a judge to allow a trial to continue and the jury to render a verdict even though the jury has been exposed to an improperly obtained confession. In *Fulminante*, the U.S. Supreme Court held that the introduction of the coerced confession as evidence was not harmless because of its likely impact on the verdict, and it ordered a new trial. Nonetheless, this case leaves the door open to admit confessions into evidence that violate the voluntariness standard (Zalman, 1991).

PART FIVE: SOME PERTINENT CASES

Brown v. Mississippi
287 U.S. 278 (1936)

Brown, an African American suspect in a murder, was visited at his home by a deputy sheriff and brought to the murder scene. Brown denied having committed the murder. The deputy and others hanged him from a tree, let him down, and hanged him again. Brown was later tied to a tree and beaten. He was then released and allowed to go home. A few days later, a deputy returned to Brown's home and arrested him. Brown was taken to jail, where he was beaten repeatedly and told that until he confessed to the murder, the punishment would continue. Brown then signed a confession. He was subsequently convicted and sentenced to death. He appealed the decision, arguing that his due process rights had been violated. The U.S. Supreme Court agreed, holding that the brutality of police officers had rendered his confession inadmissible in court. The Court also held that coerced confessions are unconstitutional. Thus, Brown's conviction was overturned.

Ashcraft v. Tennessee
322 U.S. 143 (1944)

Defendants Ashcraft and Ware allegedly conspired to kill Ashcraft's wife. Both men were arrested after her murder and were interrogated for several hours. Ashcraft was interrogated for eight hours, from 6:00 a.m. on the day of the murder until about 2:00 a.m. the next morning. A few days later, police took Ashcraft into custody and interrogated him in "relays" from Saturday evening at 7:00 p.m. until Monday morning at 9:30 a.m. During this period, Ashcraft was not given any rest and only one five-minute respite. He then confessed and was subsequently convicted. He appealed the decision to the U.S. Supreme Court. On appeal, the issue in the case was whether his confession had been coerced. The Court agreed and reversed his conviction on the grounds that his confession was not voluntary but coerced after thirty-six hours of interrogation and was thus inadmissible at trial.

Davis v. United States
328 U.S. 582 (1946)

Davis, the owner of a gas station in New York City, was suspected of selling gasoline on the black market through the unlawful distribution of gasoline coupons (the use of which was required by individuals during World War II). Two federal agents purchased gasoline from an attendant at Davis's station, using not their own coupons but those given them by the attendant. The agents arrested the station attendant, and Davis was ordered to open his gasoline pumps so that the agents could later confirm if he had the required number of coupons to cover the gasoline purchases. In this case, Davis argued that even though his records were in a locked office, the federal agents had threatened to knock the door down unless he opened it. Davis allowed the agents entry into the room, where they conducted a search without a warrant and seized evidence that was later used against him. Davis was subsequently arrested and then convicted of unlawful possession of gasoline coupons. He appealed the case and the U.S. Supreme Court granted review. The issue in *Davis* was whether the search had been coerced and therefore illegally performed. The Court disagreed, holding that the search had been consensual. Moreover, the Court reasoned that the federal agents had also wanted to inspect public documents and not private ones. Therefore, the demands that the agents had placed on Davis were valid and constitutional.

Escobedo v. Illinois
378 U.S. 478 (1963)

On the word of an informant, police searched for Ernesto Escobedo in connection with a murder. Without a warrant, police arrested Escobedo and interrogated him at the station house. He did not have an attorney present to advise him. Escobedo asked to speak with an attorney on several occasions during a long interrogation. During the interrogation, he was moved into various rooms, and at times, he could see his attorney standing in the hall at a distance. Police told Escobedo that his attorney "did not want to talk to him." Escobedo's attorney was also told that he could not see his client. After several hours of interrogation, Escobedo confessed to murder and was convicted. On appeal to the U.S. Supreme Court, the Court overturned the conviction, holding that Escobedo had been denied his Sixth Amendment right to counsel during the interrogation process and that therefore his due process rights had been violated. In *Escobedo*, the Court also stated that although the police were initially investigating a murder, at some point their investigation had shifted from the investigatory to the accusatory. When this shift occurs, the suspect (now the accused) is entitled to the benefit of counsel and can refrain from conversing with officers unless counsel is present to advise the accused to avoid making self-incriminating statements.

Miranda v. Arizona
384 U.S. 436 (1966)

Miranda was arrested on suspicion of kidnapping and raping a young girl. Though the girl was left for dead, she survived the attack and was able to identify Miranda at the police station as the kidnapper and the rapist. At the station house, Miranda was not permitted to talk to an attorney and the police did not advise him of his rights to have legal representation. Miranda was interrogated for several hours. He eventually confessed and signed a written statement admitting guilt. He was subsequently convicted. He appealed the decision to the U.S. Supreme Court and it granted review. In this case, the issue was whether Miranda's due process rights had been violated because he was not told of his right to an attorney during the custodial interrogation or of his right to remain silent. The Court agreed and created the Miranda warnings. This decision declared that any confession made by a suspect in custody who has not been notified of his or her right to an attorney or of his or her right to remain silent cannot be admitted as evidence in court to gain a criminal conviction. The Court held that suspects must be advised as follows: (1) they can remain silent; (2) they have a right to counsel; (3) they have a right to free counsel if they cannot afford an attorney; and (4) they have a right to terminate questioning at any time.

Chapman v. California
386 U.S. 18 (1967)

Chapman and a companion were charged with robbing, kidnapping, and murdering a bartender. A California statute permitted that the judge and the prosecutor could comment concerning a defendant's failure to testify in his or her own defense and that inferences about guilt could be drawn from the defendant's failure to testify. In *Chapman*, the judge informed the jury that it could draw adverse inferences from the defendant's failure to testify. Chapman was subsequently convicted. The case was appealed to the California Supreme Court. In its decision, the court cited its holding in *Griffin v. California*. In that case, the court had held that when a judge or prosecutor comments about a defendant's refusal to testify in a criminal case, the judge or prosecutor must not infringe upon the defendant's protection against self-incrimination, as guaranteed by the Fifth Amendment. In applying *Griffin*, the California Supreme Court ruled that Chapman had been denied a federal constitutional right because of the judge's instructions to the jury about her refusal to testify. However, the court held the error as harmless. The case was appealed to the U.S. Supreme Court and it granted certiorari. The Court reversed Chapman's conviction, holding that the error was not harmless when the state prosecutor's argument and the trial judge's instructions to the jury repeatedly impressed upon the jury that an inference of guilt could be drawn from the defendant's refusal to testify. As a result, Chapman was granted a new trial during which judicial and prosecutorial commentary on her refusal to testify was prohibited.

Orozco v. Texas
394 U.S. 324 (1969)

While confined to a bed in a boarding house where he lived, Reyes Arias Orozco was interrogated by police officers regarding his involvement in a murder. He was given part of his Miranda warnings. During the interrogation, he made incriminating statements. He was subsequently arrested and convicted of murder in the criminal district court of Dallas County, Texas. Orozco appealed the court's decision, contending that when the police officers had failed to read the full Miranda warnings, they had violated his Fifth Amendment protection against self-incrimination. The Court of Criminal Appeals of Texas affirmed the conviction. The case was appealed to the U.S. Supreme Court and it granted certiorari. The Court reversed and overturned the conviction, holding that because Orozco had been bedridden, his interview with the police officers constituted a complete custodial interrogation. Miranda applies both when people are in police custody (either at a station house or in another place) and when they are deprived of freedom of movement in a significant way. Therefore, Orozco should have been entitled to the full Miranda warnings, informing him of his right to remain silent and of his right to an attorney.

Michigan v. Mosley
423 U.S. 96 (1975)

Mosley was arrested on suspicion of having committed several robberies. A police officer advised Mosley of his Miranda rights, and he refused to talk to him. After Mosley had been in custody for two hours, an officer from another jurisdiction introduced himself to Mosley, gave him his Miranda warnings again, and questioned him about his involvement in a homicide. Mosley conversed with the second officer. From the testimony given to the officer regarding the homicide, Mosley was subsequently convicted of murder. He appealed his conviction, arguing that his Fifth Amendment rights had been violated by the new line of questioning by the officer from the other jurisdiction who had sought information regarding a homicide. Mosley argued that since he had stated that he did not want to talk to the first police officer about the crime against him, his rights had been violated. The U.S. Supreme Court upheld the conviction on the following grounds: (1) Mosley had been properly given his Miranda rights in the first instance of questioning; (2) the first police officer had adhered to Mosley's refusal to talk; (3) in the second instance of questioning, he had been properly Mirandized; and (4) he had voluntarily conversed with the second officer. Therefore, Mosley's Fifth Amendment rights had not been violated and the conviction stood.

Oregon v. Mathiason
429 U.S. 492 (1977)

A burglary occurred near the residence of Carl Mathiason. Aware of his place of residence and his parole status, police went to his home and left a card stating that they would like to talk with him regarding his knowledge of a recent burglary. After receiving the card, Mathiason went to the police station on his own volition. He was quickly told that he was not under arrest. He voluntarily conversed with police about the burglary. Because he was not in custody, police did not give him the Miranda warnings. After being questioned, he confessed to the burglary and was arrested and charged. At trial, he filed a motion to suppress the confession, contending that it was the fruit of an illegal interrogation since he had not been advised of his Fifth Amendment protection against self-incrimination. The trial court refused to exclude the confession since Mathiason had not been in custody when he confessed to the crime. He was subsequently convicted. He appealed the case to the Oregon Court of Appeals, and the court affirmed the conviction. However, the Supreme Court of Oregon reversed it. The case was appealed to the U.S. Supreme Court and it granted certiorari. The Court reversed and remanded, holding that in this case there was no indication that the interrogation had occurred in a context where Mathiason's freedom to leave was restricted in any way. Mathiason had voluntarily come to the police station where he was immediately informed by police that he was not under arrest. This noncustodial situation cannot be converted into one to which Miranda would apply. Police are not required to give Miranda warnings to everyone they question. Instead, Miranda extends only to cases in which a person's freedom has been restricted—namely, when the person is under arrest or in police custody. Because of the coercive environment created by a deprivation of freedom, the Miranda warnings attach.

North Carolina v. Butler
441 U.S. 369 (1979)

William Thomas Butler robbed a gas station in Goldsboro, North Carolina. He shot the station attendant and tried to escape. The attendant was paralyzed from the gunshot wounds. Butler was arrested and charged with kidnapping, armed robbery, and felonious assault. He was given his Miranda warnings. While in custody, Butler made incriminating statements to officers. At trial, he filed a motion to suppress the incriminating statements, contending that he had not waived his right to the assistance of counsel. The court denied his motion; the evidence was introduced; and he was subsequently convicted on all charges. The case was appealed to the North Carolina Supreme Court. The court reversed the conviction, holding that Miranda requires that no statement of a person under custodial interrogation can be admitted into evidence unless he or she explicitly waives the right to have a lawyer present. The prosecution appealed the ruling to the U.S. Supreme Court. The Court vacated the lower court's decision, holding that an explicit statement of waiver is not invariably necessary to support a finding that the defendant waived his right to remain silent or his right to legal counsel.

California v. Prysock
453 U.S. 355 (1981)

Prysock and another defendant were arrested for the murder of a woman. They were taken to a police station where they were given their Miranda warnings in only a general manner and were interrogated about their involvement in the crime. Prysock had earlier indicated to police officers that he wanted to talk with them but that he did not want to have the conversation recorded on tape. He had also stated that he wanted his lawyer present during the interrogation. The officers had agreed to his requests, and during the interrogation they accepted his statements regarding the crime. Prysock gave them incriminating information. He was subsequently convicted of murder. He appealed the court's decision, arguing that because his Miranda warnings had not been given to him in a precise manner, the confession he made to the police should have been suppressed and his conviction overturned. An appeals court agreed and overturned the conviction. The prosecution appealed the ruling to the U.S. Supreme Court and it granted review. The Court reversed and reinstated the murder conviction, holding that the Miranda warnings do not have to be given in their precise language. The Court added that such a rigid rule has never been mandated by the Court or by Miranda.

Edwards v. Arizona
451 U.S. 477 (1981)

Edwards was named as an accomplice to a crime on a taped confession. He was arrested and charged with robbery. He was given his Miranda warnings by the police. On January 19, 1976, he sought to strike a deal with the police, but he also wanted an attorney. After he requested an attorney, the interrogation ceased and an attorney was appointed for him. He was placed in a jail cell. The next day, Edwards was visited at his cell by two officers who read his Miranda warnings again. They asked him if he would converse with them, and he requested to hear the taped confession given by his accomplice. After hearing the recording, he made incriminating statements to the police. At trial, he sought to suppress his confession. The judge refused and he was subsequently convicted of several crimes. He appealed the case to the Arizona Supreme Court. The court held that Edwards had waived his Miranda rights and his right to counsel when he voluntarily gave his statement after having been informed of his rights. The U.S. Supreme Court granted certiorari. The Court agreed with Edwards and overturned his conviction, holding that once he had requested an attorney, police interrogations should have ceased entirely, even though Edwards had been given his Miranda rights a second time before making the incriminating statements. Furthermore, his attorney had not been present during the second custodial interrogation. The Court held that police may not continue a custodial interrogation of a suspect who is represented by an attorney and who requests to remain silent, even though the Miranda warnings are given more than once and precede any subsequent interrogation. However, the Court stated that conversation initiated by suspects may be used for incriminating purposes.

Colorado v. Spring
479 U.S. 564 (1984)

John Spring was arrested in Kansas City, Missouri, by FBI agents who gave him the Miranda warnings and interrogated him concerning his involvement in trafficking stolen firearms across state lines. FBI agents also gave Spring the Miranda warnings several times during his interrogation, and he signed several statements to demonstrate that he had received the warnings. Spring was also wanted in Colorado in connection with shooting a man during a hunting trip. Officers from Colorado traveled to Kansas City and interrogated Spring about his involvement in the murder; he confessed to the crime and signed a written statement to that effect. He was subsequently convicted of murder. He appealed the decision, arguing that his written confession to the murder should have been suppressed from trial since he had received the Miranda warnings by the FBI agents for the crime of trafficking stolen firearms across state lines. The court of appeals reversed the conviction, holding that Spring's waiver before the interrogation was invalid because a suspect cannot decide whether he or she wants counsel if knowledge of the crime is withheld. The decision was affirmed by the state supreme court. The case was appealed to the U.S. Supreme Court. The Court disagreed, holding that once the police provide a suspect with his Miranda warnings, they are not limited to asking about only one crime; officers may also ask about other crimes.

Smith v. Illinois
469 U.S. 91 (1984)

Smith was arrested in connection with an armed robbery. Upon his arrest, he was taken to a police station and interrogated about his involvement in the crime. Police officers gave him the Miranda warnings, but he was unsure whether he wanted to have a lawyer present while being interrogated. Prior to the police interrogation, Smith stated, "I wanna get a lawyer." However, when asked if he wanted to talk to police before a lawyer could be appointed, he answered, "Yeah and no." During the interrogation Smith confessed to committing the crime. At trial, Smith's lawyer filed a motion to suppress the confession, but the judge refused. Smith was subsequently convicted of armed robbery. He appealed the decision. The conviction was affirmed by both the Illinois Appellate Court and the Illinois Supreme Court. The courts held that Smith's subsequent responses to continued police questioning rendered his initial request for counsel "ambiguous" and that the officers were therefore not required to terminate their interrogations. The case was appealed to the U.S. Supreme Court and it granted certiorari. The Court overturned Smith's conviction, holding that on several occasions during the interrogation, Smith indicated that he wanted his lawyer to be present. At that time, the police interrogation should have ceased until the lawyer arrived. The Court ruled that when suspects who are in custody request a lawyer, counsel must be provided to them and no interrogation is to occur until the attorney can consult with the defendant.

Minnesota v. Murphy
465 U.S. 420 (1984)

In 1980, Murphy pleaded guilty to a sex-related offense and was given probation. As a condition of probation, he had to participate in a treatment program for sexual offenders, report to a probation officer, and be "truthful with the officer in all matters." While serving three years on probation, Murphy had to attend sexual therapy and counseling sessions. At one of the sessions, Murphy confessed to a counselor that he had committed a rape and murder in 1974. Shortly afterward, the counselor contacted Murphy's probation officer and told him about the confession. The probation officer confronted and questioned Murphy about the confession. He admitted to the probation officer that the confession was the truth. The officer contacted the local police and provided them with the incriminating testimony given by Murphy. He was later charged with a rape and murder committed in 1974. At trial, Murphy filed a motion to suppress the confession, arguing that it had been obtained in a manner that violated the Fifth and Fourteenth Amendments. He argued that during his therapy session, he was not provided his Miranda warnings. The trial court ruled that Murphy was not in custody at the time he confessed and that the confession was neither compelled nor involuntary despite the absence of Miranda. He was subsequently convicted of rape and murder. He appealed the case to the Minnesota Supreme Court. The court reversed, holding that Murphy was not in custody in the usual sense; that because of the conditions of his probation, he was required to respond truthfully to the officer; and that because the probation officer had substantial reason to believe Murphy's answers were likely to be incriminating, the Fifth Amendment protection against self-incrimination should have attached. The case was appealed to the U.S. Supreme Court and it granted certiorari. The Court held that the Fifth and Fourteenth Amendments did not prohibit Murphy's admission to his probation officer of the truth of his earlier confession. The Court reasoned that Murphy's obligation to appear before his probation officer did not convert his voluntary statements into compelled ones. Nor could Murphy invoke a claim of self-incrimination. There had been no formal arrest and no restraint had been placed on his freedom of movement. Therefore, there was no need for Murphy to have been given the Miranda warnings.

Arizona v. Mauro

481 U.S. 520 (1986)

When police approached the crime scene, they discovered Mauro and arrested him for the murder of his son. He claimed that the murder occurred in a store. At this time, Mauro admitted to killing his son and led police to the body. The police arrested him and took him to the station where they interrogated him. Before they questioned Mauro, they give him the Miranda warnings twice. He told officers that he did not want to answer further questions without having his lawyer present to advise him. Mauro asked the police if his wife could visit him at the detention station. Police agreed to allow Mauro's wife to visit him but stated that an officer would be present who would tape record the entire conversation. During the conversation with his wife, Mauro made several incriminating statements that the police later used against him. At trial, Mauro argued that the incriminating statements should be suppressed as evidence. The court refused and he was subsequently convicted of his son's murder. The Arizona Supreme Court reversed the ruling of the trial court, holding that the police had impermissibly interrogated Mauro within the meaning of Miranda since the police had admitted knowing that Mauro might make incriminating statements if he saw his wife. The U.S. Supreme Court granted certiorari. In *Mauro*, the Court reversed and remanded, holding that the actions of the police following Mauro's refusal to be questioned without a lawyer did not constitute an interrogation or its functional equivalent. In this case, the respondent was not subjected to compelling influences, psychological ploys, or direct questioning. There was also no evidence that suggested the police had allowed the wife to meet with Mauro so that they could secretly obtain incriminating statements. Moreover, the police had testified to a number of reasons why an officer needed to be present at the meeting with Mauro and his wife. The reasons included security considerations, and chief among them was a concern about the wife's safety. The Court also held that while the police were aware that the respondent could incriminate himself when talking to his wife, the police do not interrogate a suspect by simply hoping that he or she will confess. Hence, the Mauro's incriminating statements were voluntary and were therefore not protected by the Fifth and Fourteenth Amendments.

Colorado v. Connelly
479 U.S. 157 (1986)

Francis Connelly approached an on-duty Denver police officer and confessed to a murder he committed in 1982. The officer gave Connelly his Miranda warnings. Connelly stated that he understood the warnings, and he continued to give his confession. A detective arrived on the scene and he also gave Connelly the Miranda warnings. Again Connelly continued with his confession. Connelly then led officers to the murder scene and provided them with incriminating evidence. When asked why he had confessed to the crime, Connelly stated that he was "following the advice of God." A psychiatric examination revealed that Connelly suffered from chronic schizophrenia at the time of the confession. He was also found incompetent to assist in his own defense. But after six months of treatment, doctors found him competent enough to stand trial. At trial, Connelly filed a motion to suppress the confession he had made to the police, and the trial court agreed, on the grounds that the confession had been made involuntarily. As a result, the evidence was ruled as inadmissible. The prosecution appealed to the Colorado Supreme Court. The court held that the confession was involuntary since it was the product of hallucinations. Therefore, the court ruled Connelly was not competent to waive the Miranda rights. The case was appealed to the U.S. Supreme Court and it granted review. The Court held that taking Connelly's confession did not violate the due process clause since it did not involve governmental coercion. The Court held that suppressing statements in cases where suspects are not coerced does not have a deterrent effect on future violations of the Constitution by the police, since Miranda protects against government coercion. The Court thus reversed the decisions of the lower courts.

Kuhlman v. Wilson
477 U.S. 436 (1986)

Wilson was arrested and charged with a robbery and murder that occurred in 1977 at a taxi company in the Bronx, New York. After he was arraigned, he was placed in a cell with a government informant named Lee. Wilson made incriminating statements to Lee, who turned the information over to police officers. The testimonial evidence was introduced at trial. Wilson argued that the evidence should have been suppressed because it had been illegally obtained. Lee argued that the statements made by Wilson had been unsolicited and spontaneous. Wilson was subsequently convicted. Wilson petitioned the court for a writ of habeas corpus, arguing that his incriminating statements to Lee had been illegally introduced as evidence. Wilson also argued that his Sixth Amendment right to counsel had been denied when the police had elicited incriminating statements from him through Lee. The state court refused to set aside the conviction. Wilson appealed the case to the circuit court of appeals. The appeals court reversed the conviction. The state of New York appealed the ruling to the U.S. Supreme Court, which reversed the appellate court's ruling and reinstated the robbery and murder conviction. The Court argued that despite testimony from the government informant, sufficient additional inculpatory evidence existed to convict Wilson. Furthermore, the Court argued that a police officer had simply instructed Lee to listen to Wilson and not to elicit statements of guilt. The Court held that unsolicited statements made by a suspect do not violate the Sixth Amendment right to counsel during police interrogation.

Moran v. Burbine
475 U.S. 412 (1986)

Burbine was arrested in Cranston, Rhode Island, for suspicion of breaking and entering. Police also suspected him of murdering a woman in Providence a year earlier. After taking him into custody, the police phoned officers in Providence, who arrived in Cranston to question Burbine about the murder. That same night, Burbine's sister (unaware of his involvement in the murder) contacted the public defender's office to obtain a lawyer for him. The lawyer phoned the police department and informed the police that she had been retained to represent Burbine, so if the police intended to question him, they should refrain from doing so until she could assist him. She was told that they did not intend to question Burbine until the next morning. The lawyer was not told that there were police from Providence at the station, and she was not aware that Burbine was wanted on suspicion of murder. Providence police interrogated him after reading his Miranda warnings. They obtained a signed confession admitting to the murder. Since Burbine was unaware that his sister had retained a lawyer to represent him, he never requested an attorney. At trial, he moved to suppress the confession, but the court denied the motion, holding that he had waived his protection against self-incrimination and his right to counsel. He was subsequently convicted of first-degree murder. He appealed and the Rhode Island Supreme Court affirmed. Burbine then petitioned the federal district court for a writ of habeas corpus; the petition was denied. The court of appeals reversed, holding that when the police had failed to inform Burbine of his attorney's phone call, the failure tainted the waiver of his Fifth Amendment protection against self-incrimination and of his right to counsel. The case was appealed to the US Supreme Court and it granted review. The Court upheld the conviction, holding that Burbine had been properly given the Miranda warnings and therefore knew that he was volunteering incriminating statements to the police.

Connecticut v. Barrett
479 U.S. 523 (1987)

Barrett was arrested in connection with a sexual assault. The police gave him the Miranda warnings on three separate occasions. Each time he received the Miranda warnings, he signed and dated acknowledgement. He told the police that he would not make any written statements without his lawyer present but that he would provide oral statements. Officers agreed to accept the statements and provided Barrett with his Miranda rights. Because the police department had a defective tape recorder, officers made a written record of the interrogation. At trial, Barrett sought to suppress the confession since he had not agreed to having his confession written, but the court refused, finding that the defendant had fully understood the Miranda warnings and had voluntarily waived the right to an attorney. Barrett was subsequently convicted. The decision was appealed to the Connecticut Supreme Court. The court reversed, holding that when Barrett had expressed his desire for the presence of his counsel before making written statements, he had invoked his right to counsel and had not waived that right. The evidence should not have been admitted. The case was appealed to the U.S. Supreme Court and it granted certiorari. The Court disagreed, holding that voluntary confessions are admissible even when a suspect has not waived his right to an attorney or to making a written confession. The Court also held that the respondent's statement to the police demonstrated his willingness to talk about the sexual assault. In this case, there was no evidence that he had been "threatened, tricked, or cajoled" into speaking to the police. His actions, therefore, constituted a voluntary waiver of his right to counsel.

Arizona v. Roberson
486 U.S. 675 (1988)

Roberson was arrested for a burglary and given his Miranda warnings. He told police that he wished to remain silent until after consulting with his attorney. Three days later, while still in custody, a different police officer approached Roberson about his involvement in another crime unrelated to the current charges pending against him. Before interrogating Roberson about the new charges, the officer gave Roberson the Miranda warnings. Roberson made a full confession and was subsequently convicted. He appealed the decision, arguing that his confession should have been suppressed. The prosecution's position was that he had confessed to a separate crime after receiving his Miranda warnings from another officer. Nevertheless, the U.S. Supreme Court set aside Roberson's conviction on the grounds that police may not interrogate a suspect after he or she has invoked the right to remain silent or without his or attorney present. The Court warned that the ruling does not bar defendants from initiating further conversations with police on their own. To do so would make their confessions and incriminating statements admissible in court. Moreover, the Court argued that although Roberson's confession had involved another crime, the confession was immaterial.

Patterson v. Illinois
487 U.S. 285 (1988)

Patterson was arrested on suspicion of murder. He was interrogated twice by the police, and each time, he was read his Miranda rights and signed a waiver of them in order to converse with the police voluntarily. During this period, he made several incriminating statements. At trial, he filed a motion to suppress the statements. The motion was denied and he was subsequently convicted of murder. He appealed the case to the state supreme court. His conviction was affirmed by the court, which disagreed with his contention that while he had been properly Mirandized under the Fifth Amendment, he had been inadequately informed of his Sixth Amendment right to counsel. The U.S. Supreme Court granted certiorari. The Court held that the defendant's claim that his Sixth Amendment right to counsel had been violated because he had not "knowingly and intelligently" waived his right was without merit. The Constitution only requires that the accused be sufficiently made aware of his or her right to have counsel present and of the possible consequences of a decision to proceed without counsel. The Court also held that since the right to counsel is included in the Miranda warnings and since the Miranda warnings had been given to Patterson twice, he had twice waived his right to counsel. His conviction was therefore upheld.

Pennsylvania v. Bruder
488 U.S. 9 (1988)

Bruder was stopped by police officers after they had seen him driving erratically and running a red light. Before the officers exited their car to approach Bruder, they were approached by Bruder, who smelled of alcohol and was stumbling. The officers quickly administered several field sobriety tests, which Bruder failed. The officers asked Bruder if he had been drinking and he said that he had but that he was on his way home. Police placed him under arrest and gave him the Miranda warnings. At trial, his statements and conduct were admitted into evidence and Bruder was subsequently convicted of DWI. On appeal, the Pennsylvania Supreme Court reversed the conviction, holding that Bruder's statements made during the roadside interrogation had been given prior to his arrest and before he was provided the Miranda warnings. Thus, the evidence should have been suppressed. The U.S. Supreme Court granted review. The Court ruled that since Bruder was not in a coercive situation when answering police questions before the arrest, he was not entitled to the Miranda warnings. Therefore, any statements made before his arrest were legally admissible in court. His DWI conviction was ruled valid and upheld.

Duckworth v. Eagan
492 U.S. 195 (1989)

Gary Eagan was arrested in connection with a stabbing. He was interrogated by Indiana police who gave him a general Miranda statement to sign. The form provided Eagan with a general understanding of his rights according to Miranda, but the Miranda warnings explained on the form were not as specific as the warnings usually given to suspects before an interrogation. The form specified that Eagan had a right to an attorney and that if he could not afford one, an attorney would be provided free if and when the case went to court. Eagan made incriminating statements to police officers. The next day, he was again given a Miranda form to sign, and he signed it. Again, he was interrogated by officers and confessed. He led officers to a site where they recovered relevant physical evidence. At trial, Eagan filed a motion to suppress the statements, but his motion was denied. He was subsequently convicted of attempted murder. On appeal, the Indiana Supreme Court upheld his conviction for attempted murder. Eagan sought a writ of habeas corpus from the district court, claiming that his confession was inadmissible because the first Miranda warnings form had not complied with the requirements created by Miranda. The district court denied the petition, holding that the record conformed to Miranda. The court of appeals reversed on the grounds that the phrase "if he could not afford [an attorney], an attorney would be provided free if and when the case went to court" was constitutionally defective. The U.S. Supreme Court granted review. The Court reversed, holding that the Miranda warnings do not have to be given in the exact form as indicated in *Miranda*; rather, they must reasonably convey to a suspect his or her rights.

Minnick v. Mississippi
490 U.S. 146 (1990)

Shortly after escaping from a Mississippi county jail, Minnick and James Dyess murdered two men while committing a burglary. Minnick fled to California, where he was arrested four months later by the Lemon Grove Police. The next day, FBI agents advised Minnick of his right to an attorney and his right not to answer their questions. During this time, Minnick made a partial confession to FBI agents (though he advised them to come back Monday when he would have an attorney present). On that same day, Minnick was appointed an attorney who advised him to say nothing. The following Monday, a deputy sheriff from Mississippi flew to the San Diego jail where Minnick was held. Minnick was told by the jailers that he had to talk. As a result, he related all the incidents following his jail escape and admitted to committing one of the murders. At trial, Minnick moved to have the confessions suppressed, but the court denied the motion. He was subsequently convicted on two counts of capital murder and sentenced to death. On appeal, Minnick moved to suppress his statements given to the FBI agents and to the deputy sheriff on the grounds that the confessions had violated his Sixth Amendment right to counsel. The state supreme court rejected his motion, holding that Minnick had already been assigned and had consulted with an attorney. The U.S. Supreme Court granted review. The Court reversed and remanded the decision, holding that when counsel is requested, interrogations must cease and officials may not reinitiate interrogating the suspect without the attorney present.

Pennsylvania v. Muniz
496 U.S. 582 (1990)

Police stopped Muniz because they had suspected him of driving under the influence of alcohol. The police then gave Muniz several field sobriety tests, which he failed. Muniz told police that he had failed their tests because he had been drinking. Muniz was then arrested and taken into police custody. At the station house, police asked if he would be willing to take the same tests again but this time to be recorded on video. He agreed, and again he failed all of their tests. Muniz was also asked to submit to a breathalyzer test, which he refused. At this time, police read Muniz his Miranda rights for the first time, and he stated once more that he had been drinking and driving. At trial, the videotape and his confession were introduced into evidence. He was subsequently convicted. He appealed, arguing that he should be entitled to a new trial because the court should have excluded the videotape. Muniz argued that the videotape should have been suppressed because it had been made before he had been given the Miranda warnings. The Pennsylvania Superior Court reversed, holding that Muniz's answers to questions and his other verbalizations were testimonials and that therefore the audio portions of the tape should have been suppressed in their entirety. The case was appealed to the U.S. Supreme Court and it granted review. The Court upheld Muniz's DWI conviction, holding that the videotaping and questioning of Muniz before he had been given his Miranda warnings constituted routine questioning and other procedures common to DWI stops. Moreover, police may videotape suspected drunk drivers and ask routine questions.

Illinois v. Perkins
496 U.S. 292 (1990)

Perkins was arrested and jailed for having committed aggravated battery. While in jail, he was approached by his cell mate, Parisi (an undercover agent), and questioned. Perkins began to talk voluntarily to Parisi and provided him with information about crimes he had committed that were unrelated to his incarceration. When Parisi asked him if he had ever killed anybody, Perkins made statements implicating himself in a murder. These statements were used to charge him with the murder. At trial, Perkins contended that the undercover agent had failed to provide him with his Miranda warnings before the interrogation and that therefore Perkins's statements should not have been introduced into evidence. The court agreed and granted Perkin's motion to suppress the confession. The case was appealed, and the appellate court of Illinois affirmed, holding that Miranda prohibits all undercover contacts with incarcerated suspects that are reasonably likely to elicit incriminating responses. The case was appealed to the U.S. Supreme Court and it granted review. The Court rejected this ruling, holding that the Miranda warnings are not required whenever suspects provide voluntary statements to persons they do not believe are law-enforcement officers. Miranda warnings should be provided in coercive environments. However, in this case, an environment dominated by police was lacking.

Michigan v. Harvey
494 U.S. 344 (1990)

Harvey was arrested for having committed a rape. He was arraigned and provided legal counsel. Initially, he wanted to make a statement to police, but he did not know if he should wait for his lawyer to be present. Police officers advised Harvey that his lawyer did not have to be present for him to make a statement since his lawyer would later be provided with a copy of the interrogation. Harvey signed a waiver form and made incriminating statements to police without his lawyer present. At trial, Harvey gave conflicting accounts about his involvement in the crime; the police then introduced his earlier statements. He was subsequently convicted of first-degree criminal sexual conduct. The case was appealed. The Michigan Court of Appeals reversed, holding that Harvey's statements were inadmissible, even for impeachment, because they had been taken in violation of Harvey's Sixth Amendment right to counsel. The case was appealed to the U.S. Supreme Court and it granted review. The Court disagreed with the appeals court and reinstated Harvey's conviction, holding that statements to police taken in violation of the *Jackson* rule may be used to impeach a defendant's testimony in court. The Court argued that Harvey's statements had been initiated by Harvey and not by the police.

Arizona v. Fulminante
499 U.S. 279 (1991)

Fulminante was suspected of having killed his eleven-year-old stepdaughter. After questioning him for committing an unrelated felony, the police lacked adequate evidence to charge him, so they released him. He subsequently left Arizona and moved to New York. He was arrested and convicted for another crime. While in prison, his cell mate (Anthony Sarivola, a paid informant) told him that the talk in prison was that Fulminante was a "child murderer" and that he should be careful because his life was in jeopardy: inmates have a disdain for inmates who have preyed on youth. Fulminante's cell mate offered him protection from the other inmates in exchange for his confession to the murder of his daughter. Fulminate accepted the protection and confessed to his cell mate and later to his cell mate's wife. Fulminante was later charged with first-degree murder in Arizona. At trial, Fulminante filed a motion to suppress the confessions he had made to Sarivola and his wife, contending that they had been coerced and had therefore violated his Fifth and Sixth Amendment rights, but the court denied the motion. He was subsequently convicted of murder and sentenced to death. On appeal, the state supreme court held that the confession had been coerced. It remanded the case for a new trial without the confession. The U.S. Supreme Court granted review. The Court held that the "harmless error" doctrine exists to govern involuntary confessions but that the government had failed to show harmless error beyond a reasonable doubt. In this case, the Court argued that the trial judge had erred by permitting a coerced confession to be used against Fulminante.

McNeil v. Wisconsin
501 U.S. 171 (1991)

Paul McNeil was arrested and charged with committing armed robbery in West Allis, Wisconsin. He requested and was represented by a court-appointed lawyer. While in police custody, McNeil signed a waiver of his Miranda rights and began to talk to police officers about his involvement in the robbery in West Allis. He also made incriminating statements about his involvement in a murder committed in Caledonia, Wisconsin. After the interrogation, he was charged with the murder. During the pretrial motion, he asked that his incriminating statements be suppressed. The request was denied and McNeil was subsequently convicted. On appeal, the state supreme court affirmed his conviction, holding that a suspect's request for counsel at an initial appearance does not constitute an invocation of his Sixth Amendment right to counsel that precludes police interrogation concerning unrelated offenses. McNeil argued that he should have been told his rights for each of the crimes for which he had been charged. The U.S. Supreme Court granted review. The Court affirmed the decision of the state supreme court by rejecting McNeil's claim that the Sixth Amendment right to counsel also implies invoking the Miranda rights and the Fifth Amendment protection against self-incrimination. The Court argued that such a hard and fast rule would seriously impede effective law enforcement by precluding uncoerced admissions of guilt pursuant to valid Miranda warnings.

REFERENCES

Adler, F., Mueller, G., & Laufer, W. (1996). *Criminal justice: The core.* New York: McGraw-Hill.

Black, H. C. (1979). *Black's law dictionary: With pronunciations.* St. Paul: MN: West.

Bohm, R. M. & Haley, K. N. (1999). *Introduction to criminal justice* (2nd ed.). New York: Glencoe/McGraw-Hill.

Champion, D.J. (1999). *Criminal Justice in the United States* (2nd. ed.). Chicago: Nelson-Hall.

Fagin, J. A. (2003). *Criminal justice.* Boston: Allyn & Bacon.

Gaines, L, & Miller, R. L. (2004). *Criminal justice in action: The core.* Belmont, CA: Thomson/Wadsworth.

Grilliot, H. J. (1983). *Introduction to law and the legal system* (3rd ed.). Boston: Houghton Miffin.

Inciardi, J. A. (1987). *Criminal justice* (2nd ed.). Orlando, FL: Harcourt Brace Jovanovich.

Inciardi, J. A. (1999). *Criminal justice* (6th ed.). Orlando, FL: Harcourt Brace.

Klotter, J. C. (1996). *Legal guide for police: Constitutional issues* (4th ed.). Cincinnati: Anderson.

Klotter, J. C. (2002). *Legal guide for police: Constitutional issues* (6th ed.). Cincinnati: Anderson.

Light, S.C. (1999). *Understanding criminal justice.* Belmont, CA: West/Wadsworth.

Meltzer, M. (1972). *The right to remain silent.* San Diego: Harcourt.

Moskovitz, M. (2000). *Cases and problems in criminal procedures: The police* (3rd ed.). New York: Lexis.

Neubauer, D. W. (1999). *America's courts and the criminal justice system* (6th ed.). Belmont, CA: West/Wadsworth.

Peoples, E. E. (2003). *Basic criminal procedures* (2nd ed.). Upper Saddle River, NJ: Prentice Hall.

Robin, G. D. (1987). *Introduction to the criminal justice system* (3rd ed.). New York: Harper & Row.

Samaha, J. (1994). *Criminal justice* (3rd ed.). St. Paul, MN: West.

Scheb, J. M., & Scheb, J. M. (1999). *Criminal law & procedure.* Belmont, CA: West/ Wadsworth.

Schmalleger, F. (2001). Criminal justice today: *An introductory text for the twenty-first century* (6th ed.). Upper Saddle River, NJ: Prentice Hall.

Senna, J. J., & Siegel, L. J. (1998). *Essentials of criminal justice* (2nd ed.). Belmont, CA: West/Wadsworth.

Stuckey, G. B., Robinson, C., & Wallace, H. (2004). *Procedures in the justice system.* Upper Saddle River, NJ: Pearson-Prentice Hall.

Wasby, S. L. (1989). *The Supreme Court in the federal judicial system* (3rd ed.). Chicago: Nelson-Hall.

Weston, P. B., & Wells, K. M. (1976). *Criminal evidence for police* (2nd ed.). Englewood Cliffs, NJ: Prentice Hall.

Zalman, M. (1991). Reflections on *Arizona v. Fulminante*—Harmless error, coerced confessions and precedent (working paper, November 1991).

Cases Cited

Arizona v. Fulminante, 499 U.S. 279 (1991)

Arizona v. Mauro, 481 U.S. 520 (1986)

Arizona v. Roberson, 486 U.S. 675 (1988)

Ashcraft v. Tennessee, 322 U.S. 143 (1944)

Brewer v. Williams, 430 U.S. 387 (1977)

Brown v. Mississippi, 297 U.S. 278 (1936)

California v. Prysock, 453 U.S. 355 (1981)

California Attorneys for Criminal Justice, et al. v. Butts, et al., Ninth Circuit Court of Appeals No. 97-56499

Chapman v. California, 386 U.S. 18 (1967)

Colorado v. Spring, 479 U.S. 564 (1984)

Colorado v. Connelly, 479 U.S. 157 (1986)

Connecticut v. Barrett, 479 U.S. 523 (1987)

Pennsylvania v. Bruder, 488 U.S. 9 (1988)

Pennsylvania v. Muniz, 496 U.S. 582 (1990)

Rhode Island v. Innis, (No. 78-1076; decided 12 May 1980)

Smith v. Illinois, 469 U.S. 91 (1984)

Twining v. New Jersey, 211 U.S. 78 (1908)

United States v. Blocker, 354 F. Supp. 1195 (D.D.C. 1973)

United States v. Carra, 604 F.2d 1271 (10th Cir. 1979)

United States v. Leon, 82 Led 677 (1984)

United States v. Tingle, 658 F. 2D 1332 (9th Cir. 1981)

CHAPTER 9

Suspect Identification Procedures

Focal Points

- Legal Basis for Suspect Identification Procedures
- Identification Procedures Defined and Classified
- External and Internal Identification Procedures
- External Identification Procedures
    - Computer-Generated Composites
    - Showups
    - Photographic Arrangements
    - Lineups
    - Lineups: Self-Incrimination Challenge
    - Lineups: Right-to-Counsel Challenge
- Internal Identification Procedures
    - Blood Samples
    - Dental Examination
    - Voice Exemplars
    - Handwriting Exemplars
    - Fingerprint Analysis
    - Footprint Samples
- Deoxyribonucleic Acid Tests or DNA Profiling
- Some Pertinent Cases

Introduction

Some legal experts argue that there is nothing more compelling than for police officers to get suspects to sign a confession stating that they are guilty of the charges pending against them. If a prosecutor presents a signed confession to a judge presiding in a bench or jury trial, it is highly likely that the state will prevail in its case and win a criminal conviction against the accused. However, when police are unable to get a suspect to confess to his or her involvement in a crime, police usually rely on several investigative techniques to link the suspect to the crime. These methods include the use of forensic science and procedures to determine if victims and witnesses can identify the suspect. While some of the identification procedures are more intrusive than others (e.g., DNA, surgery, blood samples), police officers must be aware of the constitutional protections the U.S. Supreme Court has provided for each procedure. A failure to be thus aware could mean that a suspect's conviction will be overturned during the appeals process on a legal technicality, since some procedures of identification are more limited and restricted than others.

Concerning identification procedures, suspects often raise a number of constitutional challenges that stem from the Fourth, Fifth, and Sixth Amendments. For example, suspects often allege that the police search-and-seizure of evidence used in the identification process presents an unreasonable intrusion, thus violating their Fourth Amendment right. Suspects often argue that if the state requires them to participate in any investigation in order to assist the state in proving its case, the requirement violates their Fifth Amendment right to be free from self-incrimination (the Amendment guarantees that suspects or defendants cannot be compelled to be witnesses against themselves). The Sixth Amendment provides suspects with the right to an attorney to represent their legal interests. However, an issue that sometimes emerges is whether suspects are entitled to legal representation during the pretrial stage or the identification process. In addition, two other issues emerge: Is the identification process a critical stage of police investigation that requires the presence of an attorney? Is the presence of an attorney required only when police have focused on a particular suspect and have shifted from the investigatory phase of the criminal justice process to the accusatory one?

Chapter 9 is divided into four parts. Part One explains the legal basis for suspect identification procedures. Part Two defines and classifies identification procedures. Part Three explains both external and internal identification procedures used in police investigations. Part Four presents some pertinent cases related to various court rulings on suspect identification procedures.

PART ONE: LEGAL BASIS FOR SUSPECT IDENTIFICATION PROCEDURES

A *lineup* is a police identification procedure used when a suspect in a criminal investigation is kept in custody at a police station. The suspect is exhibited before the victim or witness to determine if he or she can be identified as the person whom the victim or witness recognizes as having committed the offense. While the U.S. Constitution has not provided law-enforcement officers with any explicit right to conduct such a proceeding, suspects are afforded some degree of protection. In fact, the constitutional issues concerning the use of testimonial procedures such as lineups and showups have generally focused on the fairness of the identification procedures and on the suspect's rights. As a general rule, the more intrusive the procedure, the greater the degree of constitutional protection given the suspect. del Carmen (2004) contends that suspects subjected to identification procedures often invoke the right to counsel, the right to due process, the right to protection against unreasonable searches and seizures, and the right to privilege against self-incrimination. The U.S. Supreme Court has stated that identification procedures cannot be conducted haphazardly but must be performed in a constitutionally correct manner. For example, to be accepted as valid, a lineup or other identification procedure must meet certain standards and be free of undue suggestiveness (see *United States v. Wade* and *Gilbert v. California*). If the procedure is conducted properly, the person performing the identification procedure may also testify against the suspect during trial. Moreover, the Court has ruled that a postindictment lineup is a critical stage of the criminal proceedings when the accused should have his or her counsel present to represent his or her legal interests. Furthermore, courts have ruled that the use of a one-person lineup or placing a suspect in a lineup with others of different body types is prohibited (see *Dozie v. State*) because the inference can be drawn that law-enforcement officials could be leading the witness to conclude that the suspect has already been identified.

Despite the protections provided to suspects in testimonial procedures, the U.S. Supreme Court has not extended the same level of protection to suspects in nontestimonial procedures. For example, in *Schmerber v. California*, the Court ruled that the forced extraction of a blood sample from a defendant who had been accused of driving while intoxicated was admissible at trial. In *United States v. Dionisio*, the Court held that a suspect could be forced to provide voice exemplars. Also, in *United States v. Mara*, the Court held that a suspect could be compelled to provide a handwriting exemplar. Moreover, in *United States v. Ash*, the Court held that the Sixth Amendment does not grant the suspect the right to counsel at photographic displays conducted for the purpose of allowing a witness to attempt to identify an offender. Despite its earlier position on nontestimonial identification procedures, the Court held, in *Winston v. Lee*, that a suspect cannot be forced to undergo surgery to remove a bullet from his chest even though probable cause exists that the surgery would produce evidence of a crime. The Court reasoned that such an identification procedure was too intrusive and therefore deserved greater constitutional protection.

Part Two: Identification Procedures Defined and Classified

Identification procedures are defined as the strategies and techniques used by police to link suspects to crime. They can be divided into two categories: testimonial methods and nontestimonial exemplars. Testimonial methods are typically showups, lineups, or photographic arrangements. Nontestimonial exemplars include examinations of voice, blood, handwriting, and other specimens used as evidence. According to Black (1979), police engage in identification procedures to prove that "a person, suspect, subject, or article before the court is the very same that he or it is alleged, charged, or reported to be; as where a witness recognizes the prisoner as the same person whom he saw committing the crime; or where handwriting, stolen goods, counterfeit coins, etc., are recognized as the same which once passed under the observation of the person identifying them." Identification procedures include external and internal procedures.

Part Three: External and Internal Identification Procedures

Though police officers use a number of techniques to identify suspects, they typically can be placed in two general categories. First, police may apply forensic science methods to physical evidence on the suspect or to evidence left at the crime scene by the suspect to determine his or her involvement in criminal activity. Using forensic science methods means applying scientific principles to legal issues. Second, police may rely on a variety of techniques that allow victims or eyewitnesses to identify the suspects of crime (Bohm & Haley, 1999). In the past, police have used forensic practices that have included the analyses of blood samples, clothing fibers, semen, voice exemplars, and handwriting samples; comparisons between head and body hair; and dental examinations. However, two recent developments in scientific investigations have increased the likelihood that suspects will be identified after committing a crime. These methods include DNA profiling and an automated fingerprint identification system. The forensic practices—both those used in the past and those recently developed—yield what is referred to as nontestimonial identification evidence. When police use these procedures, defendants often argue that such practices constitute violations of their protection against self-incrimination, of their right to counsel, and of their protection against unreasonable searches and seizures.

Police officers rely upon several types of external and internal identification procedures to connect suspects to crime. External identification procedures include computer-generated composites, showups, photographic arrangements, and lineups. Internal identification procedures include the examination of blood samples, dental examination, voice exemplars, handwriting exemplars, fingerprint analysis, foot print samples, and DNA profiling. Though police officers prefer having both, either type of identification procedure can be an effective tool in winning a criminal conviction.

External Identification Procedures

Computer-Generated Composites

Many police departments are now capitalizing on new technology to bring criminal offenders to justice (Pliant, 1994). According to Schmitz (1994), computers allow police agencies to share information on cases, suspects, and warrants. In fact, computers can link neighboring law-enforcement agencies together to prevent crimes. By using computers, local departments now share computerized databases to record crime-related information, motor vehicle and business data, worker's compensation files, and other public records that can assist officers in tracking felons. Computers can also be used to expedite the analysis of evidence. For example, Olson (1988) reports that computer technology is so exact that offenders with brown cars and facial scars can be cross-referenced. In his research, Schmitt (1992) finds that some police departments are actually replacing antiquated mug books with computerized imaging systems. These imaging systems, or identification programs, were created to help victims and witnesses create composite pictures of the perpetrators of crime. Schmitt also reports that computer files can store the equivalent of a library of photographs and can draw facial features that can be easily accessed on a terminal screen. This technology allows victims and witnesses to scan through literally thousands of lips, eyes, noses, caps, kinds of hair, and other features until they find the features that match those of the suspect. Moreover, these computer programs allow for the addition of eyeglasses, mustaches, skin tone, and beards. When the composite has been generated, an attached camera makes a hard copy to be circulated through the law-enforcement community.

Rau (1991) argues that new technology and techniques are constantly being developed to assist law-enforcement officers in identifying criminal suspects. For example, some police departments have been introduced to genetic algorithms (mathematical models), a computerized composite image of a suspect's face that can be constructed with very little information. Moreover, officers are now being introduced to digitized photography, which allows them to reconstruct more clearly the blurred images that are commonly found on the videotapes of convenience stores and banks after they have been robbed. From the inception of this technology to the present, experts have remained optimistic over the use of computer-generated composites, believing it helps in the identification process on two fronts. First, it allows victims and witnesses to create a composite or sketch of the perpetrators of the crimes. Second, during the booking process, a computer assists in the identification of suspects since it can store an image of the suspect on its hard drive. This capability allows a police department to create a photo lineup on the computer's monitor of all suspects with particular characteristics described by victims and witnesses (Senna & Siegel, 1998). Another identification procedure that police have traditionally used to connect suspects to their crimes is showups.

Showups

A *showup* is a quick identification procedure used by police officers to determine whether or not a particular suspect has committed the crime in question (see *Jones v. State*). del Carmen (2004) defines a *showup* as a one-to-one confrontation between a suspect and a witness to the crime conducted under circumstances that make a lineup impractical. Experts argue that during a showup, a victim's or witness's identification of a suspect is more likely to be reliable than a later identification since the memory of the crime is still fresh. During a showup, a suspect matching a description of the suspect by the victim or by a witness near the scene of the crime is returned to the crime scene to be identified by the injured party or the eyewitness (Gaines & Miller, 2004). Scheb and Scheb (1999) report that in some cases, the victim or witness is brought to the suspect for possible identification. In *People v. Love*, the court established that a showup is considered an acceptable method of obtaining identification. When a showup is at issue, courts are concerned with whether they were fair and whether the defendant's right to the presence of an attorney was recognized. The suspect is entitled to the presence of an attorney and to due process rights. However, he or she has no protection against self-incrimination or unreasonable searches and seizures.

While the suspect is entitled to the presence of an attorney, several events must occur before he or she can invoke such a right. For example, if police officers accost a male fitting the description of a young male who, minutes earlier, had burglarized someone's home and stolen a television set, the officers can request that the suspect return to the scene of the crime for the purpose of identification by the victim or the eyewitness. At this point, if the suspect requests an attorney, he has no constitutional right to one because he has not yet been charged with a crime (see *Kirby v. Illinois*). (In *Kirby*, after Kirby and his alleged accomplice, Ralph Bean, were arrested, police officers brought Willie Shard, the robbery victim, to a room in a police station where Kirby and Bean were seated at a table with two other police officers. Shard testified at trial that the officer who brought him into the room had asked him if Kirby and Bean were the robbers and that he had indicated they were). If the police officer allows the suspect to drive himself to the scene of the crime for identification purposes, is the suspect in custody or is he or she under arrest? The U.S. Supreme Court has said that if police officers intend to question suspects, they must give them the Miranda warnings because the situation has progressed beyond a police lineup (del Carmen, 2004).

After suspects have been formally charged, they have the right to an attorney to represent their legal interests. The U.S. Supreme Court addressed this issue in *Moore v. Illinois*. In this case, Moore was convicted of rape according to a positive identification by the rape victim. The victim, along with a police officer, appeared in court at the preliminary hearing to determine if the case should go to a grand jury and to set bail. After the suspect appeared before the judge, the prosecutor asked the victim if she saw the perpetrator in court; the victim pointed to the suspect. Though the defense argued for suppression, the identification was admitted into trial and the suspect was subsequently convicted. On appeal, the Court overturned the conviction, holding that the admission of the identification violated the defendant's right to counsel because criminal proceedings had begun and the defendant was therefore entitled to an attorney.

In *Neil v. Biggers* and *Stovall v. Denno*, the U.S. Supreme Court addressed the issue of due process during showups. In *Neil*, Biggers was suspected of rape. The rape had occurred in full moonlight, so the victim had the opportunity to see the rapist clearly. Prior to Biggers's arrest, the victim had participated in a showup and in a lineup and had viewed photographs of other rape suspects. At no time did she identify any other suspect as her attacker. Police arrested Biggers seven months later on information supplied by an informant. Biggers was brought before the victim alone. The police showed the victim the defendant's orange shirt and asked if she could identify the defendant's voice from an adjoining room. No other voices were provided for comparison. Biggers was convicted, largely on the victim's testimony. He challenged the conviction, contending that his identification by the victim had been "suggestive." The Court held that though the confrontation procedure was suggestive, the totality of circumstances made the identification reliable. Specifically, the Court held that a station-house identification based on the viewing of a single suspect was admissible into evidence on the basis of the totality of the circumstances. The factors to be considered in evaluating the likelihood of misidentification include the opportunity of the witness to view the criminal at the time of the crime; the witness's degree of attention to the suspect during the crime; the accuracy of the witness's prior description of the criminal; and the level of certainty demonstrated by the witness at the confrontation.

In *Stovall v. Denno*, Stovall was a suspect in the murder of Dr. Behrendt. The victim's wife was severely injured and was admitted into a hospital, where her condition was critical. Police officers brought Stovall (who had been arrested the day after the murder and had not been given time to obtain a lawyer) to the hospital, where he was identified by the victim's wife as the murderer. The identification was introduced at trial. Stovall was subsequently convicted and sentenced to death. He appealed his conviction to the U.S. Supreme Court and it granted certiorari. Stovall contended that his due process rights had been violated. The Court rejected Stovall's contention, holding that under the circumstances, the victim's wife was the only person in the world who could exonerate Stovall by simply saying, "He is not the man." Under the circumstances of *Stovall*, the police identification method was proper. The hospital was not far from the courthouse and jail. The usual police lineup that Stovall believed to be appropriate was totally out of the question, given the victim's wife's condition in the hospital. Thus, traditional lineups may be circumvented depending upon the circumstances.

The Fourth Amendment protection against unreasonable searches and seizures does not extend to showups because they are not considered unreasonable searches or seizures: their level of intrusiveness is very limited in scope. For example, when suspects are taken by police to the scene of a crime, identification is relatively quick, and when searches are conducted, they are minimal. Moreover, because of exigent circumstances, officers are not required to procure a search warrant. At the same time, suspects cannot claim that participating in showups constitutes self-incrimination because a showup is physical and not testimonial or communicative. Therefore, there is no violation of a protection against self-incrimination.

Photographic Arrangements

Photographic identification is another technique police officers use to connect suspects to crimes. For some departments, however, this method has been replaced by the recent development of computer-generated composites. Other departments still use the older process of showing "mug shots" of possible offenders to victims and eyewitnesses in the hope that police officers can make a positive identification of the perpetrator. When positive identifications are made, officers make efforts to bring the suspect in for questioning. Because photographic identification is typically conducted in the absence of the suspect, some experts question whether suspects should be afforded some level of constitutional protection, such as the Sixth Amendment right to have a lawyer present or the Fifth Amendment due process considerations. Specifically, some question whether the photographic identification process is inherently prejudicial against a suspect, thereby necessitating the presence of an attorney to represent the suspect's legal interests. This issue was addressed in *United States v. Wade*. In *Wade*, the U.S. Supreme Court argued that "the dangers of mistaken identification ... set forth in *Wade* are applicable in large measure to photographic, as well as corporeal identifications." In *Simmons v. United States*, the U.S. Supreme Court established that while mistakes are common during identifications generally, the dangers of misidentification are greater in a photographic display than in a lineup. In *Simmons*, the Court stated that photographic displays are impermissibly suggestive for several reasons. First, the photography may suggest which of the pictures is that of the suspect. For example, differences in age, pose, or other physical characteristics of the persons represented, as well as variations in the mounting and background lighting or markings of the photographs, may single out the accused (Weston & Wells, 1976). Second, impermissible suggestions may lie in how the photographs are displayed to the eyewitness. For example, the danger of misidentification is increased if the police display several pictures to the witness of a single individual. The danger is also increased if the photographs are arranged in an asymmetrical pattern or if they are displayed in a time sequence that emphasizes a particular photograph. Third, gestures or verbal comments from the prosecutor during the time the photographs are displayed may lead an uncertain witness to select the "correct" photograph. For example, the prosecutor may suggest to the eyewitness that he has more evidence that one of the persons pictured committed the crime and may even point to a particular photograph and ask if any one of the persons in the picture looks familiar (Weston & Wells, 1976). Thus, an improper photographic identification procedure can often lead to a mistaken identification. When such a mistake occurs, the eyewitness is more inclined to retain the image in the photograph than to remember the actual suspect. Therefore, the witness has already determined the identity of the suspect before the trial (*United States v. Wade*).

When impermissible and suggestive identifications are made, they can be detrimental to the suspect during trial for several reasons. First, the presentation of the photographs affords little protection to and may even disadvantage the accused. For example, photographs may reveal little to the defense counsel on how they were displayed to the eyewitnesses. Second, the accused cannot rely on the witness to either detect or expose the three sources of suggestion. Third, the accused is not present at the photographic identification. As a result, irregularities in the process are not revealed. For example, in *Wade*, the Court stated:

> When the defendant is present—as he is during a lineup—he may personally observe the circumstances, report them to his attorney, and (if he chooses to take the stand) testify about them at trial.... In the absence of an accused, on the other hand, there is no one present to verify the fairness of the interview or to report any irregularities. If the prosecution were tempted to engage in "sloppy or biased or fraudulent" conduct, ... it would be far more likely to do so when the accused is absent then when he is himself being "used."

The *Wade* decision revealed that both photographic and corporeal identifications create a grave danger that an innocent defendant might be convicted simply because of his or her inability to expose a tainted identification. Therefore, the Court concluded that, considering logic, consistency, and fairness, a pretrial photographic identification is a "critical stage of the prosecution at which [the accused is] as much entitled to such aid [by counsel] ... as at the trial itself." Essentially, in *Wade*, the Court held that the Sixth Amendment right to counsel applies to indicted defendants who are required to participate in lineups. The rule is applicable to the states through the due process clause of the Fourteenth Amendment.

Lineups

Of the many types of identification techniques used by police, perhaps the one best known and most often used is the lineup identification procedure. Lineups occur at police stations when the suspect is placed together with several other persons and the victim or eyewitness is asked to pick out the suspect from the array of individuals (Inciardi, 1987). Champion (1997) argues that a lineup is a procedure in which police ask suspects to submit to being viewed together with others who resemble their personal characteristics by eyewitnesses to a crime. During this procedure, those involved in the lineup are usually similar in age, size, race and physical stature. For example, in *Foster v. California*, the suspect, who was six feet tall, was first placed in a lineup with three other men who were several inches shorter. He was wearing a leather jacket similar to the one the witness had seen worn by one of the robbers. The witness thought the suspect was the robber but was not absolutely sure. Several days later, police held another lineup, and the suspect was the only one in the second lineup who had also been in the first. The witness positively identified the suspect as the robber. The U.S. Supreme Court ruled against the identification process, stating that "in effect, the police repeatedly said to the witness, This is the man."

In most cases, suspects in a lineup may be asked to repeat earlier statements that were made at the time the crime was committed. Such statements typically include, "This is a stick up," and, "Give me your money." It is hoped that this confrontation with the suspect, along with the suspect's statements, will enable the victim or eyewitness to make a positive identification of the suspect. Like photographic identifications, some experts question whether suspects placed in an identification lineup are entitled to the Fifth and Sixth Amendment's rights to counsel and protections against self-incrimination. This issue was also addressed in *Wade*. In that case, the defendant had been shown to witnesses at a postindictment lineup without an attorney present. The U.S. Supreme Court ruled that such a condition created the chance that an unfair identification could occur. Hence, the Court ruled that a person subjected to pretrial lineup or showing is entitled to be represented by counsel during the procedure. At the same time, a lineup must represent the description given by the witness. *Wade* refers to only postindictment lineups and not to those that occur in the earlier phases of the criminal justice process (Inciardi, 1999).

Lineups: Self-Incrimination Challenge

Some defendants maintain that participation in a lineup violates their Fifth Amendment right against self-incrimination. They argue that being in a lineup makes them a witness against themselves. This challenge has not been successful in court. In *Wade*, the U.S. Supreme Court stated that requiring the accused merely to exhibit his or her person for observation by a prosecutor's witness before trial does not compel the accused to give evidence having testimonial significance. Moreover, in *Schmerber v. California*, the Court held that the mere viewing by an eyewitness of a suspect under arrest does not violate this constitutional right because the prisoner is not required to be an unwilling witness against himself or herself or to communicate ideas.

Lineups: Right-to-Counsel Challenge

The U.S. Supreme Court has stated that the postindictment lineup is a critical stage of the proceeding if the in-court identification of the accused can be jeopardized. The Court's reasoning is that if police conduct a lineup in a manner that suggests that a suspect is the one who committed the crime, there is a serious danger of misidentification at trial (see *United States v. Wade*). Despite its decision in *Wade*, the Court did not require counsel at all lineups and did not hold that the in-court identification should be disallowed (Klotter, 1996). Rather, the Court referred the case to the lower courts to give the prosecution an opportunity to show that the in-court identification was based on the crime-scene observation of the suspect that was not influenced by the lineup (Klotter, 1996). As a result, police can conduct as many lineups or confrontation procedures as they desire. However, if the eyewitness is to be used during trial, the suspect should have the benefit of an attorney to represent his or her legal interest. Under this circumstance, the failure to have an attorney for the suspect at the postindictment lineup does not contaminate the court identification. However, it could compel the prosecutor to show that the in-court identification was not influenced by a lineup without the presence of an attorney for the suspect (Klotter, 1996).

While *Wade* is considered a major case concerning suspect identification, it left several questions unanswered. For example, in *Wade*, the lineup was conducted after the indictment was handed down. After *Wade*, some experts questioned if the ruling applied to a police-station showup that occurred before the suspect was indicted or formally charged with a criminal offense. These questions were addressed in *Kirby v. Illinois*. In that case, the U.S. Supreme Court refused to extend the suspect's right to an attorney before the preindictment identification. In fact, the Court ruled:

> A showup after arrest, but before the initiation of any adversarial criminal proceeding (whereby way of formal charge, preliminary hearing, indictment, or arraignment) is not a criminal prosecution at which the accused, as a matter of absolute right, is entitled to counsel.

In *Kirby*, the Court held that the right to counsel is generally not required at the scene of arrest when an officer is merely trying to determine whether he or she has the correct suspect. However, the arresting officer must recognize that even though the presence of counsel may not be required during the preindictment confrontation, the in-court identification may be contaminated if the procedure is so suggestive that it violates the due process guarantee of the constitution (Klotter, 1996). Despite *Kirby*, some state courts extend the right to counsel to suspects at a lineup to formalize proceedings (see *People v. Bustamante, Blue v. State, People v. Jackson, Commonwealth v. Zabala*).

Internal Identification Procedures

Blood Samples

In *Breithaupt v. Abrams*, the U.S. Supreme Court demonstrated its willingness to allow blood samples to be used in criminal cases to gain a conviction. *Breithaupt* allowed reasonable bodily intrusions to ascertain evidence that a person has ingested a certain amount of alcohol. Breithaupt was the driver of a car that had collided with another vehicle, killing the occupants of the vehicle. The accident rendered him unconscious. While he received medical care in a nearby hospital, a police officer requested that a physician take a blood sample. The officer turned the sample over to the police department for analysis to determine whether Breithaupt was driving under the influence. At trial, the blood-sample evidence was entered at Breithaupt's objection. He was subsequently convicted of manslaughter. On appeal, Breithaupt argued that his constitutional rights had been violated because while unconscious, he could not give consent or waive his privilege against self-incrimination and that when the officer took his blood, his due process right had been violated. In this case, the Court held that blood was a nontestimonial body substance not protected by the Fifth Amendment guarantee against self-incrimination. Moreover, the Court claimed that there was nothing brutal or offensive in the way the blood sample had been taken by the physician and noted that many people often submit to such tests with proper medical precautions. Furthermore, the Court reasoned that though Breithaupt was unconscious, the procedure did not violate his constitutional rights (see also *Schmerber v. California*).

In *Schmerber v. California*, Schmerber was arrested for driving a vehicle while under the influence of alcohol. He was asked to submit to having his blood-alcohol content tested. On the advice of his attorney, he refused, but a blood sample was extracted by a physician at a hospital. At trial, Schmerber sought to suppress the evidence; however, the judge refused and he was subsequently convicted. He appealed the case. During the appeal, the defense claimed a violation of several constitutional rights that included the Fifth Amendment's protection against self-incrimination, the Sixth Amendment right to counsel, and unreasonable search-and-seizure within the meaning of the Fourth Amendment. In this case, the U.S. Supreme Court rejected Schmerber's claim of protection under the Fifth Amendment. The Court held that the protection against self-incrimination concerns evidence of a testimonial or communicative nature. Moreover, the extraction of a body fluid for chemical analysis was not a compelled testimony. The Court reasoned that because there was no violation of the Fifth Amendment protection against self-incrimination, there was little point in providing Schmerber with legal counsel. Nevertheless, the Court held that Schmerber was entitled to the Fourth Amendment protection against unreasonable searches. But it also held that there was no violation and that the search was reasonable within the meaning of the constitution because: (1) there was probable cause for arresting Schmerber and charging him with driving a vehicle while under the influence of intoxicating liquor; (2) the bodily intrusion could not be delayed while application was made to court for a search warrant because of the oxidation of alcohol in the human body with the passage of time; (3) there was no objection to the test on the grounds of fear, health, or religion; and (4) the search was performed in a reasonable manner.

Dental Examination

Another procedure that police use to identify suspects is a dental examination. Dental examinations typically occur when a suspect has left bite marks on the victim or the suspect has a distinctive gap or missing teeth that a victim or eyewitness can readily identify. For example, bite marks leave behind distinctive teeth patterns that are similar in many ways to fingerprints or footprints. Suspects may be required to submit to dental X-rays so that a dental examination can be used either to exclude them from or to implicate them in the commission of a crime. However, when police request that suspects submit to a dental examination, the suspects sometimes decline, contending that such a procedure would violate their protection against self-incrimination guaranteed under the Fifth Amendment. In *United States v. Holland*, the U.S. Supreme Court rejected this claim by a defendant. In *Holland*, the prosecution moved to admit dental-examination evidence after one of the witnesses remembered that the suspect had a missing tooth in a specific area of his mouth. The defense objected to the inclusion of the evidence, contending that it violated the defendant's Fifth Amendment rights. The district court, relying on *Schmerber*, concluded that the self-incrimination protection was not violated when the suspect was required to submit to a dental examination. The court also argued that there were no Fourth Amendment or due process violations. In fact, the court held that the compelled display of identifiable physical characteristics places no infringement on any constitutionally protected interests, especially not on compulsory self-incrimination (Klotter, 2002).

Voice Exemplars

Only some courts allow the admission of spectrographic evidence to link a suspect to a crime (Klotter, 2002). Courts on the federal level are divided on whether voice exemplars are reliable enough to use to identify suspects. Despite

United States v. Dionisio, in *United States v. Marvia*, the District Court of Hawaii concluded that the use of spectrographic evidence to identify voices is no longer considered unreliable and that expert testimony is admissible for voice-comparison purposes. In *Marvia*, the court proposed several protections when spectrographic analysis is offered: (1) two or more minutes of each speech sample; (2) a signal-to-noise ratio in which the signal is higher by twenty decibels; (3) a frequency of 3,000 hertz or higher; (4) an exemplar consisting of the same words spoken at the same rate and in the same way and spoken naturally and frequently; and (5) a responsible examiner (see also *United States v. Williams*). Moreover, in *United States v. Smith*, the Fifth Circuit Court of Appeals upheld the use of spectrographic voice identification and stated that expert testimony concerning the use of spectrographic voice analysis is admissible in cases in which a proponent of the testimony has established a proper foundation. Defendants who disagree with the admission of such evidence often contend that it is unreliable and that it violates constitutional protections, especially the protection against self-incrimination concerning evidence of a testimonial or communicative nature, as established in *Schmerber*. However, in several cases, the U.S. Supreme Court and circuit courts have argued that the admission of voice exemplars to establish a suspect's identity does not violate the Fifth Amendment protection against self-incrimination (see *United States v. Dionisio*, *Burnell v. Collins*, and *State v. Frasier*). In *Dionisio*, the U.S. Supreme Court argued that in keeping with the *Schmerber* decision, to compel a suspect to submit to a voice exemplar does not violate the Fifth Amendment because the exemplars were to be used for identification purposes and not for their testimonial or communicative content. Stated another way, a suspect can be compelled to provide a voice exemplar on the grounds that the recording will be used only to measure the physical properties of the suspect's voice as distinct from the content of what the suspect has said.

Handwriting Exemplars

Another procedure that police use to identify a suspect of a crime is to require him or her to submit a handwriting sample. Defendants often object to submitting such a sample on the grounds that it violates their Fifth Amendment protection against self-incrimination and the tenets of *Schmerber* that protect evidence of a communicative nature. They also argue that submitting such a sample deprives them of their Sixth Amendment right to have a lawyer present. The legality of admitting handwriting samples into evidence was addressed in *Gilbert v. California*. In that case, the U.S. Supreme Court ruled that a suspect can be compelled to provide a handwriting exemplar. The Court reasoned that the sample is not a testimony but an identifying physical characteristic. In fact, a mere handwriting exemplar, in contrast with the content of what is written, is an identifying physical characteristic, like the voice or body itself, and therefore outside the protection of the Constitution (see *United States v. Wade*). Moreover, the Court held that when police request that a person accused of a crime give a handwriting sample for analysis, this procedure does not represent a critical stage of the pretrial proceeding and therefore the petitioner is not entitled to an attorney since no indictment has yet occurred. Also, any threat to a fair trial can be addressed and corrected at the trial itself. Furthermore, unlike police-station lineups, there is nothing that police or prosecutors can do that is suggestive to witnesses. In addition, numerous additional handwriting samples can be made for comparison (Weston & Wells, 1976). The Court also held that while a person's handwriting is a means of communication, when identifying the physical characteristics of the handwriting rather than its content is of primary concern, compelling a person to write does not violate protections against self-incrimination since handwriting samples are nontestimonial evidence.

Fingerprint Analysis

Perhaps the oldest method of identifying a suspect as connected to a crime is the use of fingerprinting. Fingerprints are often found at the crime scene in some form: latent, partial, plastic, and other forms (Weston & Wells, 1976). While fingerprints stored at a police station can be compared without debate, some question whether police officers can request suspects to submit to fingerprint analysis. Critics contend that such a procedure must be guided by constitutional protections, namely, the Fourth and Fifth Amendments. This matter was first addressed in *Holt v. United States*. In *Holt*, the U.S. Supreme Court distinguished between compelling a person to give verbal evidence and requiring a person to have his or her fingerprints taken. Some legal experts argue that unless taken from police records, fingerprints used for comparisons must be taken by methods that are reasonable within the meaning of the Fourth Amendment. As a general rule, when fingerprints are not available for comparison, Weston and Wells (1976) argue that the safeguards of the Fourth Amendment apply to any intrusion to obtain them.

After *Schmerber*, the U.S. Supreme Court held that fingerprinting does not violate the self-incrimination protection of the constitution if the suspect is in custody and is requested to submit to photographing and fingerprinting as part of the routine identification process (*United States v. Smith*). Moreover, *Davis v. Mississippi* established that fingerprints can be taken if the suspect has been legally arrested. However, if the sole purpose of detention is to obtain fingerprints and the arrest is unjustified, the Fourth Amendment search-and-seizure protection is violated because the search is unreasonable. Nevertheless, in *Davis*, the U.S. Supreme Court stated that police can seek authorization from a judge to schedule a time for fingerprinting a suspect even when the suspect has not been formally arrested. However, police cannot engage in any form of interrogation.

There has been a new development in fingerprint technology. The automated fingerprint identification system allows investigators to sort through thousands of stored fingerprints for a match with those taken from criminal suspects. The older process required several people and thousands of man-hours (Bohm & Haley, 1999). Some experts argue that were it not for this new technology, many suspects would escape apprehension and avoid being identified and brought to justice.

Footprint Samples

While not as popular as fingerprinting, footprint samples are used to identify suspects when such evidence is found at the crime scene. For example, when the suspect steps into mud, onto a wet lawn, or into the victim's blood and leaves behind a shoe print, it may be the only clue or source of evidence that the police have to build a case. However, this type of evidence has not always been accepted. Prior to *Schmerber*, some courts prohibited the use of footprint-comparison evidence on the grounds that the suspect had been forced to place his or her foot in a print at a police station (Klotter, 2002). These courts viewed forced or active participation by the suspect as a form of self-incrimination prohibited by the Fifth Amendment since the suspect would be aiding the prosecution in making a case against him or her. However, after *Schmerber*, all courts accepted footprint-comparison evidence since this procedure does not require testimony or communicative evidence from suspects. Put differently, *Schmerber* allowed the inclusion of footprint evidence when police officers were trying to establish the identity of the perpetrators of crime.

Deoxyribonucleic Acid Tests or DNA Profiling

As stated earlier, one of the most innovative and recent procedures that police use to identify the perpetrators of crime is Deoxyribonucleuic Acid or DNA profiling (Senna & Siegel, 1998; Bohm & Haley, 1999; Klotter, 2002; del Carmen, 2004). DNA is a molecule that is present in every living organism. Researchers have made a significant breakthrough in using DNA sequences that are present in blood and other bodily fluids. These sequences are unique since they include a genetic profile that can be taken from blood, saliva, hair, semen, and other bodily substances found on a suspect or victim or at a crime scene. In fact, blood and other bodily fluids can be used as evidence to link a suspect to a crime since such evidence has an extremely high probability of identifying the perpetrators of a crime (Bohm & Haley, 1999). DNA experts contend that, depending on the technique used to analyze the DNA, tests can determine the degree of certainty (of up to 99.99 percent) that the DNA matches evidence taken from a suspect, victim, or crime scene. A DNA match indicates a four-billion-to-one chance that the suspect is the offender (Senna & Siegel, 1993). For this reason, proponents contend that DNA testing, when used properly, can easily exclude or isolate a suspect as the perpetrator of a crime.

Critics argue that if a laboratory performs sloppy procedures while conducting DNA and other forensic tests, lawyers should challenge the reliability of the evidence (Scheb & Scheb, 1999). Nevertheless, some wonder how courts have responded to the use of forensic-science technology to help gain a criminal conviction. According to articles in the *Pocono Record* (Stroudsburg, PA) (Associated Press, 1999a, 1999b; Associated Press, 2001a, 2001b, 2001c) and the *Honolulu Advertiser* ("DNA Tests Clear 3,000 Suspects," 1997; "Two Inmates Freed," 1997), by 1997, the FBI crime lab's DNA analysis unit had exonerated 3,000 suspects believed to have been the perpetrators of crime. Moreover, DNA evidence has been instrumental in the release of wrongfully convicted felons.

According to the decision in *Frye v. United States*, in admitting expert testimony deduced from a well-recognized scientific principle or discovery, the assumption from which the deduction was made must have been sufficiently established to be generally accepted by the specific field to which it belongs. Since 1923, *Frye* has been applied in federal and most state courts faced with the issue of whether new scientific tests should be admitted into evidence in a criminal trial. However, in 1993, the U.S. Supreme Court rejected *Frye* in *Daubert v. Marrell Dow Pharmaceutical*.

In light of discoveries and advances in DNA testing, several state supreme courts and some circuit courts have embraced the use of DNA in analyzing evidence as well as in establishing a suspect's identity. For example, the Minnesota Supreme Court ruled in *State v. Swartz* that forensic DNA typing is heralded as a significant breakthrough because it promises greater specificity of results and permits analysis of samples too small to be identified by traditional means. In *United States v. Bonds* and *United States v. Martinez*, the Sixth and Eighth Circuit Courts, respectively, ruled that while some states continuously allowed DNA tests in the 1980s, by the 1990s, the use of DNA profiles and identification was widespread and accepted as a credible technique. In *Martinez*, the Eighth Circuit Court stated:

DNA profiling is still relatively new as a forensic tool and has been the subject of heated controversy in both the legal and scientific communities. However, it is generally conceded that the principles of DNA profiling are recognized as reliable and the procedures are not so new or novel as to warrant this disagreement.

In *Martinez*, the court of appeals cited the ruling that the U.S. Supreme Court handed down in *Daubert v. Marrell Dow Pharmaceutical*. In that case, the Court argued that the admissibility of scientific evidence must be based on several factors, including whether the evidence can be tested and whether it can be subjected to peer review. As a result of *Daubert*, the Court requires that trial judges make a preliminary assessment of whether the methodology underlying the expert's testimony is scientifically valid and whether the methodology can be applied to the facts at issue. After the court determines admissibility, a jury determines the weight of the evidence. Despite the ruling in *Daubert*, most states still follow the ruling in *Frye*. During trial, there have been some criticisms concerning DNA evidence. They have not targeted DNA evidence per se but have focused on the procedures and methodologies of conducting DNA testing. Critics contend that sometimes DNA testing may fail to meet acceptable standards (see *United States v. Bonds*). However, as long as scientific evidence meets the conditions established in *Frye*, it is generally accepted.

Part Four: Some Pertinent Cases

Rochin v. California
342 U.S. 165 (1952)

Rochin, a suspect allegedly trafficking in narcotics, was visited by three Los Angeles sheriff's deputies one evening. The officers found him sitting on his bed partially dressed. Several white capsules were on a nearby nightstand in plain view. When the officers attempted to seize them, Rochin grabbed the capsules and swallowed them. The officers immediately brought Rochin to a nearby hospital and ordered physicians to give him an emetic solution to cause him to vomit. The capsules were obtained through a stomach pump and turned out to be morphine. At trial and without a jury, Rochin objected to the admission of the evidence, arguing that it violated his due process rights. The capsules were used against him in court, and he was subsequently convicted of violating California Health and Safety Code, 1947, 11,500. He was sentenced to sixty days in jail. He appealed his conviction, but the district court of appeals affirmed it. The Supreme Court of California denied Rochin's petition for a hearing. The U.S. Supreme Court granted review and reversed the decision, holding that the police officers had violated Rochin's Fifth Amendment protection against self-incrimination and the due process clause of the Fourteenth Amendment. Rochin's conviction was overturned because of the unreasonableness of the manner of the officers' search-and-seizure of the capsules. The Court labeled the police tactics offensive and "conduct that shocks the conscience."

Schmerber v. California
384 U.S. 757 (1966)

After a traffic accident, Schmerber was arrested in California for driving under the influence of alcohol. He was arrested and taken to a hospital to receive treatment for injuries he had sustained during the accident. At the direction of a police officer, a physician drew a sample of Schmerber's blood against his will. The chemical analysis of the sample revealed that Schmerber was intoxicated at the time of the accident. At trial, Schmerber objected to the introduction of the chemical analysis, arguing that the seizure of his blood had been unreasonable and had violated his Fourth Amendment rights. He also argued that his own blood used against him was tantamount to self-incrimination and that this action violated his Fifth Amendment rights. Furthermore, he argued that at the time the blood was taken, the state had not afforded him the opportunity to consult with an attorney, an action which violated his Sixth Amendment rights. The chemical analysis was allowed into court and Schmerber was subsequently convicted. The case was appealed, but the appeals court affirmed the conviction. The case was appealed to the U.S. Supreme Court and it granted review. The Court held that at the time of the arrest the police had probable cause and that therefore that same degree of certainty justified the police having Schmerber submit to a test of blood-alcohol content. Because of the time required to bring the petitioner to a hospital, the consequences of the delay in performing a blood-alcohol test, and the time needed to investigate the accident scene, there was no time to procure a warrant. These circumstances made the search incidental to an arrest.

United States v. Wade
388 U.S. 218 (1967)

Wade was a participant in a bank robbery. He drove away from the bank with an accomplice. Eyewitnesses saw them in the bank and gave descriptions to police. Wade was arrested and indicted for robbery. A lawyer was appointed for him. Later at the jail, police placed Wade in a lineup with other men for two bank employees to identify. Wade's attorney was not notified of the lineup. Each man wore strips of tape on his face, as the robber had allegedly done, and was directed to repeat the same words as those the robber had allegedly uttered during the crime. Both bank employees identified Wade as the robber. Later, at Wade's trial, the same bank employees again identified Wade as the robber. He moved to suppress the lineup identification from being admitted into evidence at trial on the grounds that it had violated his Fifth Amendment protection against self-incrimination and his Sixth Amendment right to counsel. His motion was denied, and he was subsequently convicted upon the testimony of the eyewitnesses. Wade appealed and moved to suppress their testimony because he had been subjected to a lineup without the benefit of his appointed counsel. The court of appeals reversed his conviction, holding that there had been no Fifth Amendment deprivation but that Wade had been denied the right to counsel during the lineup, which had violated his Sixth Amendment right. The case was appealed to the U.S. Supreme Court. The Court agreed with the court of appeals, holding that merely exhibiting the accused for observation by witnesses and using his or her voice as an identifying characteristic require no compulsion of the accused. Such actions do not violate the Fifth Amendment. The right to counsel is a Sixth Amendment guarantee that not only attaches during trial but also extends to any critical confrontation by the prosecution during pretrial proceedings when the result of the confrontation might determine one's fate.

Gilbert v. California
388 U.S. 263 (1967)

Gilbert was arrested by an FBI agent on charges that he had robbed a bank in Alhambra, California, and had killed an investigating police officer. During the robbery, Gilbert had given the bank teller a note demanding money. When the FBI agent interviewed Gilbert following his arrest, without an attorney present, Gilbert gave the agent some handwriting samples. These were incriminating because they matched the writing in the note at the scene of the bank robbery. Gilbert was subsequently convicted. He appealed, contending that his Fifth Amendment right against self-incrimination had been violated when he gave samples of his handwriting to the FBI agent. The U.S. Supreme Court granted review. The Court upheld Gilbert's conviction and rejected his Fifth Amendment claim, noting that handwriting samples are mere physical evidence, not evidence of "self-incrimination." Self-incrimination pertains to utterances and not documents that contain incriminating statements or content-specific information.

Simmons v. United States
390 U.S. 377 (1968)

Simmons was suspected of armed robbery of a federally insured savings and loans association. Following the robbery, witnesses were shown photographs of various suspects, including Simmons. A description of the getaway car yielded information leading to Simmons's mother's residence, which FBI visited and entered. They found inculpatory evidence in the home, including a gun holster, a sack similar to the one used in the robbery, and several bill wrappers from the bank that had been robbed. Simmons was charged with and convicted of the armed robbery. He appealed, contending that the search of his mother's home had not been performed by consent or with a warrant and that the photograph lineup of him was suggestive. The U.S. Supreme Court granted review. The Court rejected Simmons's contention that the lineup was suggestive and noted that at the trial five of the witnesses had positively identified Simmons. Simmons's conviction was upheld as valid.

Foster v. California
394 U.S. 440 (1969)

Clay Foster confessed to police the day after a robbery of a Western Union office and gave information about the other two robbers who had participated. He was subsequently placed in a lineup with other men, all of whom were shorter. Foster was wearing a jacket similar to the one he had worn during the robbery. The eyewitness could not be sure that Foster was the robber and asked police if he could speak with Foster. Foster was taken into a room and was seated across from the witness at a table, with no other person in the room. After conversing with Foster in the room, the witness could still not make a positive identification. A week later, the witness viewed another lineup, this time with Foster and four men different from those in the first lineup. This time, the witness made a positive identification of Foster. Foster was subsequently convicted of robbery. He appealed the case, but the California Court of Appeals affirmed the conviction. The state supreme court denied review, but the U.S. Supreme Court granted certiorari. The Court reversed and remanded the case, holding that in the first lineup arranged by police, the petitioner stood out from the other two men by the contrast of his height and clothing. After this attempt to identify Foster as the offender failed, officers arranged that the witness was the only person in the room with the suspect. When this attempt also failed, the officers arranged that the petitioner was the only person placed in the second lineup who had also participated in the first lineup. The suggestive nature of the identification procedure made it inevitable that the petitioner would be identified as the offender. Thus, the procedure had violated due process.

Kirby v. Illinois
406 U.S. 682 (1972)

Kirby and a companion were stopped on the street by a police officer who asked Kirby for his identification. The identification shown to the officer was that of another man named "Shard," who had been robbed of his wallet a few days earlier. Suspicious of Kirby and his companion, the officer asked them to accompany him to police headquarters where he would check the identification. Kirby and his companion were not placed under arrest, and the officer did not know of the earlier robbery. While checking records at the police station, the officer discovered the robbery report. He sent for "Shard" and asked him to come to the police station. When "Shard" saw Kirby in the station, he identified Kirby as the robber. When confronted by the robbery victim, Kirby and his companion had not been advised of their right to counsel and they had not received legal assistance. Kirby and his companion were arrested and charged. At trial, the defense moved to suppress the testimony of the witness, questioning the identification procedure used by police and claiming that the defendants should have had an attorney present at the identification. The court refused the motion and "Shard" testified to the identities of Kirby and his companion. The two were subsequently convicted. They appealed and the court upheld the conviction. The case was appealed to the U.S. Supreme Court and it granted review. The Court disagreed with Kirby and his companion, holding that there is no right to counsel at police headquarters, during police lineups, or during identification sessions when suspects have not been formally charged with a crime, since, under such a circumstance, suspects are not being prosecuted for crimes.

Neil v. Biggers
409 U.S. 188 (1972)

Biggers was suspected of rape. The crime had occurred during full moonlight; the victim had spent over thirty minutes with the attacker; and she had

had an opportunity to see the rapist clearly. Prior to Biggers's arrest, the victim had participated in a showup and a lineup and had viewed photographs of several rape suspects. Police stated they had used the showup procedure because they could not find any suspects who had the same physical description as the rapist. During several identification procedures, the victim at no time identified any of the suspects as her attacker, but when Biggers was subjected to a showup, the victim immediately said she had "no doubt" that he was the rapist. He was convicted of rape, largely on the basis of her testimony, which occurred seven months after the confrontation. He challenged the conviction, contending that his identification by the victim had been "suggestive." The Tennessee Supreme Court affirmed the conviction. The case was appealed to the U.S. Supreme Court and it granted certiorari. The Court held that a station-house identification based on the viewing of a single suspect was admissible into evidence on the basis of the totality of the circumstances. In this case, the victim had spent a considerable amount of time with her attacker. She had been with him under adequate light in her house and under a full moon outdoors. Her description to the police—which had included the attacker's approximate age, height, weight, complexion, skin texture, build, and voice—was thorough. The victim, a practical nurse, had had the unusual opportunity to observe and identify her attacker. The factors to be considered in evaluating the likelihood of misidentification include the opportunity of the witness to view the suspect at the time of the crime; the witness's degree of attention to the suspect during the crime; the accuracy of the witness's prior description of the accused; the level of certainty demonstrated by the witness at the confrontation; and the length of time between the crime and the confrontation.

United States v. Ash
413 U.S. 300 (1973)

Charles Ash, an African American male, along with several accomplices, was suspected of robbing a federally insured bank. A government informant, McFarland, told the FBI that he and Ash had conversed about Ash's involvement in the robbery. The FBI circulated color photographs of Ash and other blacks involved in the crime to witnesses at the bank. They made uncertain identifications of Ash. Before the trial, which was held almost three years after the robbery, the prosecution and an FBI agent showed several color photos to the four witnesses who had tentatively identified the black and white photographs as those of Ash. Three of the witnesses selected the color photo of Ash and one was unable to make any identification. None of the witnesses were able to select his accomplices from any of the other photographs. At trial, Ash argued that this postindictment identification procedure had violated his right to counsel since he viewed this procedure as a critical stage in the criminal justice process. Therefore, the evidence should be excluded. Most witnesses could not positively identify Ash, but McFarland testified against him. The testimony was admitted as evidence, and Ash was convicted and given concurrent sentences of eighty months to twelve years. Ash appealed the conviction. The court of appeals held that Ash's Sixth Amendment right to counsel had been violated since his counsel had not been allowed to be present during the photographic display conducted before trial. The case was appealed and the U.S. Supreme Court granted certiorari. The Court reversed and remanded the case, holding that the Sixth Amendment does not guarantee the right to counsel during a photographic display conducted by the government for the purpose of allowing the witness to attempt to identify offenders.

United States v. Dionisio
410 U.S. 1 (1973)

Dionisio and twenty others were advised that they were suspects in an illegal gambling investigation. They were subpoenaed before a grand jury and ordered to submit recordings of their voices for comparison with various messages police had intercepted through telephonic wiretapping. Dionisio refused and argued that to submit to a voice exemplar would violate his Fourth Amendment protection against unreasonable searches and seizures and his Fifth Amendment protection against self-incrimination. He was held in contempt of court and was ordered to jail for eighteen months. He appealed, contending that no one could compel him to give evidence against himself, pursuant to the Fifth Amendment protection against self-incrimination, and that the "seizure" of his voice pattern through a vocal recording was unreasonable within the meaning of the Fourth Amendment. The court of appeals agreed in part but reversed the district court's decision on the grounds that the Fourth Amendment requires a preliminary showing of reasonableness before a suspect can be compelled to furnish a voice exemplar and that in this case the proposed "seizure" was unreasonable because of the large number of suspects subpoenaed to produce exemplars. The appeals court also found that the Fourth Amendment applies to grand-jury processes. The case was appealed to the U.S. Supreme Court and it granted review. The Court reversed and remanded the case, holding that grand juries can compel a suspect to give vocal recordings and that such an intrusion is not an unreasonable seizure within the meaning of the Fourth Amendment.

United States v. Mara
410 U.S. 19 (1973)

Richard Mara was subpoenaed twice by a grand jury to submit a handwriting sample for comparison with words written on paper during a commission of a crime. He refused to comply, contending that to submit such a sample would constitute an unreasonable search-and-seizure within the meaning of the Fourth Amendment. A district court judge placed him in civil confinement until he agreed to submit the writing sample. He was subsequently convicted, partially on the basis of this handwriting comparison. He appealed the decision. The Seventh Circuit Court of Appeals reversed the decision of the lower court, citing *Dionisio* and holding that the Fourth Amendment applied to such handwriting comparisons and that therefore the government had to make a preliminary showing of reasonableness. The government appealed to the U.S. Supreme Court and it granted review. The Court reversed and remanded the circuit court's ruling, holding that a grand-jury subpoena is not a seizure within the meaning of the Fourth Amendment and that therefore the Amendment is not violated by a grand-jury directive compelling production of "physical characteristics" that are constantly exposed to the public. Handwriting, like speech, is repeatedly shown to the public, so there is no more of an expectation of privacy in the physical characteristics of a person's script than there is in the tone of his or her voice.

Winston v. Lee
470 U.S. 753 (1985)

Lee claimed to have been shot in the left side of his chest and robbed by someone fleeing down the street. Police officers were simultaneously investigating a robbery and shooting during which a store owner had been shot but had wounded the assailant in return. The store owner advised police that he thought that he had shot his assailant in the chest. While both men were being treated at the same hospital, the store owner recognized Lee as the robber. The officers obtained a court order for doctors to remove a bullet from Lee's chest to be used as evidence, but the doctors advised police that surgery might be dangerous. Lee sought to bar doctors from removing the bullet because the act would be an unwarranted bodily intrusion. The Commonwealth of Virginia moved in state court for an order directing the respondent to undergo surgery to remove the lodged bullet under his left collarbone. After hearing expert testimony that the procedure would not be dangerous or threatening, the court granted the motion. The Virginia Supreme Court denied the respondent's petition for a writ of prohibition and a writ of habeas corpus. The respondent later brought an action in the federal district court to enjoin the pending operation on the grounds that it violated his Fourth Amendment rights. The court refused to issue a preliminary injunction. Before surgery, X-rays revealed that the bullet was lodged substantially deeper than had been thought when the state court granted the motion to compel surgery. The respondent unsuccessfully sought a rehearing at the state trial level, and the Virginia Supreme Court affirmed. The respondent returned to the federal district court to enjoin the surgery. The court of appeals affirmed. The case was appealed to the U.S. Supreme Court and it granted review. The Court held that compelled surgery into an individual's body for evidence is an "unreasonable" intrusion within the meaning of the Fourth Amendment since it offends one's expectation of privacy—even if such an intrusion is likely to produce evidence of a crime. In this case, compelled surgery would threaten the respondent's safety since it would pose an unknown medical risk. In any case, however, a surgical intrusion on any suspect's privacy interests and bodily integrity can be characterized as severe. In sum, the Court held that states cannot compel surgical intrusions into one's body, even if that intrusion would produce evidence of a crime.

REFERENCES

Associated Press. (1999a, April 16). DNA testing frees two inmates imprisoned 12 years for murder. *Pocono Record* (Stroudsburg, PA), p. A6.

Associated Press. (1999b, September 2). DNA test frees 60-year-old inmate. *Pocono Record* (Stroudsburg, PA), p 3A.

Associated Press. (2001a, March 16). Convicted killer freed on new DNA evidence. *Pocono Record* (Stroudsburg, PA), p. B6.

Associated Press. (2001b, April 5). Convicted murderer finally acquitted. *Pocono Record* (Stroudsburg, PA), p. A4.

Associated Press. (2001c, October 19). DNA clears man jailed for 13 years for rape. *Pocono Record* (Stroudsburg, PA), p. C10.

Black, H. C. (1979). *Black's law dictionary: Definitions of the terms and phrases of American and English jurisprudence, ancient and modern* (5th ed.). St. Paul, MN: West.

Bohm, R. M., & Haley, K. N. (1999). *Introduction to criminal justice* (2nd ed.). New York: Glencoe/McGraw-Hill.

Champion, D. (1997). *Criminal justice in the United States.* Chicago: Nelson-Hall.

del, Carmen, R. V. (2004). *Criminal procedure: Law and practice* (6th ed.). Belmont, CA: Wadsworth/Thomas Learning.

DNA tests clear 3,000 suspects. (1997a, November 30). *Honolulu Advertiser,* p. A2.

Gaines, L., & Miller, R. (2004). *Criminal justice in action: The core* (2nd ed.). Belmont, CA: Wadsworth/Thomson Learning.

Inciardi, J. (1987). *Criminal justice* (2nd ed.). Orlando, FL: Harcourt Brace Jovanovich.

Inciardi, J. (1999). *Criminal justice* (6th ed.). Orlando, FL: Harcourt Brace.

Klotter, S. C. (1996). *Legal guide for police: Constitutional issues* (4th ed.). Cincinnati: Anderson.

Klotter, S. C. (2002). *Legal guide for police: Constitutional issues* (6th ed.). Cincinnati: Anderson.

Olson, K. (1988). LAPD's newest investigative tool. *Police Chief, 55,* 30.

Pliant, L. (1994). Information management. *Police Chief, 61,* 31-35.

Rau, R. (1991). Forensic science and criminal justice technology: High tech tools for the 90s. NIJ Reports.

Scheb, J. M., & Scheb, J. M. (1999). *Criminal law and procedure* (3rd ed.). Belmont, CA: West/Wadsworth.

Schmitt, J. B. (1992). Computerized ID systems. *Police Chief, 59,* 33-45.

Schmitz, J. (1994). Criminals versus computers. *Law & Order, 42,* 80-84.

Senna, J. J., & Siegel, L. J. (1998). *Essentials of criminal justice* (2nd ed.). Belmont, CA: West/Wadsworth.

Two inmates freed after new DNA tests. (1997b, December 7). *Honolulu Advertiser,* p. A6.

Weston, P. B., & Wells, K. M. (1976). *Criminal evidence for police* (2nd ed.). Englewood Cliffs, NJ: Prentice Hall.

Cases Cited

Blue v. State, 558 P.2d 636 (1977)

Breithaupt v. Abrams, 352 U.S. 432 (1957)

Burnell v. Collins, 982 F.2d 922 (5th Cir. 1993)

Commonwealth v. Zabala, 456 A. 2d 622 (Pa. 1993)

Crawford v. Commonwealth, 534 S.E. 2d 332 (Va. 2000).

Daubert v. Marrell Dow Pharmaceutical, 509 U.S. 579 (1993)

Davis v. Mississippi, 394 U.S. 721 (1969)

Dozie v. State, 49 Wis. 2d. 209 (1989)

Foster v. California, 394 U.S. 440 (1969)

Frye v. United States, 293 F. 1013 (D.C. Cir. 1923)

Gilbert v. California, 388 U.S. 263 (1967)

Holt v. United States, 218 U.S. 245 (1910)

Jones v. State, 600 P.2d 247, 250 (Nev. 1979)

Kirby v. Illinois, 406 U.S. 682 (1972)

Moore v. Illinois, 434 U.S. 220 (1977)

Neil v. Biggers, 409 U.S. 188 (1972)

People v. Bustamante, 643 P.2d 727 (1981)

People v. Jackson, 217 N.W. 2d 22 (Mich. 1974)

People v. Klinger, 713 N.Y. S. 2d 823 (2000)

People v. Love, 443 N.E. 2d 948 (N.Y. 1982)

Rochin v. California, 342 U.S. 165 (1952)

Schmerber v. California, 384 U.S. 757 (1966)

Simmons v. United States, 390 U.S. 377 (1968)

State v. Frasier, 341 S.C. 546 (2000)

State v. Swartz, 447 N.W. 2d 422 (Minn. 1989)

Stovall v. Denno, 388 U.S. 293 (1967)

United States v. Ash, 413 U.S. 300 (1973)

United States v. Bonds, 12Fd 540 (6th Cir. 1993)

United States v. Dionisio, 410 U.S. 1 (1973)

United States v. Holland, 378 F. Supp. 144 (E.D. Pa. 1974)

United States v. Mara, 410 U.S. 19 (1973)

United States v. Martinez, 3 F.3d 1191 (8th Cir. 1993)

United States v. Marvia, 928 F. Supp. 1471 (D. Haw. 1990)

United States v. Smith, 869 F2d 348 (7th Cir. 1989)

United States v. Wade, 388 U.S. 218 (1967)

United States v. Williams, 583 F.2d 1194 (2d Cir. 1978)

Winston v. Lee, 470 U.S. 753 (1985)

Index

Note: Case names are in italic font.